Scaling Teams

Strategies for Building Successful Teams and Organizations

Alexander Grosse and David Loftesness

Beijing · Boston · Farnham · Sebastopol · Tokyo

Scaling Teams

by Alexander Grosse and David Loftesness

Copyright © 2017 Alexander Grosse & David Loftesness. All rights reserved.

Published by O'Reilly Media, Inc., 1005 Gravenstein Highway North, Sebastopol, CA 95472.

O'Reilly books may be purchased for educational, business, or sales promotional use. Online editions are also available for most titles (*http://oreilly.com/safari*). For more information, contact our corporate/institutional sales department: 800-998-9938 or *corporate@oreilly.com*.

Editor: Laurel Ruma	**Indexer:** Ellen Troutman-Zaig
Production Editor: Melanie Yarbrough	**Interior Designer:** Monica Kamsvaag
Copyeditor: Jasmine Kwityn	**Cover Designer:** Randy Comer
Proofreader: Rachel Monaghan	**Illustrator:** Rebecca Demarest

January 2017:   First Edition

Revision History for the First Edition

2017-01-10:   First Release

See *http://oreilly.com/catalog/errata.csp?isbn=9781491952276* for release details.

The O'Reilly logo is a registered trademark of O'Reilly Media, Inc. *Scaling Teams*, the cover image, and related trade dress are trademarks of O'Reilly Media, Inc.

978-1-491-95227-6

[LSI]

Contents

Introduction

Growth is never by mere chance; it is the result of forces working together.

—JAMES CASH PENNEY

Leading a fast-growing team is a uniquely challenging experience. Management techniques that seemed so effective last month can suddenly fail in surprising ways. The adjustments you make might carry you six months into the future, or maybe only six weeks. Meanwhile, your new team members have an increasingly difficult time coming up to speed, and you wonder whether all the effort you've put into recruiting might actually be slowing down the team.

Such experiences can be humbling, but they can also be thrilling and rewarding for those who successfully navigate the inflection points that come from rapid growth. Looking back on our own careers, we wish that we had been given a practical guide to those inflection points, to help us see the warning signs of dysfunction before they grew into full-fledged crises. Rather than pivoting rapidly in response to scaling problems, we'd prefer to have used proven solutions from successful companies, adjusting them to the unique challenges of our own situation. This book is the toolbox we wish we'd had, and we hope it proves useful to you.

Who Should Read This Book?

We wrote this book for leaders of technology companies, particularly those involved in product development: software and hardware engineering, product management, design, QA, and so on. Our advice will be most helpful to teams ranging from 10 to 250 members, either in the context of a startup company, or a newly formed team within a larger organization.

We have focused on the needs of teams experiencing a dramatic increase in size, often referred to as *hyper-growth*. While there is no strict definition for what distinguishes "hyper" from normal growth, it's most often used to describe increases greater than 50% in a 6- to 12-month period. During times of hyper-growth, scaling challenges are amplified, with less time to react and craft solutions, but we expect that teams with slower growth will be able to apply our suggested strategies as well.

Leaders of teams that interact closely with product development, such as technical sales, marketing, or customer success, should also find value in this book. And we hope our suggestions are useful to leaders in fields outside of technology as well.

Why We Wrote This Book

Although we the authors, Alexander Grosse and David Loftesness, took different paths to engineering leadership, we share similar experiences of how growth can overwhelm an otherwise high-functioning team:

Alexander's story

In 1999, I was hired by a startup as a senior software engineer. After a few months, I came to the office and found a letter on the CTO's desk stating that he had quit, effective immediately. The CEO turned to me and said "Congratulations, Alex. You are the CTO now." At first, I was in full panic mode and had no idea what to do. So I spent the coming months concentrating on the technical work, as I had no clue what other things needed to be done. When the dot-com economy crashed, we went bankrupt. I later read an article outlining the typical mistakes that startups make. Each point the author made applied to our startup...

David's story

I joined Geoworks in 1993, my first job out of college. One year later, my boss, a Director of Engineering, asked me to manage the team I was working on. As a dutiful and ambitious young software engineer, I accepted the challenge immediately and set to work trying to emulate what I'd seen my boss do—hold one-on-ones and team meetings, build project schedules, hire more engineers, and work like crazy. I really had no idea what I was doing, but did my best and tried to keep things moving forward, making many mistakes along the way. After a period of explosive growth, Geoworks's momentum faltered. I eventually had to lay off almost half my team, many of them good friends, one of the worst experiences of my career. Looking back, I can't help wondering what might have been... Had we managed our growth better, could we have kept our key clients, continued to grow, and become the successful company we aspired to be?

After we met and compared notes, we recognized a shared ambition: to provide future leaders with the guidance we lacked early on, and learned mainly through hard-won experience.

The content of this book is based on that experience, from managing rapidly growing teams at a number of different companies. But the combined experience of two people can only cover so many situations, so we also interviewed founders and executives from a number of different high-growth companies. And we incorporated and referenced the written work of dozens of other industry leaders whose ideas have influenced our careers.

The Context for Growth

We have all heard stories of high-flying technology companies that doubled, tripled, or even more in a very short time. In his book *The Hard Thing About Hard Things* (HarperBusiness), Ben Horowitz recalled that his company LoudCloud grew from 4 founders to 200 employees in less than 6 months, and then grew to 600 in less than a year!

Such growth is an impressive achievement, but no matter how talented their leaders are, teams that grow by 300% in 12 months almost never see a 300% increase in the output of the team. Typically such rapid growth leads to diminishing returns (see Figure P-1).

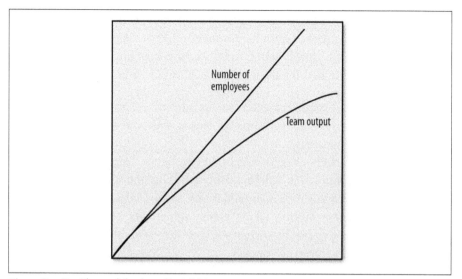

Figure P-1. Rapid growth leads to diminishing returns

For reasons we will explain, the challenges that come from growing fast often limit the productivity gained from each new employee, and side effects can even lower the overall effectiveness of the team. Kate Heddleston describes an extreme case:

> When the new Senior VP of Engineering took over at a major Silicon Valley tech company a few years back, the first thing he had to do was freeze hiring. The company had been growing rapidly and their engineering team had hired aggressively, but they had reached a point where each new engineer they added to the team decreased overall productivity.[1]

How frustrating would it be to expend effort and money recruiting and training a new employee, only to decrease the output of your team!

But this begs the question—how fast is too fast? The answer depends on many factors, particularly the size and maturity of the team in question. A 10-person team with a well-established on-boarding and mentorship program could probably triple in size over the course of a year without much difficulty. But for a less prepared team this could be a recipe for chaos, and would certainly not be

---

1 Kate Heddleston, "Onboarding and the Cost of Team Debt" (*http://bit.ly/2hLlwGb*), Kate Heddleston's blog.

sustainable over the long term. We hope that the advice and techniques in this book can help you significantly raise the effective growth rate limit for your team.

A rule of thumb derived from our experience and from conversations with leaders of hyper-growth companies is that once your development team is larger than 20, trying to double the team in less than a year is likely to lead to trouble. Expect to waste time on personnel issues, product flaws introduced by poorly trained new hires, flagging morale, and inefficient meetings instead of moving your product forward and keeping customers happy.

HIRING: ONE OPTION AMONG MANY

A commonly observed pattern in technology startups is that they try to solve every problem through hiring. Instead of understanding why productivity has slowed or product quality is slipping and then crafting an appropriate solution, many companies simply crank up the hiring machine and "throw people at the problem." Unfortunately, the complexity of managing a larger team often makes the problem worse, or introduces new ones.

Alex once worked at a company with a buggy product and unhappy customers. In response, the company hired more developers and focused them on fixing bugs. But these new hires lacked insight into the overall system. They ended up causing more problems than they fixed, leading to even more hiring and a downward spiral of quality.

A better approach would have been to *suspend* hiring and understand why quality was slipping. Were new employees not getting the training they needed? Was the development process that worked for 5 engineers starting to break down at 25? Perhaps instead of hiring, adding rigor to their development process or training in better testing techniques would correct the problem. If so, the team would then be in a much better position to resume hiring once new hires could contribute without reducing the quality of the product.

Despite our focus on scaling teams, **we recommend considering alternatives to hiring first.** Process improvements, organizational changes, or canceling unnecessary projects may allow you to meet your goals with fewer new hires. This costs less, simplifies your job, and adds less risk to your business. In our experience, the complexity of managing a 100% growth rate team is more than twice as difficult as managing a 50% growth rate team.

If after looking at alternatives you decide that you still need to hire, then the rest of this book is for you. Sometimes you simply can't deliver what the business demands with the team you have. And it's clear that another month of "crunch mode" will cause your old-timers to burn out and quit. When you reach this point, we hope to prepare you for the challenges that come with a fast-growing team and help you manage it more effectively.

Structure

In *Scaling Teams*, we cover strategy, tactics, and stories of growth across five dimensions. These are the areas where we've seen the greatest challenges during hyper-growth:

Hiring
>Chapter 1, *Scaling Hiring: Growing the Team*
>Chapter 2, *Scaling Hiring: Interviews and Hiring Decisions*
>Chapter 3, *Scaling Hiring: How to Close, On-Board, and Beyond*

People management
>Chapter 4, *People Management: Getting Started*
>Chapter 5, *People Management at Scale*

Organization
>Chapter 6, *Scaling the Organization: Design Principles*
>Chapter 7, *Scaling the Organization: Delivery Teams*
>Chapter 8, *Scaling the Organization: Reporting Structure*

Culture
>Chapter 9, *Scaling Culture*

Communication
>Chapter 10, *Scaling Communication: The Complexity of Scale and Distance*
>Chapter 11, *Scaling Communication: Communicating at Scale*

Hiring is how you build the foundation of the company. You must hire people to grow. Ideally, your new recruits share your vision and values, and have the talents needed to help the company succeed. Hiring poorly is often worse than not hiring at all, and investments in the other four areas are unlikely to make up for it.

Next, we address *people management*. Hiring provides the raw materials for your team, but people management is needed to ensure that team members are happy and productive over the long term. An effective manager uses coaching, feedback, work assignments, dispute resolution, and other techniques, adjusting their approach based on the needs of each individual.

If hiring and people management are the essential ingredients of productivity, *organization* acts as the framework for boosting and channeling that productivity. An effective organization removes barriers to delivering work output, bringing together the right team members to solve challenges for the business.

Finally, *culture* and *communication* are the glue that keeps the other three dimensions together. A strong culture includes aspects of the other dimensions and helps reinforce the best parts of them. Communication provides the necessary context for the team to be effective in the other dimensions.

In the the book's final chapter, we tie together the warning signs and the most essential guidance from the preceding chapters, and propose building a *scaling plan* to help you navigate the growth challenges ahead.

How to Read This Book

We tried to write a book that could be read cover to cover while still allowing the reader to drop into a single section of particular interest. If you're considering whether to add a layer of management to your team, for example, we invite you to drop into the chapters on people management as soon as you finish this introduction.

Because every organization is different, we don't often prescribe one-size-fits-all solutions. Many factors can influence the direction to go when things break: the size of the team, the growth rate, the number of offices (and time zones), the number of remote employees, and so on. In the few cases where a specific approach is likely to work, we describe it in more detail. In the other cases, we broadly cover possible solutions and provide examples of how other companies have approached the same issues.

A time-pressured reader might focus on Chapter 12. There we list our *scaling essentials*, the most important things you can do to prepare for rapid growth. It also contains a collated list of the *warning signs* from each chapter. Reviewing the warning signs, finding those that are evident on your team, and applying the suggested remedies would be a very surgical way to make use of the recommendations in this book.

Acknowledgments

Scaling Teams would not exist without the contributions, feedback, and support from our many friends, colleagues, and family members. Alex and David are overwhelmed with gratitude. We would like to extend our heartfelt thanks to:

- The reviewers who convinced O'Reilly that our proposal wasn't crazy talk and that our final draft was worth printing. They called bullshit when needed, gave us insightful suggestions, and made the book better in so many ways: Kellan Elliott-McCrea, bethanye McKinney Blount, Mike Loukides, Marcy Swenson, Kevin Goldsmith, Oren Ellenbogen, Alexander Kong, Anna Sulkina, Kevin Way, Naomi Chin, and Dillion Tan.

- The colleagues and friends who let us interview them, pick their brains, or quietly jot down the smart things they said about scaling teams. They gave us illuminating stories and examples, and helped us expand our limited range of experience to cover so many other situations and challenges: Mike Krieger, Marcy Swenson, Chris Fry, Raffi Krikorian, Michael Lopp, Eric Bowman, David Noel, Jesper Pascal, Oren Ellenbogen, Kevin Goldsmith, Phil Calcado, Duana Stanley, Kellan Elliott-McCrea, Dale Harrison, Nick Weaver, Laura Bilazarian, and Marc Hedlund.

- Many more colleagues and friends who reviewed drafts of the book or contributed in other ways. We'd like to highlight specific contributions from each one, but they all offered many helpful comments, perspectives, and suggestions, so you can mentally append the phrase "and many other things" after each one: Joy Su suggested tech talk rotations; John Kalucki improved the logical flow; Glen Sanford fixed the sports metaphor for predicting manager success; Penny Campbell made myriad outline improvements and suggested the section on how the behavior of leaders influences team culture; Sylvain Grande helped us improve the initial structure of the book; Joanne Yee turned many overly obtuse phrases into readable prose; Joe Xavier provided the perfect summary of the people manager role; Mike Sela reminded us that poor management and the absence of management are not the same thing; Ryan King provided veteran insights on core values and culture; Aaron Rothman reminded us that recruiting requires closing; Scott Loftesness fixed the sequencing of the people management chapters (thanks, Dad!); Stefan Gross-Selbeck suggested a better structure for the "Scaling the Organization" chapters; Soren Thompson helped clarify several sections in "Scaling Organization"; John Sturino added some important concepts to "Delivery Teams"; Ben Linders improved "Scaling the Organization"; Jan Lehnhardt provided valuable input on diversity in "Scaling Hiring"; Erik Engstrom contributed two stories and valuable input to "Scaling Hiring"; Charmilla Kasper helped with diversity in the hiring chapters; Oliver Hookins survived providing our first top-to-bottom in-depth review, which was hugely valuable; Peter Vida reviewed "Scaling Hiring"; Philipp Rogge gave a great review of "Scaling the Organization"; Simon Munich-Andersen reviewed the whole book and provided useful and motivating feedback; David Parmenter gave us a lot of advice on the overall structure of the book; Sonya Green and Robert Slifka provided the tree metaphor that connects values and culture; and Mike Pierovich provided a perfect quote for the "People Management" chapters. We've probably missed a few of you. Please accept our apologies and our gratitude.

- Many people were present for the origin of the book, when David and Alex met at the Hive Summit 2015 in Yerevan, Armenia. They provided encouragement and support then and along the way: Laura Bilazarian, David Singleton, Lennon Day-Reynolds, and Dale Harrison. We are grateful to the Hive Group, the Tumo Center, and the Armenian tech community for hosting us and providing such an inspiring beginning to our journey. And ultimately, it was Raffi Krikorian who invited us to the 2015 Hive Summit and set us on the path that led here.

- Special thanks to Laurel Ruma for sponsoring this project and convincing us to work together as coauthors; Tim Howes for the idea of breaking down scaling challenges into discrete dimensions; Robert Hoekman for help turning ideas into wonderfully readable prose; and especially Colleen Toporek, who wrangled our words, our ideas, and our schedules with a gentle confidence that we sorely needed.

- David cannot express how much support and patience Penny Campbell provided throughout the writing process, not to mention her numerous corrections and additions. Thank you, Penny, and thank you, Z and L, for putting up with your busy and distracted dad for so many months. This book is dedicated to you. I know someday you'll read it and send me improvements for the nth edition.

- Alex promises to spend more time with his family for the foreseeable future. Without the support of May-Britt Frank-Grosse and the patience of our three kids, this book would not have been possible.

Scaling Hiring: Growing the Team

Great vision without great people is irrelevant.

—JIM COLLINS, *GOOD TO GREAT* **(HARPERBUSINESS)**

Growing a team requires dedicated effort by team leaders to identify, recruit, and hire the best candidates, and probably a lot more effort than you think. You need a well-designed recruiting process that channels this effort to yield the results you want: great hires. This is especially critical in a team's early days, since the founders and early employees form the bedrock of what the company hopes to become. Hiring poorly is often worse than not hiring at all.

In this and the next two chapters, we outline a scalable hiring process that can take a team from single digits to hundreds of employees. We'll explain how to evaluate candidates efficiently and accurately, minimize bias in the recruiting process, and maximize the chance that your new hires will be strong contributors. But first, let's discuss the principles that form the foundation of any effective recruiting process.

Hiring to Scale

Teams that need to hire are trying to bridge the gap between what they can do today and what they need to do in the future. These could be *skill gaps,* such as the group of hardware engineers who realize their product needs a major software component. Or they could be *capacity gaps,* such as when the founding team realizes they are unable to keep up with customer demand for new features and support requests. In either case, what should team leaders do to best fill those gaps and help the team succeed?

KEY PRINCIPLES

Before outlining the full recruiting lifecycle, let's cover the key principles for hiring.

Hire for talent

It goes without saying that you want to hire the best employees you can. By "best," we mean the employees that can contribute the most to team success over the long term. Often, teams focus too much on filling specific short-term skill gaps, or simply getting a "warm body" on board who can handle the work that isn't currently getting done. It's critical to remember that the hires you make at your current stage will set the tone for hires you make in later stages.

Hire for the team

Every team is different, and in larger companies, so is the organization that surrounds them. The best person for your team may be very different than the best person for your friend's team at a nearby startup. We often hear the advice that you should only hire "A" players, but we believe that building an "A" team is more important. A super-talented hire who has very different values can pull a team apart rather than bringing it together. We will share insights on how to identify individuals who can magnify the team's strengths, who are genuinely passionate about the product and will reinforce the value of being an open, product-focused organization.

Minimize bias

A biased interview process is a flawed interview process. Besides the inherent unfairness to the individuals involved, bias reduces the chance of finding the best hire for your team by allowing irrelevant factors such as race, gender, or age to influence the hiring decision. This chapter explains why diversity matters when you're building teams, and what simple changes can be made to reduce the impact of hidden bias in the interview process.

Don't cut corners

A rigorous interview process is analogous to a rigorous code review process. Finding bugs in code review is much less expensive than finding them in production, and similarly, rejecting a candidate that is wrong for your team during the interview process is much less expensive than hiring them and dealing with the resulting problems later. This is sometimes described as "optimizing for false negatives." Later in this chapter, we discuss how to do this appropriately, as well as cover when it's strategically sound to take a risk on a candidate who may not seem like a perfect fit.

Treat candidates with respect

Candidates often talk to friends, family, and colleagues about their interview experience, and may even post summaries on sites like Glassdoor and Quora. Providing a great experience will improve your chances of landing the candidate you want and may encourage others to apply. A bad experience can not only lose you a candidate but might also prevent their entire network from interviewing with you! Your goal should be to have every candidate walk away from the interview wanting to work for your company, whether you decide to make an offer or not.

Word of Mouth: A Story from Alex

Candidates talk to one another, which can be good or bad for you depending on their recruiting experience. One candidate we were trying to hire, who was really a great fit for my team, decided not to move forward with us, as he couldn't relocate to Europe. But two weeks later, another engineer from the same company applied, citing the awesome hiring experience his colleague had gone through. We ended up hiring that engineer.

Another time, I visited a conference and was very impressed by one of the speakers. I tried to convince her to apply for a position at my company, but she declined, saying that she had actually thought about it a while ago, but had heard from a friend that our hiring process was very chaotic. She chose to go with a different company.

It's much easier to hear about the positive side of your recruiting process because candidates who have a negative impression may not apply in the first place. By actively seeking out candidates and listening to their opinions, you can learn what is being said about your company and your recruiting process and make changes accordingly.

Know how much risk to take

In times of hyper-growth, you may feel pressure to take risks in order to meet your growth targets. You might take a chance on a borderline candidate or blindly hire a referral because one of your cofounders heard good things about them. But we advise a more cautious path. There are enough distractions in your organization already without the added disruption of having to terminate the new hire that didn't work out. Firings will happen regardless, but they happen even more frequently when you take more risk in the hiring process.

There are certainly arguments for taking more risk and tolerating false positives in order to find a diamond in the rough. As Henry Ward explains in his article, "How to Hire" (*https://medium.com/swlh/how-to-hire*): "Do not be afraid of hiring false positives. Give people chances. Be afraid of missing the 20x employee." It's certainly possible to construct a system in which hiring decisions are made more loosely, relying instead on a more rigorous on-the-job evaluation process that identifies bad hires quickly. But even when you make a quick decision that someone needs to leave, it takes time and energy to manage those people out, and time and energy are especially precious resources during hypergrowth. This is why our default advice is to not take too much risk.

Know when to listen to your gut

Experienced interviewers often develop a strong gut feeling that kicks in 10 or 15 minutes into an interview. Because gut feelings can be a source of bias, they should not replace a thorough hiring decision; instead, they are an indicator that you should dig deeper—into the candidate, and your own reactions.

When Your Gut Is Right...and When It Isn't

Consider the following story from Alex:

> At one of my former companies we were hiring a VP of Product and in the hiring sync everybody was in favor of the candidate except one product manager, who said that he had a strange feeling that he was a poor collaborator. Because of that we checked more references and those heavily advised against hiring that person—so we didn't.

On the other hand, the following story from bethanye McKinney Blount is an example of how your gut can be misleading:

> There was a guy who was great on paper and who answered my questions well during the interview, but there was something

about him that bothered me and made me want to not hire him. I couldn't figure out why, until I realized he had an uncanny resemblance to an ex-boyfriend who was a jerk. After some reflection, I realized this guy wasn't a jerk, he just reminded me of my ex. So I voted to hire him.

HIRING FOR DIVERSITY

Because bias can affect every stage of the process, each chapter on scaling hiring includes suggestions about how to reduce bias and minimize its impact. But before getting into specifics, let's first define what is impacted by bias: team diversity. Some characteristics of team diversity are race, ethnicity, gender, age, religion, physical ability, and sexual orientation. A more complete list can be found at CodeOfConduct.com. Too often, discussions of diversity narrow in on one or two characteristics rather than taking a broader view.

Beyond the inherent unfairness to those affected, bias reduces the effectiveness of your recruiting efforts by unnecessarily narrowing the field of qualified candidates. From a purely pragmatic view, excluding certain groups only serves to limit the size of an otherwise huge talent pool.

The result is a less diverse team which is likely to perform worse than more diverse teams, particularly in situations that require creativity and innovation. For a more complete discussion of the research, see the McKinsey reports "Why Diversity Matters" (*http://bit.ly/mckinsey-diversity*) and "The Case for Team Diversity Gets Even Better" (*http://bit.ly/2gFkmwi*).

Diverse teams are also more likely to understand the perspectives of their customers. A homogeneous workforce (typically young, white, heterosexual males in the tech industry) might not question product decisions are insensitive or hurtful to their users. There are plenty of examples we can cite, such as Snapchat releasing "anime" and "bob marley" filters that were immediately condemned as harkening back to the days when white artists performed in "yellowface" or "blackface" makeup.

In general, the problem you face when scaling a startup is that you naturally tend to hire people who are similar to one another from the very start, in part because it's often the referral networks of the founding team members that lead to early hires. This intimacy quickly becomes a disadvantage. Once you have a homogeneous core team, people with other traits and backgrounds are less likely to join the company. As an example, let's say you have 50 employees, none of whom have kids. Will someone with three children join that team, especially if there are often meetings at 8:00 p.m., when they need to put their kids to bed? And who wants to be the first woman on a "bro" team? Unreflective homogeneity can prove daunting and prohibitive to potential new hires, and quite reasonably so.

Form the founding team and choose early hires based on who shares values and ideas with you—people who are passionate about the mission of the team. If all these people are white and male, so be it. If they are black and female, so be it. After that, however, diversifying the team must be a high priority. We'll talk about how to accomplish this goal throughout this chapter.

Also note that creating an inclusive workplace is essential to maintaining team diversity. It doesn't much help to hire a diverse team if you can't retain them. Inclusion is covered in more detail in "Building an Inclusive Workplace" on page 102.

The Hiring Process

With this overview in place, let's dive into the details of a typical hiring process, describe some warning signs that indicate that the process isn't scaling, and discuss some ideas for how to adjust as you continue to grow.

Figure 1-1 illustrates a typical hiring process. Candidates come in from three different sources and go through a set of screens and interviews. Next, a "hire" or "no-hire" decision has to be made. If it's a "hire" and the candidate accepts, they go through on-boarding before settling into their new role. We also include the off-boarding process because it can help you gain valuable insights into your hiring and organization. This isn't the only way to hire, but the broad strokes shown here are how the majority of tech companies approach hiring.

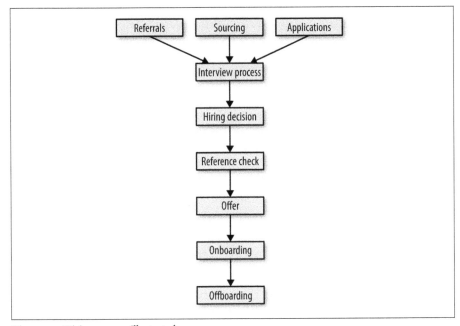

Figure 1-1. Hiring process illustrated

FINDING PEOPLE

There are three main sources for new candidates: a candidate applies directly, is sourced by a recruiter, or is referred by someone. In Chapter 3 we will discuss another way of getting candidates—acquiring a company in order to hire some or all of their employees. But in the following sections, we'll examine in detail the three most common ways to find people.

Referrals

Arguably the most effective method for finding new candidates is through referrals. A referral means that current employees (or other friends of the company, such as advisors, investors, and board members) identify potential candidates from their existing networks.[1] Ideally, this is someone the referrer has worked with in the past, so the referrer knows the person's qualifications, talents, and values. Referrals have a lot of advantages over other channels, but also a few caveats you should be mindful of. The advantages include:

---

1 Paul Petrone, "Here Is Why Employee Referrals Are the Best Way to Hire" (*http://bit.ly/2hNYNxx*), LinkedIn Talent Blog, August 3, 2015, *http://bit.ly/2hNYNxx*.

Reduced cost and effort

> Although you may pay a referral bonus, which we'll cover later, you don't have to pay a recruiter to source the candidate. And the process tends to be much faster than when you hire from other sources.[2]

Retention

> Referred employees stay longer at the company, and employees who made successful referrals stay longer than employees who didn't.[3]

Success rate

> Referred candidates are usually already motivated when entering the hiring process, as they have already spoken with current employees about the company beforehand. They come in much better informed about the company than other candidates, and because of this tend to have compatible values, work quality, work style, and a good fit with the culture. And perhaps most importantly, people tend to refer people they think will do a good job and are thus hired at a higher rate than other sources.[4]

A high rate of referrals can be a very good indicator of company health. Conversely, a lack of referrals can mean employees are unhappy with their jobs or unsure about the future of the company. Tracking referral data can provide insight into the morale of the team. Watch for trends here!

But there are also disadvantages to relying too much on referrals in the hiring process; essentially, groups tend to become groups because they're relatively alike. White males are likely to know other white males. So hiring more diverse team members through referrals alone becomes extremely difficult. Referrals, in other words, can dilute diversity right out of the gate, especially if the founding team itself lacks diversity. Research from Freada Kapor-Klein[5] shows that, statistically, if we are white, then 90% of our friends are also white. If we are African American, 85% of our friends are as well.

---

2 This is discussed more fully in "Why Employee Referrals Are the Best Source of Hire" (*http://bit.ly/2gFIX5g*).

3 Ibid.

4 Ibid.

5 Kim-Mai Cutler, "What the Kapors Have Learned from Years of Working on Diversity in Tech" (*https://techcrunch.com/2015/04/02/kapors-2/*), TechCrunch, April 2, 2015.

Be careful to avoid creating subgroups comprising friends who were already friends before they joined. They can end up building their own culture, and then maybe even leaving the company together.

Handling referrals in the hiring process

Though a referral is a strong sign, it's important to ensure that everybody goes through the same hiring process. If a candidate gets a softball interview, then the rest of the team may question whether they are truly qualified, which is not a good starting point.

Although all candidates should be treated respectfully during the hiring process, this is especially true for referrals. A bad hiring experience can seriously annoy the person who made the referral and discourage them from making any more in the future. If your hiring experience needs improvement across the board, consider focusing your efforts on referrals first and expanding from there. And don't forget to keep the referring employee up to date on the candidate's status, which will help them feel included and encourage them to make more referrals.

Generating referrals

It is amazing how many referrals you can get if you just ask employees for them. Set yourself up to regularly communicate job openings and ask everyone on the team to refer qualified candidates. This can be handled by the recruiting team or by the manager (who could then use one-on-ones for referrals).

You should also decide whether to pay a bonus for successful referrals. Most companies do. It's a simple approach, and it works well. Consider the following points:

- No referral bonus should be paid to managers who refer someone for their own team. Hiring for your own team is part of your job and shouldn't generate extra pay.

- When considering how much to give as a referral fee, consider how much an external recruiter might charge. That dollar amount should be the upper limit. Most companies pay in the $2,000–$5,000 range.

- Some companies (such as Amazon) have a progressive scale where the bonus gets larger for each referral generated. This can motivate employees to keep thinking of referrals and not stop after one or two, assuming that they've done their part.

Companies that don't offer bonuses often state that referrals are just part of the job, and employees should refer great colleagues so that they can work with the best people. One can imagine that a bonus might encourage someone to refer less qualified colleagues, but hopefully your interview process is rigorous enough to filter out those who aren't a good fit.

APPLICATIONS

Applications are one of the most straightforward methods of finding new employees. Candidates simply apply directly to the company, mainly by using a form on the company's website. But this method is not effective for most small companies as they are unlikely to be known by many qualified applicants.

There are techniques that can help raise awareness of a new company, such as advertising on job boards or getting mentioned in the press. Another way is to publish blog posts about the company's social values or engineering culture. Besides being a positive thing to do, it attracts like-minded future staff. Stewart Butterfield, for example, sent a letter (*http://bit.ly/2gFiDqQ*) to all Slack employees urging them to take time to reflect on Martin Luther King, Jr. Day despite the fact that not all businesses observe it as a holiday.

The downside of applications is the high level of noise—applications that clearly are not a good fit for the advertised position. There is no easy remedy for this issue; reading CVs simply takes patience and time.

SOURCING

Sourcing is a proactive recruiting technique in which you search social networks, open source hosting sites like GitHub, or other relevant sites for potential candidates and then contact them directly. This can be done internally by dedicated recruiters or hiring managers, or externally by contractors, often called "head hunters."

In the beginning, sourcing might be handled by the founders or other senior leaders, with the task of scheduling interviews being handled by the office manager. This illustrates very nicely the two main roles in recruiting:

- A *recruiter* does the actual sourcing work, approaching candidates through various methods.

- A *recruitment coordinator* is responsible for organizing the candidate experience—that is, scheduling interviews, welcoming candidates, and making sure interviews happen as planned. It's easy to underestimate how much work this is.

The recruitment work can also be done by an external recruiter, which can get you access to a large, preexisting candidate pool. External recruiters tend to use one of these three approaches:

Commission
> Depending on the market, an external recruiter might take 10%–25% of a new hire's first-year salary as a commission. Usually, no up-front payment is required.

Executive (fixed fee)
> An executive recruiter usually works for a fixed fee. The fee structure varies from firm to firm, but often they are paid in three installments, one at the beginning of the search, one when candidates start interviewing, and the last when a candidate they sourced is hired. Note that the first two payments are often required, even if you hire someone from a different source or decide to give the job to an internal candidate. Executive recruiters charge more than other recruiters, but their fee often gives you access to an exclusive candidate pool.

By effort
> Alternatively, a recruiter may charge by the effort it takes to find candidates, usually just an hourly rate.

Table 1-1 shows the pros and cons of these approaches.

Table 1-1. Pros and cons of recruitment approaches

	Pros	Cons
Commission	• No up-front financial commitment.	• No identification/association with the company. • Often a bad candidate experience (such as when a recruiter is more interested in bringing a candidate into the process than ensuring the person is a good fit). • Often a low signal-to-noise ratio; in many cases, it requires more work to deal with external recruiters.
Executive	• Access to candidates you wouldn't be able to contact otherwise. • Up-front payments come with the expectation that the recruiter will invest more time in understanding your needs.	• Searches are not always successful despite the cost. • Substantial financial investment necessary without any success guarantee.
By effort	• No pressure to hire the wrong candidate, as the recruiter is paid hourly.	• No incentive for the recruiter to close candidates quickly, so the process can drag out longer than necessary.

When selecting an external recruiter, we recommend the following:

1. Ask your network to refer you to recruiters they've used successfully in the past.

2. Check references; ideally, they've worked with companies that have a strong hiring process. A proven track record of unbiased (or less biased) hiring is important if you want to get diversity right.

3. Interview them on how they calibrate with hiring managers, as this can tell you how well the recruiter will be able to find appropriate candidates. A recruiter who doesn't understand what you need will have a hard time finding good people.

General recommendation

For roles with titles held by only one person, such as a VP of Product, it makes sense to hire an external recruiter, as there isn't likely an existing pipeline of candidates. If that position is relatively senior, consider using an executive recruiter. In other cases, use a recruiter who is working on commission or on an hourly basis. For positions you constantly recruit for, such as a Junior Programmer, we recommend building internal expertise.

Calibration between hiring manager and recruiter

The most important aspect of the relationship between a recruiter (external or internal) and the hiring manager is *continuous calibration*. This means that the recruiter and the hiring manager are in regular contact to review the requirements for potential hires. If these two people are misaligned, you are likely to waste effort interviewing and rejecting candidates that don't fit the role. You can tell you need to work on calibration if you hear from interviewers that the interviews they are doing are not worth their time, and the quality of candidates is not good enough.

To align the hiring manager and the recruiter, you can use a calibration exercise, in which the recruiter prepares a list of 10–20 hypothetical candidates with different backgrounds, seniority levels, and strengths and weaknesses. The hiring manager and the recruiter then spend approximately one hour together, during which the hiring manager screens the CVs and explains to the recruiter why certain CVs are interesting and others are not. Usually, this helps both sides tremendously; the hiring manager often gains a clearer understanding of what they are looking for, which helps the recruiter do a better job of searching for and filtering candidates. Executive recruiters commonly use this technique at the beginning of a search to get a clearer understanding of the ideal candidate.

The first calibration exercise (finding 10–20 candidates with different backgrounds) requires significant effort, but after it's done, a weekly, in-person review of CVs by the recruiter and the hiring manager can efficiently keep them in sync. Instead of simply saying "yes" or "no" for each candidate, the hiring manager should try to understand where the recruiter was coming from so the two are in agreement about which qualities are important and can adjust their expectations. Best is to have the recruiter explain: "I said 'no' to this candidate because of X and Y, and I presented you this other candidate because I thought Z was interesting." Over time, the recruiter will get a better sense of what's attractive to the hiring manager. We recommend taking this approach for every open position.

When to hire an internal recruiter

The right time to hire an internal recruiter depends on a couple of factors: how much time hiring managers are spending on recruitment work, and your overall recruiting strategy. Look for these warning signs:

- The process of scheduling interviews, booking flights, and so on takes so much time that the team office assistant or a department lead spends most of their time arranging these details, and as a result ends up neglecting the tasks they were actually hired to do. Administrative arrangements like these can be delegated to a recruitment coordinator.

- The same is true for screening calls. At one company, there was only one person in engineering screening CVs and doing the initial calls with candidates. This took more than half of their time. Only after the company hired a recruiter was the original person able to focus on other tasks. You can delegate these calls to engineers, but without proper calibration, it might not end well. A well-calibrated recruiter, who does most of the screening work, can help here.

One full-time recruiter typically hires one to two candidates each month for companies with rigorous hiring standards and adequate organizational support for the recruiting effort. Assuming the same rate applies to a hiring manager, you can calculate the time it takes for a hiring manager to be successful in recruiting. In the first stages of building a recruitment team, it is very important to focus on the quality of the recruiter, and to make sure the recruiter and hiring manager maintain a very close relationship.

The right time to hire a recruitment coordinator depends on how long the team assistant, executive assistant, or hiring manager can deal with the work associated. An experienced and talented first hire can often act as both recruiter *and* coordinator for some time.

The First Recruiter

Erik Engstrom worked at SoundCloud with Alex and has been a great go-to person for recruitment questions that require deeper thinking. He believes that just as the first engineer/designer/product manager you hire sets the tone for the future of the team, the same is true for the first recruiter. Here is Erik's view on the preferred qualities of a first recruiter, in order of importance.

Strong emotional intelligence

Recruiting is the face of your company in the talent pool. You want a recruiter who understands people—someone you enjoy talking with, who you can have an interesting conversation with, who puts you at ease, who you look forward to working with. Someone thoughtful. If you feel that way about someone, it's very likely that candidates will as well. A recruiter is the only person that many people outside the company will communicate with—they represent your company to many talented and connected people. The recruiter's initial note of outreach may be thoughtful or a carbon-copy. A rejection letter may be constructive or tactless. An offer may be pleasant or tone-deaf. Your first recruiting hire will set the tone for your company's employer brand.

A promising candidate is more likely to successfully navigate the interview process if your recruiter preps them effectively, rather than leaving them completely in the dark. And a good deal of your ability to close a candidate, also, will come from your recruiter's relationship with the candidate (if they're thinking ahead, they will build one) and a solid understanding of their motivations. The recruiter should make sure to communicate how your company can fit into that person's plan, by enabling them to have conversations with the right people at the right time, and by being specific about things like role and compensation. A weak hiring manager might be oblivious to all of these factors. But a good recruiter, on the other hand, can be one of the main reasons that candidates join your team. Ask your new hires about their recruiter. Most people join a company despite their recruiter, but you can do better. Look for emotional intelligence first and foremost.

Organized and quick

The first recruiter may be expected to help with Engineering first, but will likely have 10 or more other roles to consider across the company very quickly. Their ability to prioritize and stay on top of communication is key.

Expertise with hiring process

In a typical startup, many people will be in roles where they are hiring for the first time and have no idea what they're doing. A recruiter should be the subject matter expert. They should be able to help establish best practices, understand startup equity and the business, know how to effectively present offers, push back on hiring managers who make candidates sit on the sidelines for months while they interview more and more candidates, help set up a comprehensive and unbiased interview process to make clear hiring decisions, pick an Applicant Tracking System, help develop criteria for evaluation, understand what motivates candidates and what candidates will say to a recruiter as opposed to a future boss or a founder (hint: it will be different things for all three scenarios), and more. Don't just hire someone who has "experience." Ask them about their thoughts on all of the above and anything additional that you are wondering about. Finally, don't base your first hire merely on the idea of someone being metrics-oriented. Your first recruiter won't have time for metrics, and you won't have enough data with one recruiter covering multiple roles to make any sense of it anyway.

Bonus: Ability to screen candidates

It's a major bonus if the recruiter can reduce work for the initial interviewers by screening the candidates. Recruiters who can do this usually are not screening for subject matter expertise, but other related predictors of success, such as the person's ability to talk through a complex project and their process and decisions with regard to business goals and outcomes. If you can offload the must-have hiring factors to your recruiter (strategic thinking, communication, etc.), you have a true winner.

Building an Employer Brand

You might think, "There are so many things to do—why should I invest in an employer brand?" But a strong brand can help you tremendously with recruiting. High-quality candidates are often motivated to apply by insightful posts on the company's blog. It can also boost retention; when you give your employees the opportunity to promote their work, either through public posts or conference appearances, it helps them build their careers and feel recognized for their work.

ENGINEERING/PRODUCT/DESIGN BLOG

If the nature of your business allows you to share internal stories, set up a blog to talk about them. Beyond the points just described, many candidates will read your posts to get an impression of your team culture, the technologies and methodologies you use, and so on. Just make sure you keep up a regular cadence of posts. A stale, outdated blog is a disadvantage when it comes to recruiting.

MEETUPS

Meetups are an easy way to connect to local candidates. If your office allows it, consider hosting meetups related to your business or to the technologies your team has chosen. The organizers are often very grateful for the space and will give you a few minutes to talk about your team and any relevant job openings. The costs of sponsoring meetups are very low compared to conferences and therefore a good way for smaller companies to gain some exposure. Finally, speaking at meetups about interesting things going on at your company can help motivate candidates to apply.

SPEAKING AT CONFERENCES

Speaking at conferences can give you a lot of publicity, assuming you choose the conferences wisely. Preparing a talk requires a lot of time, so letting your employees talk at irrelevant conferences makes no sense. Look for one of these two conditions before approving a conference talk:

- Do potential candidates visit the conference, and is the topic of the attendee's talk likely to be interesting to them?
- Are there talks or speakers the attendee can learn from?

In short, a conference has to be either a recruiting opportunity or a learning opportunity.

OPEN SOURCE CONTRIBUTIONS

Many engineers value the ability to contribute to open source software (OSS), especially if the company allows them to contribute during work time. But keep in mind the needs of your company's business before agreeing to open source your team's work. A reasonable policy is to encourage contributions during work time for OSS products used internally and to allow engineers to open source technologies that don't provide a competitive advantage. But keep in mind that an open source project requires ongoing maintenance and support. Simply dumping some code into a repository and then never updating it or accepting pull requests might end up damaging your engineering brand.

A Pragmatic Approach to Open Source

Kellan Elliott-McCrea is the former CTO of Etsy and a respected writer on engineering practice and culture. As one of the original authors of OAuth, he is passionate about the importance and power of the Open Web. Here is Kellan's view on how to approach open sourcing your company's software.

The ongoing maintenance requirements of company-sponsored open source projects are easy to underestimate. Your speed of response to pull requests becomes part of your public brand, as does the quality of the code, the language it is written in, and other factors. A GitHub repository of abandoned projects can be a warning sign for savvy prospective employees, especially if none of the contributors still work at the company.

Consider only open sourcing tools that can be useful to other teams *and* that you've had in production for a significant amount of time. You want to head off the energy that can be spent on designing a tool specifically to be open sourced rather than for your business needs. Additionally, you can write a much better blog post about a tool that has been in production for a considerable time, including some of the surprising ways it's failed and helped.

Don't be afraid to allow engineers to open source projects on their own, unrelated to your company. You should have a process by which engineers notify you of significant side projects, but these side projects should be encouraged and can be a good outlet for interests that would be disruptive at work.

Finally, when thinking about open source consider how you can support key projects that your company uses. While the initial prestige of pitching in on an existing project can be lower, an employee who has the blessing of his company to help improve infrastructure the company relies on will often rise to an influential and prominent role in the project.

Conclusion

Hiring great people is essential to building a great team. In this chapter, we've covered the key principles that underlie a scalable recruiting process, and the best ways of getting qualified candidates into your recruiting pipeline. The next step is to sort through the candidates, evaluate which ones best fit your needs, and make a hiring decision, all of which we will cover in Chapter 2, *Scaling Hiring: Interviews and Hiring Decisions*.

Additional Resources

- Tammy Han's "A Primer for Startups and Job Seekers to BOTH Win the Talent War" (*http://bit.ly/2gFpiBl*) gives advice to companies and candidates on how to make the right choices.

- In "Thoughts on Diversity Part 2. Why Diversity Is Difficult" (*http://bit.ly/2gFtPnw*), Leslie Miley reflects on his time at Twitter and the problems faced while trying to build a more diverse workforce.

- The Wikipedia entry for "Diversity (business)" (*http://bit.ly/2gFqGnL*) gives a good overview of the business advantages of diversity.

- Riley Newman and Elena Grewal's "Beginning with Ourselves—Using Data Science to Improve Diversity at Airbnb" (*http://bit.ly/2gFrnxe*) describes how Airbnb's Data Science team improved diversity using some of the techniques they are using for customers.

2

Scaling Hiring: Interviews and Hiring Decisions

This chapter continues our discussion of the hiring process, focusing on how to select the right new hire from a pool of candidates. These steps include interviewing, decision making (a vastly underrated part of the process), and reference checks (Figure 2-1).

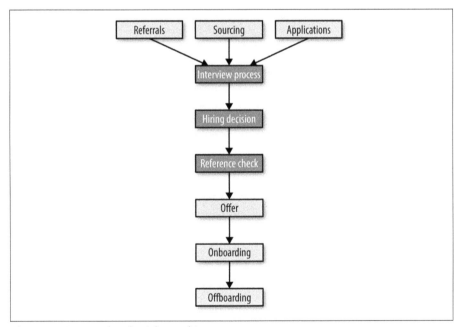

Figure 2-1. Steps to select the right new hire

As your company grows, you may notice these warning signs that your hiring process is not scaling:

- Negative feedback about the hiring process from candidates themselves. This can come from candidates who went through the same interview multiple times, encountered unprepared interviewers, or waded through general disorganization.

- Difficulty closing candidates due to delays in the offer process. When the management team doesn't trust the decision-making process, they may dig into details of the interview feedback and require additional interviews or reference checks before a final decision can be made.

- Veteran employees complain that the quality of new employees has decreased. This may indicate that your hiring process lacks rigor or is failing to scale with team growth.

- Your team lacks the diversity needed to be successful, and/or your candidate pipeline closely matches the demographics of the existing team members.

- Hiring managers bring on poorly qualified new hires because they are desperate for help. This can further erode upper management's trust in the hiring process.

In this chapter, we'll examine some useful techniques for solving these issues as you scale up your hiring process.

Interviewing

Once you've found candidates for the positions you're hoping to fill, the next step is to evaluate them. Figure 2-2 shows our recommended process. There are other approaches, such as skipping the challenge step and instead evaluating coding skills during the on-site interview, but what we've outlined has worked well for numerous technology companies.

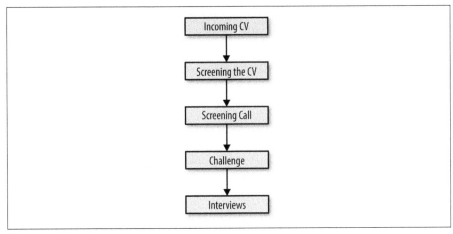

Figure 2-2. Interview process

SCREENING A CANDIDATE'S CV

Screening CVs is an imperfect science at best. For every guideline we propose here, we personally know candidates who failed to meet it but who performed well as employees anyway. Many junior candidates won't know the right format for a CV. And people switching careers may be coming from a background with different expectations about the right way to present themselves. So, use the guidelines below as suggestions and use feedback and evaluation to develop your instincts over time.

First, try to identify specific achievements. It doesn't say much if a candidate "was member of the X team, where we used Ruby." Prefer CVs that highlight specific accomplishments, such as, "Designed and implemented feature X, which positively impacted user satisfaction by N%."

Next, consider how long the candidate stayed at their previous companies. While we have absolutely no problem with people leaving some of their employers after just a short while, leaving *every* company after just a few months means the chances are slim that their tenure at your company will be any longer. We once screened a CV that showed the candidate left every company (and there were 10 of them) after exactly 2 years. Look for candidates who don't merely see the next job as another step in their career. You want candidates who choose their next company carefully, who try to find a good fit in the hopes of staying there for quite some time. (This is relative, however; typical employment durations in Silicon Valley, for example, tend to be much shorter than they are in, say, Denmark.)

Professional activities outside of the workplace demonstrate that a candidate is engaged in their profession. Check, for example, if the person has any public code contributions available, either on a GitHub profile or an open source platform. Look for past speaking appearances at conferences or meetups, and any online courses the person has taken. Continuing education (e.g., Coursera) indicates that candidates have an interest in learning new things. These details don't rule anybody in or out necessarily, since not everyone has the time or resources to participate in these activities—imagine a college student who has to work nights to support an ailing parent—but they may give you helpful perspective for those that do.

If the candidate is senior level, look carefully at their previous employers. If the candidate has worked a long time for an employer with a different culture, it might be difficult for them to adopt yours. Somebody who has worked for the last 20 years at a large multinational corporation might have a hard time adapting to a startup culture.

THE INITIAL SCREEN

When a person's CV interests you, the next step is to make sure it's worth it for both sides to invest the time for an on-site interview. This is obviously more important when the candidate has to be flown in from another location. The best way to accomplish this goal, assuming the person lives nearby, is to meet them in person. When that's not possible, the next best option is to hold a screening call.

Such in-person meetings and live screening calls are advantageous because they are high bandwidth—the screener can learn more in less time and can pick up on subtle cues that might otherwise be lost. But this format also allows bias to alter the process. There are a number of new online tools emerging that attempt to make the screen and practical challenge (described in the next section) more impartial by making the screener "blind" to the candidate while maintaining accurate evaluations. No specific approach has emerged as the clear winner, but readers may want to investigate these options in case one seems right for their team.

Becoming accurate and efficient in this step is critical for scalability. On-site interviews are expensive for your team as well as the applicant. The earlier either side realizes that it might be a bad fit, the more time everyone saves.

During a screening call, it's important to ask candidates about their timeline. Do they have outstanding offers? How soon do they plan to make a decision? If they are halfway through another interview process and eager to decide, you'll want to fast-track them. They won't always volunteer this info, but you can waste a lot of time or end up in a frenzy if you don't know what their situation is from the beginning.

Here are some things to watch out for during a screening call.

Preparation

Did the candidate do any research on your company? Candidates should come prepared. Even if they were approached by a recruiter, preparation on their side is a must. Start a conversation with, "What have you heard about our company so far? Do you have any questions?" The answers you get can reveal if somebody is truly interested. If the answer is something like, "Yeah, I think everything is good," it's a sign that person has not looked at your product and is not really passionate about it, nor motivated enough to do their research. Look for people who say things like, "Yeah, this is awesome, but please improve these features because then it will fill this need and these use cases for me." We like it when a candidate tells us about their ideas. That helps us say, "OK, this person is either already passionate about the product, or is using it and can become passionate about it."

Culture

The more experienced a candidate, the more they might be accustomed to other company cultures. Ask about the cultures and values at their previous employers, and what they liked or didn't like. Reflecting on this is very important. Great candidates who have a luxury of choice will sometimes make it a point to ask proactively about culture and explore the fit from that standpoint. For more information about how to interview for culture and values fit, see "Hiring, Values, and Culture" on page 181 in Chapter 9.

Job history

Always ask candidates why they left their previous jobs. Many candidates with a history of short-term positions have well-rehearsed stories about what happened (depending on the emotional intelligence of the screener, this may or may not be apparent, however). Ask what they're looking for in their next role. Many people won't be able to speak specifically about what they're looking for, and don't expect such a question. You can find out a lot about their interest and what's currently not working for them by asking this question.

Knowledge and fit

Your first screening call should reveal whether the candidate is a good culture and values fit for the team and whether they meet the minimum requirements of the job. Sometimes a single screen is sufficient, but you can certainly do more. Multiple screens (ideally scheduled back-to-back to make it easier on the candidate) can be a good way to train new interviewers without having them be the sole data point prior to an on-site interview. If the person doing the screening is a subject matter expert, they can also ask questions that reveal the candidate's depth of knowledge.

Regardless, continue until both sides have substantial interest in working together and it is worth the time to do a practical challenge. Once the screening is complete, a recruiter can exclude any details about gender, race, or anything else in conversations about the candidate to help reduce bias.

PRACTICAL CHALLENGE

What will the candidate be doing all day if they are hired? An engineer, for example, writes code, and you want to see concrete examples of that work. Failure to verify a possible hire's abilities would be a major oversight in the hiring process.

Several approaches exist for verifying abilities:

- Send candidates a *challenge* they can work on at home. This mirrors normal working conditions as the candidate can use any resources they need to solve the challenge—web search, reference manuals, online tutorials, and so on. We recommend establishing a time limit; you'll receive fewer replies when there is no time limit. Also, consider asking probing questions about their solution during on-site interviews to confirm they actually did the challenge, and to find out how they react to constructive critique.

- Challenges can also be done on-site. The advantage is that it's easier to verify that they completed the challenge on their own, and you can evaluate their ability to collaborate with another engineer.

- If some public contributions are available (in the case of an engineer, open source code, for example), you can skip the practical tests and look over the code and how they communicate in issues and pull requests yourself. For a designer, you might look at products they designed that are publicly accessible.

Reduce bias by having reviewers evaluate the practical challenge either without a CV or with an anonymized CV. Recruiters can help anonymize a CV and make sure that the hiring process contains as little bias as possible.

Advice on Challenges

Kellan Elliott-McCrea is the former CTO of Etsy and a respected writer on engineering practice and culture. As one of the original authors of OAuth, he is passionate about the importance and power of the Open Web. Here is Kellan's view on how to approach practical challenges in your interview process.

If you give a practical challenge, make sure you communicate expectations that the effort the candidate spends on it will be time-bounded (e.g., "Don't spend more than four hours on this"). Explain why you chose this challenge (e.g., "This is a simplified version of a key scaling challenge we have," or, "We think this challenge allows us to evaluate candidates on the key skills we use every day, including X"). Make the criteria clear: don't tell candidates that they can choose any language and then mark them down for not choosing your preferred language. If you tell them it must be language X, don't mark them down for not writing idiomatic X, unless that's what you value in your company and you don't think you can teach it. If you're going to evaluate whether the challenge comes with unit or integration tests, then tell the candidate that.

Finally, asking a candidate to commit to doing a challenge means you are committing as the interviewing company to evaluating the work they produce. Great candidates who choose to do the challenge will want to talk to people about their solution and will be disappointed if no one is interested in talking about it.

INTERVIEW STRUCTURE

According to Google, using too many interviewers in the hiring process leads to diminishing returns. Google's research found that, after the fourth interview, each additional interview only increased their "decision accuracy" by a mere 1 percent: "In other words, after four interviews the incremental cost of conducting additional interviews outweighs the value the additional feedback contributes to the ultimate hiring decision."[1] This research is most applicable to your company if you already have well-structured interviews.

The risk, though, of having "only" four to five interviews is that it can lead other employees to feel excluded from hiring decisions. A lunch session with more team members can increase inclusion at a lower cost, but may also cause more stress for the candidate.

Another option for including more people is to interview candidates in pairs, but this strategy can also add stress to the process for the interviewee.

The Same Interview Five Times: A Story from Alex

As the head of engineering at SoundCloud, I was always the last person to interview a candidate. Interviewing every candidate could have easily taken all of my time. I started interviewing last so I didn't have to interview candidates who'd already gotten negative feedback. An additional benefit was that I could get feedback from the candidate about the interview process so far.

In the beginning (until we had around 30 engineers), this seemed to work fine, but at a certain point, I started to notice a trend in the feedback: "It was nice, but I basically had the same interview five times." When the company was smaller, interviewers aligned with one another about who should focus on what; during hyper-growth (a phase where we tripled within a year), this informal alignment got lost.

We agreed to limit the number of interviews so as to avoid overloading the candidate and to spend less time on interviews that had questionable gains. Additionally, we started structuring the interviews, so that each interviewer covered different topics. The result was that our hiring process was just as accurate in identifying great candidates with significantly less effort.

---

1 "Google's 11-Step Guide to Interviewing" (*http://on.inc.com/2gS5spL*), *Inc.* magazine, October 17, 2014.

Personal involvement by senior leaders

During times of hyper-growth, senior leaders such as founders or department heads can easily spend 50% of their time on recruiting. The time investment is usually worth it given the importance of hiring the right people for the team.

So, in the beginning, it's quite appropriate to personally interview every candidate so you can get an overview of the whole hiring process, make sure the right people are being hired, and figure out who among your reports are the best interviewers. But your ultimate goal should be to create a hiring process that could work *without* you.

Choosing the interview panel

Usually, you can identify good interviewers during *hiring syncs*, meetings in which you discuss feedback and coordinate expectations (see "How to Gather and Discuss Feedback" on page 36). You may be surprised to find that there are people who say "thumbs up" or "thumbs down" to every candidate. Others give only superficial feedback. It won't take long to identify those who give thorough feedback and understand the situation the candidate is in, while continuing to hold a high bar.

To make sure you have a breadth of perspectives when interviewing, choose interviewers at different levels of seniority, who come from different teams. This is especially important in engineering departments where engineers usually switch teams often, and therefore hires need to fit to the whole department and not just a specific team. To strengthen diversity, make sure that the interview panel is as diverse as possible (but beware of burnout; if you only have one woman on staff, for example, she could end up on *a lot* of panels).

Choose one of the decision-making processes we outline later in this chapter. Make sure to revisit the hiring syncs from time to time, in order to make sure everything works well. But once you feel things are running smoothly, you should be able to leave the job of reinforcing the process to recruiters and members of your organization. In the end, you should only have to interview managers and senior candidates. If your company grows slowly, the approach we've outlined can be introduced slowly as well.

Ensuring interviews are complete

To avoid the "same interview five times" feedback and ensure all necessary topics are covered, define which areas are the most important ones for your organization and assign these to specific interviewers in each panel. This step should be the responsibility of the hiring manager, though an experienced recruiter can help out if needed.

To ensure interviewers have sufficient context to evaluate candidates and there is no duplication of focus areas, consider having hiring managers hold a "pre-brief" before each interview. This is particularly helpful at the beginning of rapid growth when team members are less familiar with the hiring process. For small teams, this preparation step could be part of a regular staff meeting or standup. For larger teams, an email to the interview panel is more efficient. The typical structure of the pre-brief consists of context on the candidate (how you found the person), what role and seniority level you are trying to fill, and the assignment of specific areas of focus for each interviewer. Here is a (far from complete) list of potential topics and questions. Obviously, you should customize this to the requirements of the role you're trying to fill.

For engineering candidates and those with specific technical skills:

- Computer Science 101 (data structures, algorithms, order of complexity, etc.)
- Architecture (availability, horizontal versus vertical scaling, etc.)
- Problem solving (approach to problem diagnosis and resolution)

For design candidates:

- Taste/eye (influences, aesthetics)
- Product thinking (process, problem solving, prioritization, working against goals, success metrics, etc.)
- Team (collaboration with Engineering and Product)

For everyone, communication skills and values fit:

- When pairing on a practical challenge, see how candidates respond to critique
- Ask, "What would you do differently if you could do project X again?" Can the candidate reflect on what went well and what didn't? Are they able to learn from the experience? If someone answers that they would do nothing differently, then this means their project went perfectly, which never happens.

- Ask, "What was your favorite project/least favorite project so far, and why?" General questions like this can help reveal what the candidate is passionate about and what they want to avoid, which may or may not be a fit with what your team needs. You should also look for whether they can reflect on their work and learn from it.

For more details on how to interview for values fit, see "Hiring, Values, and Culture" on page 181 in Chapter 9.

HOW TO HIRE MANAGERS

The recommended process for hiring managers shares many core elements with the process for individual contributors, but there are a few subtle differences. This topic is covered in detail in "Hiring Managers Externally" on page 83 in Chapter 4.

Making a Hiring Decision

Do you hire for the company or for a single team? Hiring is undoubtedly one of the most important things a manager does to build a team and an organization. At the end of any hiring process, a decision has to be made, and how it is made can make or break the whole process. There are several well-known approaches, each of which has pros and cons. An effective hiring process satisfies the following objectives:

- Confirms that a candidate's skill set is a fit
- Ensures that a candidate is a culture and values match
- Gathers thorough feedback to create a comprehensive view of each candidate
- Ensures that everyone involved in the hiring process is heard
- Avoids hiring for the wrong reasons: desperation, favoritism, or otherwise

The ultimate goal of any hiring process is to maximize the probability that a new hire will be a successful, long-term contributor to the team. In the following sections, we describe the advantages and disadvantages of common approaches to the hiring decision process.

FULLY ACCOUNTABLE HIRING MANAGER

In this model, the hiring manager makes the final hiring decision, and is fully accountable for it. Although the hiring manager takes interviewers' feedback into consideration, they can veto a majority vote.

The advantage to a hiring manager is that accountability for the hiring decision is clear. If the interviewers inconsistently vet a candidate's qualifications, the hiring manager can eliminate feedback that is based on irrelevant hiring criteria and extend an offer anyway. When many people are involved in the interviewing process, the hiring manager can break the tie to make a quick decision. Experienced managers who feel strongly about a candidate for some reason (perhaps a trusted referral, their gut instinct, or strong qualifications), or who simply want to take on a "flyer," have the flexibility to override the panel, knowing that they are on the hook for the success or failure of the candidate.

But there are disadvantages to this approach. Sometimes the needs of the manager and the organization are misaligned, leading them to hire a candidate for the wrong reasons. This might occur, for example, when the manager is a recent hire, or when the manager is under extreme pressure to expand the team.

Or worse, when hiring managers override their interviewers, they are basically saying they don't trust the panel's decision making, which is a message the interviewers carry with them to the rest of their jobs. Additionally, it is possible for the hiring manager to make a decision out of desperation, which is more likely for an individual than it is for a group.

HIGH-RANKING HIRING MANAGER

There is a pattern we've seen in quite a few companies where, say, the VP of Engineering hires all the engineers and then assigns them to different groups—basically, one person does all the hiring, but the hired candidates then report to other managers. The process can be really fast, as only one person is responsible for making a hiring decision, and it can be done after just one interview.

But the hiring manager may not understand the actual needs, skill pool, and culture of the team for which they are hiring. The actual manager faces unnecessary surprises that can negatively affect resource planning and cause tension within the team. This can indicate trust issues—one person thinks they're the only one qualified to hire new people and cannot delegate, so they just hire people and assign them to teams.

This is a flawed approach. If the high-ranking hiring manager does not understand the culture of the team for which they're hiring, the team may be really surprised by their new candidate's working style. We have seen a manager come to work and say, "Hey, here's your new hire from yesterday's interviews." It's very difficult for a candidate to report to a person who didn't hire them, as the candidate has no established relationship with their new manager, and can end up feeling pretty detached from what their new team is actually doing.

CONSENSUS

The interview panel, which includes the hiring manager and any technical experts, reaches an agreement; the interviewers, either unanimously or by majority, agree to the hiring decision.

The advantage is that multiple interviewers have discussed and reached agreement on the hiring decision. For example, sometimes an individual who is unconvinced that someone is a good fit will trust their coworkers' decision after hearing their feedback. And several of the candidate's future peers get to meet the candidate before they join the team, so there are no surprises. This strategy allows the team to self-manage. By following this approach, the team better understands their own needs, as opposed to having someone impose things upon them.

There are disadvantages to the consensus approach. If one or more interviewers are unsure about what kind of talent the organization is looking for, the feedback criteria may be inconsistent. And it can be difficult to come to an agreement if a lot of interviews take place. When compared to other strategies, there is a higher probability that politics and personal relationships will adversely affect a decision to hire or not hire a candidate.

HIRING COMMITTEE

Google is the company perhaps most responsible for spreading the hiring committee model. This is how Google explains their approach: "An independent committee of Googlers review[s] feedback from all of the interviewers. This committee is responsible for ensuring our hiring process is fair and that we're holding true to our 'good for Google' standards as we grow."[2]

What is the difference between this strategy and one where the interviewers reach agreement by majority? Most significantly, the hiring committee does not interview the candidate. Instead, it relies on written feedback from the panel, and

---

2 Google, "How We Hire," *https://www.google.com/about/careers/how-we-hire/*.

provides feedback to the interviewers if the written feedback is not clear enough to make a decision or is otherwise flawed in their judgment.

Don Dodge (a Developer Advocate at Google) explains:

> Hiring decisions are made by hiring committees. This means that no single hiring manager can make a potentially bad decision by themselves. This doesn't guarantee 100% success, but it does reduce bad decisions. There must be consensus that the candidate is a great hire. Doesn't this slow down the process? Not really, in fact the process ensures that candidate status is reviewed by the committee every week. There is no opportunity for the hiring decision to get delayed by personal deadlines for other work. The consensus approach avoids 'blind spots' or biases by an individual hiring manager, and results in better hiring decisions. Candidates are compared across several groups to make sure the acceptance criteria remain high.[3]

Former Google employee Piaw Na writes anecdotally, "When the committee found feedback on hiring to be ambiguous, it would assign another interview to an engineer well-known to be decisive [...] many people dislike rejecting people, and occasionally, someone would write feedback that wasn't really informative enough."[4]

The advantage of a hiring committee is that the chance of a single person making a poor hiring decision is significantly reduced. Through the fact that a hiring committee is responsible for a lot of groups, the acceptance criteria for hiring a candidate is broadly applied. The hiring committee can also send feedback to the panel members about the quality of their interview questions and write-ups, hopefully improving them over time.

But there are also disadvantages to this approach. The members of the hiring committee rely only on written feedback, which can be incomplete or misleading and the candidate's future team is not in control of the hiring process, and thus cannot ensure that there is a cultural fit with the candidate. A hiring committee can also introduce a delay, as the decision can't be made until the next hiring committee review.

---

3 Don Dodge, "How to Get a Job at Google, Interview Questions, Hiring Process" (*http://bit.ly/2gSdYET*) September 14, 2010.

4 Piaw Na, "Hiring Committee Stories" (*http://bit.ly/2gS71nt*), April 5, 2010.

BAR RAISERS

Amazon uses what they call *bar raisers* in the hiring process. Bar raisers play a special role to help ensure that good hiring decisions are made. As Ivan Gevirtz explains, "The bar raisers had generally been at Amazon long enough to know what the corporate values and culture [were] like, and generally were the best employees in terms of productivity, inventiveness, and technical acumen. And they were authorized to spend up to 25% of their time on recruiting. [...] Amazon felt that making good hiring decisions was the most important thing the company needed to do successfully. Every employee hired was required to interview with a bar raiser from another team. And hiring decisions had to be unanimous."[5]

Including a bar raiser in the process has the advantage that someone who knows the requirements of the organization is always part of the hiring decision. Chosen wisely, bar raisers have a proven track record of making good hiring decisions.

There is one concern about having bar raisers: top-performing employees can end up committing a sizeable percentage of their time participating in interviews (like the 25% Amazon allowed) rather than working on projects. In the long term, the benefits gained by such a rigorous vetting process can be positive for the team and the company. In the short term, however, this can be really burdensome. And it can become worse if the same few people remain involved in interviews for a sustained period as the company continues to grow. The time commitment is worth considering.

Choosing a Process That Works for You

There are a lot of different approaches to hiring and interviewing, and no clear-cut winner for every organization. There is pretty convincing data that having more than one person involved in the decision-making process results in better hires, but we haven't seen any data indicating that total agreement between the interviewers is better or worse than hiring by committee.

While other departments tend to have a clear-cut hiring manager, for engineering departments, for example, this isn't always true. In one former situation, one of our goals was to find a common approach for engineering/design/product and other departments alike.

---

5 Ivan Gevirtz, "The Most Important Thing" (*http://bit.ly/2gSf5o3*) October 11, 2005.

We agreed on the following core concepts (which is basically the "interviewers reach agreement" approach combined with a bar raiser):

- Interviewers are all either decision makers or advisors. The decision makers' votes have to be unanimous, and any single decision maker can veto a hire. Advisors are heard, but have no veto ability.

- The bar raiser is always a decision maker, and is usually a senior employee from a group not directly involved in hiring the candidate.

Usually, everybody is a decision maker, but there are some exceptions, such as employees doing their first interviews. And interviews for high-level positions (VP of Engineering, for example) often include so many interviewers that giving each one a decision maker role would make consensus nearly impossible.

How you make a hiring decision can seriously impact your organization. This wise principle applies: as a senior leader, rather than make every hiring decision, install a process that ensures good decisions are made.

HOW TO GATHER AND DISCUSS FEEDBACK

A common problem in discussing interview feedback is that the highest-ranking interviewers tend to speak first, and their opinions can influence the feedback of the rest of the group. Not everybody is comfortable disagreeing with their boss openly. To avoid letting interviewers influence one another, follow these two suggestions:

- Ask interviewers to write up their feedback about the candidate before discussing it with the other interviewers.

- Let the highest-ranking interviewer speak last, so that person's authority isn't a factor in anyone's feelings about the candidate.

Set up a hiring sync in which the interviewers discuss everyone's feedback and make a decision. This approach lets people learn how a more experienced interviewer approaches an interview. By discussing candidates, you can align the team's expectations and approaches. This also enables the hiring manager to see who is a good interviewer. And knowing their feedback will be read or heard by their peers encourages interviewers to do a thorough job.

ADDRESSING DIVERSITY

You should work on minimizing all forms of bias throughout the process, from the initial review of candidates through to hiring and on-boarding.Try to establish a transparent, consistent interview process in order to:

- Mitigate the fast-tracking of referrals, making sure that referrals are interviewed consistently with other candidates and not given preferential treatment.

- Ensure referral feedback is incorporated appropriately, as another data point but not as an override for any interviewer concerns.

- Make sure job postings are inclusive and avoid biased language. One option is to ask underrepresented groups internally to review job descriptions before they go live. The editing process can help recruiting/leadership learn some of the basics about what is considered neutral and attractive to a wider talent pool. Because this might prove to be a burden (see "Don't focus the burden of diversity on your "diverse" team members" on page 104 in Chapter 5), consider using an online tool like Textio before asking employees to review.

- Regularly remind the team to be aware of unconscious bias before they leave feedback, and call out stereotypical evaluation/feedback not based on merits but rather on differences (i.e., "lack of presence" for female candidates, "communication skills" for underrepresented minorities, etc.). To create awareness, we recommend you conduct an unconscious bias training with recruiters and hiring managers.

A recruiter with strong EQ and experience running high-quality, rigorous interview processes will do a lot of these things naturally, but it is also a good idea to bring someone in who specializes in this area to take a look at your process early on before you develop bad habits. A headcount policy, for example— wherein each manager has a certain number of reports and wants to *maintain* that number—can cause teams to focus only on candidates with more experience. Because many underrepresented groups make up an even smaller percentage of senior candidates, consider taking headcount out of the equation. If your overall headcount allows some flexibility, you can state that new hires with less overall experience and from an underrepresented group don't count against the headcount of that specific team.

For additional information about removing bias, have a look at Facebook's anti-bias program (*https://managingbias.fb.com/*) and Project Include (*http://projec tinclude.org*).

REFERENCE CHECKS

Every minute devoted to putting the proper person in the proper slot is worth weeks of time later.

—JIM COLLINS, *GOOD TO GREAT*

Reference checks are basically the validation of your internal process and an important chance to catch problems before they slip through. To see if your impression of a candidate matches their performance at a previous job, you must talk to their former coworkers. This is usually the last step of the interview process; references are usually busy people, so it's important to only interrupt them once it becomes truly necessary. Reference checks should be mandatory for managers but can be optional for individual contributors.

Be aware that candidates tend to list people who will speak positively about them. Try to get a 360-degree view by asking the candidate for references from people who worked above them, alongside them, and beneath them (if applicable).

Don't try to merely confirm your impression of the candidate by asking leading or shallow questions. As one colleague described, "The typical call I get lasts five minutes with the reference checker basically saying, 'We adore this candidate. You love 'em, too, right?' They make the call hoping I won't say anything that will cause concern about the candidate which would throttle their company back to square one of the hiring process." Instead, clearly explain the position you're hiring for to the reference and then ask concrete questions, such as: "Do you think X is a good candidate for this position?" and "Why is X no longer with the company?" This is also a good opportunity to inquire about any concerns or "yellow flags" raised by interviewers during the hiring sync.

Prefer to talk to references over the phone when you have the opportunity; people are often less open when asked to respond in writing (for legal reasons or otherwise). Be aware, however, of country-specific legal requirements (in Germany, for example, a written reference has to be benevolent).

It's likely that speaking to references will confirm your hiring decision. But what happens if the references raise concerns? What if they were negative about the candidate's fit for the role? We recommend discussing the results of the reference calls with the other decision makers in your hiring process so the group can then decide whether or not to change their decision.

Conclusion

In this chapter, we described how to select the right candidates from your pipeline and build a scalable approach to making a hiring decision. By testing candidates thoroughly, making decisions with as little bias as possible, and emphasizing the candidate's fit with company values, you will be able to build a strong team. After choosing the right candidates, you still need to convince them to join by making the right offer. Chapter 3, *Scaling Hiring: How to Close, On-Board, and Beyond* explains how to convince candidates to accept your offer and how to on-board them once they join the company.

Additional Resources

- Hcareers.com's "Checking References: Top 10 Questions to Ask" (*http://bit.ly/2gSeD9u*) gives detailed advice on how to do reference checking.

- Facebook published the videos of its internal anti-bias training (*https://managingbias.fb.com*).

- Y-Vonne Hutchinson's "Biased by Design" (*http://bit.ly/2gS9LRE*) shows how exclusion hurts tech companies.

3

Scaling Hiring: How to Close, On-Board, and Beyond

You've interviewed a great candidate and decided to make them an offer to join your team. Successfully closing a new hire, especially in a competitive market, requires a clear and compelling offer, presented the right way. It's important that you:

- Make sure the candidate understands their future role at the company.

- Set clear expectations for the candidate's first few months at the company.

- Make sure the candidate understands the financial aspects of the offer, especially any elements beyond the base salary. Bonuses and equity can be very difficult to understand, and candidates will appreciate any clarity you can provide.

If you're successful in convincing a candidate to join your team, the next step is to on-board them. *On-boarding* is the process of providing your new hires with the detailed knowledge they need to be a happy and productive employee, and is often an overlooked part of the hiring process.

In addition to closing and on-boarding we will also cover *off-boarding*, which, when done well, provides a great opportunity to improve your hiring process and your work environment (Figure 3-1). We will also cover *acqui-hires*, as there are some important considerations to address when merging an entire team into your own.

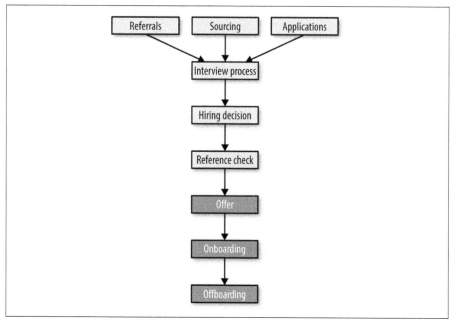

Figure 3-1. The part of the hiring process covered in this chapter

Making an Offer

Preparing and presenting an offer is one of the most critical yet subtle steps in the hiring process. You are asking someone to make a major change in their life, and therefore they will likely scrutinize every detail of the offer and how it was presented before making a final decision.

To that point, it's quite important who actually *presents* the job offer to the candidate. A common anti-pattern is having a hiring manager contact candidates and lead them through the hiring process, but then have somebody else, often the recruiter or someone in HR, make the offer. This can be a strange experience for candidates. At a very crucial moment, after lengthy discussions with the hiring manager about their next career move, somebody else takes over the process —a person they don't know who might not be aware of all the conversations the hiring manager previously had with the candidate. In our experience, the closing rate is much higher when the same person leads a candidate all the way through the process. Likewise, when a recruiter leads a candidate through the process, they should at least be involved in presenting the offer (see the following sidebar).

Full-Cycle Recruiting: A Story from Erik Engstrom

Note: This story only applies when you have a recruiter on staff.

Full-cycle recruiting is a process that starts from sourcing a candidate, screening, leading them through the interview process, and making the offer. The idea behind it is that the more time you spend with a candidate, the more trust you can develop, and the more you know about what that person is looking for in terms of their next step.

The key thing here is to avoid handing the candidate off from one person to the next, as information and trust can be lost in the process. Usually, a recruiter should lead the candidate all the way through the process, including making the offer. The hiring manager can certainly be involved, but while the hiring manager can explain the concrete role and the technical challenges better, a recruiter understands the soft aspects of an offer better. Quite a lot of offers have been rejected because the hiring manager struggled to explain the equity part of an offer, or was too busy to spend enough time with the candidate to ask about competing offers, make a case against them, find out what the person was looking for in their next role (specific types of projects, better work–life balance, a great team, leadership possibilities, etc.), explain the company culture and vision and benefits, walk through monetization strategy, and so on.

One additional aspect here is that a tough salary negotiation with the hiring manager might be a bad start to their relationship. Especially with regard to compensation or other soft factors (work–life balance, working remotely, better work hours to accommodate young families), candidates are instinctively more conservative with their future boss about bringing up what was lacking in their past role and what they hope will be different in their new role, for fear that they'll look less passionate or dedicated.

Hiring managers, typically, should not be involved in compensation negotiations, for several reasons. They may know less about negotiation. They may not have visibility into salaries on other teams, which can cause them to throw off compensation for similar roles across the company, something that can have disastrous consequences very quickly. With regard to cash, a new hire will often be compensated equally or less than their direct reports at certain stages of growth if they joined a small team early (low salary, high equity, high responsibility). This is because new hires receive much less equity and, in certain cases, more cash, so their offers remain competitive in the market.

At larger companies, HR should have a compensation specialist looking into compensation across the company, establishing standards and adjusting them quarterly to maintain internal equity among employees at the company, as well as to stay competitive in the market. A hiring manager's instinct is to use their own salary as the upper limit for their own team's compensation, which may not necessarily be the best point of reference depending on when and for what they were hired. Compensation standards, then, should be set by someone else.

CLOSING

You can safely assume that once you find a great candidate and are about to make an offer, there will be competing offers from other companies. Here's some advice on how to make sure that the candidate actually accepts your offer.

Start by getting to know the candidate during the interview and finding out what they care most about. Is it their manager, the team, cash compensation, equity, title, or something else? Design the offer according to those priorities. Be ready to adjust the offer if needed (within reason). And you must move quickly: some candidates can be lost when they have time to talk to other companies. Other candidates are in a hurry, maybe because of a competing offer that's about to expire. Keep informed of such factors (ask the candidate!) and accelerate the process if needed. Make it a point to stay in touch. *Recency bias* definitely exists, and candidates are more likely to accept an offer from their most recent interview. Be aware of consistency, and don't hand the candidate from person to person, except to escalate. And follow up quickly after escalation by specifically asking, "How did your conversation with the CEO go?"

Of course, one of the most significant parts of the offer is the compensation package. Although many companies are cash-sensitive, especially early on, we don't recommend trying to lowball the candidate. Make the first offer a fair one, and communicate this, along with your thought process that went into the numbers. Don't rely on the possibility of additional requests to up the offer—a substantial percentage of candidates don't like to negotiate, and for them the first offer is the final one. If they do negotiate, try to avoid a lengthy back-and-forth process by asking them to provide you the numbers that they will definitely sign.

You may not be able to match them, but better to know this sooner rather than later.

Especially important during this process is to *create meaning*. Often a meaningful job with a lower salary will be chosen over a less meaningful job with a higher salary. Your effort to get to know the candidate earlier in the process will help you know what is meaningful to them. It could be potential career progression, challenging work, wider impact, or something else. Outline how the role can progress through the company (only if you know it actually can). What challenges will the role be tackling? How does the company as a whole, and that role in particular, make a difference in the world? These are all aspects of a role that can convince a candidate to choose your offer over others.

Finally, make the offer clear and understandable. Try to be as open as possible about the financial aspects of the offer—equity in the form of stock options or stock units, in particular, is often poorly explained. The company eShares has a fantastic offer letter (*http://bit.ly/2gSqDrq*) that clearly lays out its approach to compensation and provides guidance on how to think about the future value of the equity grant.

Later, as more layers of management are introduced, there are two additional things you'll need to do: educate hiring managers on techniques to use in closing, and establish guidelines on how to escalate to senior leaders when needed. There's a saying in sales: "Always be closing." It's relevant to hiring as well. Every step of the process should be geared toward increasing the candidate's desire to work for your company, whether you decide to make an offer or not. Even a candidate you decide not to hire may still refer their colleagues to your company—but only if they had a positive recruiting experience.

Follow the advice in "Matching compensation to job levels" on page 110 to make sure you make a fair offer and minimize bias.

Acqui-Hires

Another way to hire more people is an *acqui-hire*. In many cases, this is the only method to achieve significant growth in a short time, though it can be both costly and risky. In a normal acquisition, you buy a company for its products and/or services. In an acqui-hire, you do so to recruit its employees, but not to continue the operation of its product.[1]

---

1 For more on this, see Miguel Helft's *New York Times* article "For Buyers of Web Start-Ups, Quest to Corral Young Talent" (*http://nyti.ms/2gSctGW*), May 17, 2011.

There have been many successful acqui-hires, but failures are also common. A frequent failure pattern occurs when companies don't pay attention to whether the culture of the acquired company is compatible with their own.

Let's say BigCo decides it wants to acqui-hire SmallCo. BigCo has a clear business model and its employees are focused on delivering business value within that model. The SmallCo team, on the other hand, is driven more by passion for their product than by business sense. Despite the mismatch, the deal goes through but integrating the teams proves difficult. One year later, most of the staff of SmallCo has left, only making it that long thanks to a retention bonus.

ACQUI-HIRE ANTI-PATTERNS

The most important concerns in an acqui-hire are actually the same as with normal hiring. You have to ask: are the potential employees motivated to work in your company? And are they a good fit in terms of talents, skills, culture, and values?

When an acqui-hire fails, it's often because these basic assumptions were not carefully considered. Leaders at the acquiring company may have been too focused on closing a deal, or investors in the acquired company were overly eager to facilitate a "face-saving" exit.[2]

Here we list a few anti-patterns we have seen so far:

Interviewing only the founders

By not putting all the acquired employees through your standard interview process (assuming you acquire the company for more than just one or two specific people), you risk bringing on employees that don't match your team's talent standards. This will lead to costly performance and morale issues down the line, undermining the value of the acquisition.

Assuming interest

A comprehensive interview process can also confirm that the acquired team (beyond the founders) actually wants to work within your company, and make sure that the values and cultures of the two teams are compatible. When a large company acquires a much smaller one there are often many cultural differences, but if the teams share the same values you have

---

2 Liz Gannes, "The Vanity of the "Acqhire": Why Do a Deal That Makes No Sense?" (*http://bit.ly/2gtm9Ec*), All Things D, August 10, 2012.

a much higher chance that the acquired team can adjust to the new culture. For a deeper discussion of values and culture, see Chapter 9.

Assuming founder retention

It's very common for the founders of an acquired company to leave as soon as they reasonably can. Entrepreneurs often don't like being employees, and are eager to start working on their next venture. So if the founders are a key reason for making the acquisition, make sure you consider the best way to retain them, whether through vesting cliffs, retention bonuses, or a motivating work assignment.

Bait and switch

You or someone in corporate development paint an unrealistic picture of life at the new company ("We will absolutely use your technology!"), leading to a morale hit after on-boarding. This happens when an acquisition is presented as a products-and-services acquisition, but is in reality an acqui-hire. Don't oversell the new situation.

Dispersing the acquired team without announcement

The acquired team, which is accustomed to working together and expects to remain that way, instead gets distributed without preparation into many existing teams of the acquiring company. This means new jobs for everyone—potentially jobs they did not interview for. This creates a high likelihood of turnover.

None of these are guaranteed to lead to failure, but in our experience they increase the chance that the acqui-hire will not provide the desired growth in staff or productivity.

David's Acqui-Hire Experience

In 2003, Blue Mug, a small consulting company I had cofounded, was acqui-hired by Amazon.com. In discussing the integration plan, we argued strongly that our team should stay together, to take advantage of our close working relationships and our knowledge of each other's talents. But Amazon argued even more strongly that dispersing acquired teams had benefits, citing in particular their prior experience acquiring the 30-person Geoworks Seattle engineering team. The deal sponsor told me that once dispersed throughout engineering, the tight-knit Geoworks team (later dubbed the "Geoworks Mafia") acted as a sort of communications backplane across the organization, allowing ideas and techniques to flow more efficiently between teams than they would otherwise. For this reason, they did the same with the Blue Mug team. With this explanation in place, the integration went smoothly. There was no backlash, and we noticed a similarly positive effect.

MAKING AN ACQUI-HIRE THE RIGHT WAY

Here are the steps to take to ensure you're making acqui-hires the right way:

- Interview *all* the employees so you can get a good impression of the complete team. To make the acquisition worth it, a large majority of the team should make it through the standard interview process you use for individual candidates.

- Get an impression of whether or not your company is interesting to the other company's team. Talk about upcoming projects and current challenges and see if they get excited.

- Discuss how the existing products and services of the acquired company will be handled. The acquirer wants to minimize the effort required, but it is often hard to simply revoke support or turn off services without angering customers or partners. This could harm the reputation of the acquirer and the morale of the acquired team.

- Find a good balance between keeping the team together versus distributing them all over the company.

The real work starts after the acquisition

We have seen many acquisitions where people high-fived each other after the deal was done because they thought the hard work was behind them. In reality, most of the work happens after the paperwork is signed. It's important to on-board the acquired employees the same way as those you hire through normal channels. Assign buddies who can help them get accustomed to the new company. And make sure you don't discourage the acquired employees from maintaining their sense of "our team," even if they have been dispersed into different groups. You don't need to encourage it, either—just recognize that this is a big transition, so it's natural for them to stick close to the people they know. Over time, if there is a good fit, their sense of "our team" will shift from the acquired one to their new ones.

An Acqui-Hire Success Story

In 2009, Nokia acquired a company called bit-side. The acquisition was successful, presumably because bit-side was a professional services and software company with nearly half of its staff already supporting projects at Nokia and enjoying their work. So for nearly 50% of the employees, it was already clear that they'd like the company culture and the actual work. Acquiring the company was a straightforward move.

Evaluating Your Hiring Process

An important technique in building a scalable hiring process is to use data to understand how well it is working. Many companies rely on just a few simplistic metrics, like the median time to fill an open position. Because the process can break down at any stage and the underlying reasons may not be obvious, you need to take a more detailed look, such as:

- Median time between first contact and offer, and for each stage of the process in between
- Most common reasons given for not accepting an offer
- Percentage of new hires by source (referral, organic, recruiter)
- Percentage of candidates that make it through each stage of the pipeline, particularly percentage of on-sites that receive offers (since this is such an expensive step)

And because new hires that don't stay at the company are so costly, we recommend taking a holistic view and analyzing the full lifecycle of the employee:

- Surveys of new hires about their candidate experience
- Performance data on how new hires are doing 6 and/or 12 months after their start date
- Percentage of employees who refer candidates, and median number of referrals

- Regretted versus non-regretted attrition (defined later in this chapter). At larger companies, break this down by the source of the candidate and their tenure at the company to look for trends.

Attrition data is particularly important, and there is quite a bit of data about turnover rates in various industries. The rule of thumb (which matches our experience) is that a turnover rate of 10% per year or less is fairly healthy.[3] When your company is growing quickly and your hiring process is struggling to scale, not every hire will be a perfect fit.

As with all metrics, it's important to look at the underlying data from time to time. You could have a turnover rate of 10% and think everything is fine, but then notice that it's only your top performers who are leaving. That is definitely not healthy. You need to look at everybody who leaves and decide whether it was regretted attrition (a solid performer that you wanted to keep) or non-regretted attrition (a failed hire or someone who did not scale with the company).

High rates of non-regretted attrition often indicate a problem in your hiring process. Because bad hires can be so costly, it's worth investigating whether this is the case. But there could be other explanations. For example, someone who does a very good job for three years and then struggles for a year before leaving the company doesn't necessarily mean your hiring process has flaws—it could just mean the company isn't the right place for them anymore. There's more on regretted versus non-regretted attrition in "Off-boarding" on page 56.

On-Boarding

On-boarding is a very important part of the overall hiring process. Anyone who has worked a few jobs has probably experienced a disorganized or even nonexistent on-boarding process. You get assigned a desk, and from then on it's "good luck!" On-boarding constitutes the new employee's first impression of what it's really like to work at the company. If that impression is one of chaos, or of "we don't care about new employees," just imagine the impact that will have on employee tenure. Additionally, a bad on-boarding process results in new employees taking longer to become productive, which is not in your interest. And, as Kate Heddleston points out in "The Null Process" (*http://bit.ly/2gSjkQF*), the absence of a strong on-boarding program can make your work environment less

---

3 For more on this, see Benson Smith and Tony Rutigliano's article "The Truth About Turnover" (*http://bit.ly/2gSmlAi*), February 4, 2002.

inclusive. New hires who are members of the dominant group can acquire knowledge more easily from social interaction, creating a disadvantage for new hires outside this group, ultimately leading to higher attrition rates.

Let's look at how on-boarding might evolve as your company grows. Remember that the bigger and the more mature your company, the higher the expectations are for your on-boarding process.

Figure 3-2 shows how to organize on-boarding at different stages of the company.

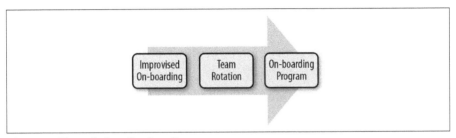

Figure 3-2. The evolution of on-boarding

IMPROVISED ON-BOARDING

In the first stage, your company is small and all of your employees are probably in the same office or on the same floor. On-boarding here usually starts with you simply handing them a laptop and asking one of the team members to be their mentor and help them get going. You rely on the fact that communication is still easy and that people will talk to each other anyway. But there are still some things you should do proactively:

- It may seem obvious, but make sure the new hire has a one-on-one meeting with their manager during their first week, ideally on their first day. This is a great way to set expectations for the rest of the on-boarding process and make the new hire feel welcome.

- Ask someone to write up a brief on-boarding document, which can start with just a few notes to help orient the new hire. Then have each new hire update the document with anything that has changed or any helpful tips to pass on to the next new hire. Over time this will evolve into a fairly comprehensive guide with just a little effort from each hire.

- Make it clear to the mentor that it is their responsibility to help the new hire get up to speed, and that this is part of their job expectations. Reward them with praise and positive feedback if they do it well. Letting a new hire struggle due to lack of guidance will erode their morale quickly. (More details in the section "Mentor Program" on page 56.)

- Organize a few chats with founders and senior employees who can tell the history of the company and the product to your new hires. Knowing where the company has been can be very helpful in orienting new employees and explaining the current state of affairs.

- Organize a few sessions wherein product teams present the most important parts of the product to new employees. These sessions should include:

    — Understanding the current product: why it was started, how it evolved, and plans for the future

    — Spending a day with the support team to understand how users perceive the product, and the most common complaints (if applicable)

TEAM ROTATION

As the company grows, improvised on-boarding becomes less effective. Once you have, say, five teams, simply adding hires to one team means they are less likely to know what the other teams are building. Instead of understanding how the whole system fits together, they end up with a narrow view and may lack working relationships with the engineers outside their team. Setting up an on-boarding rotation can help avoid this problem. New employees spend one or more weeks (depending on the learning curve) with each team, at least enough time to complete an easy task. By the end of the rotation, they'll have worked with nearly everybody and built personal connections, and should have a decent overview of how the various components fit together.

Note that this is in addition to everything mentioned in "Improvised On-Boarding" on page 51, not a replacement.

ON-BOARDING PROGRAM

The team rotation approach only works up to a certain number of teams, however. At some point, rotating through all of the teams takes too much time. And if you just choose a subset of teams, the new employee only gets limited visibility into the system. The logical next step is to create a formal on-boarding program. This usually contains a part that is designed for all employees and a part that is specific to engineering/product/design.

When SoundCloud had around 20 engineers, on-boarding meant having new engineers visit several teams (around five) for one week each. As the number of teams and engineers increased, it stopped making sense to have new hires visit all of the teams. Still, there were a few teams each candidate *had* to visit, because their area was so central to how the system operated. One of these teams was the core API team, which was in charge of all the core business logic. Unfortunately, the constant rotations meant that the team ended up with a different team setup nearly every week. After a while, this constant churn prevented the team from working efficiently. So we stopped this way of on-boarding, and asked Duana Stanley, an engineer who expressed interest in this area, to come up with a new approach—one inspired by Facebook's "Bootcamp" on-boarding program (*http://bit.ly/2gSnSq2*).

A Story from Duana: Rebuilding On-Boarding for SoundCloud

Our new approach to on-boarding, we thought, should accommodate our increased technical and organizational complexity. The idea was to build a structured on-boarding program that provided an introduction to the complex technical architecture and introduced key members of the organization without overloading the development teams in the process. The goal was that new engineers would be able to get up and running as quickly as possible while renewing and broadcasting the engineering culture at the same time. The culture was presented as it should be—not by misleading new hires about its current state, but by focusing on our aspirations for the future.

First approach

First, we identified the core areas in engineering and created a presentation for each of them. The presentations were given by a member of the responsible team, so that new engineers would already have one contact person within each core team.

To familiarize them with the code base and to allow them to ship something significant within their first weeks, each new engineer had to fix a bug in the "mothership" (the name for our monolithic Ruby application) in a one-day session, which was then deployed to production. The on-boarding took two weeks, and there were two sessions per day.

This first approach had some problems. There were too many sessions, with too much information to digest. The new engineers felt overwhelmed. After a series of bug-fixing successes, the bugs remaining in the mothership became too obscure. It was hard to fix them, and the impact of each fix was hardly noticeable anymore. The new engineers stopped seeing the value in touching the mothership code, as they no longer felt it was relevant to their jobs.

Second approach

The second time around, we got rid of the bug-fixing session and instead used a presentation to provide an overview of the mothership code base. We also tried to organize a mini-hackathon instead of the bug-fixing session, but decided it was too much effort.

To reduce the amount of time it took to prepare and hold presentations, we considered using recorded videos, but they ended up being too impersonal; live presentations were better at putting names to faces and establishing a meaningful connection. Instead, we changed the presentations to workshops/interactive sessions, where presenting engineers discussed the top five issues in their component, whether they were key concepts, shortcomings, or bugs. This worked much better.

Where we ended up

The first three days of on-boarding are general company presentations (legal, marketing, product, and others), attended by new employees of all departments. Following that, we do one week with one session per day about engineering topics. SoundCloud hires engineers for a specific team, so engineers join their teams right away. Because of their eagerness to contribute to the goals of their new teams, however, it becomes tough for engineers to focus on on-boarding.

Here are the key lessons we learned:

- A single individual should be responsible for on-boarding, but it takes a group of people to do it well, given the effort required and the breadth of topics covered.
- The scheduling effort should not be underestimated.

- Attendee retrospectives and feedback are helpful.

- Time should be allocated for process improvements.

- On-boarding is tremendously different when engineers are hired for a specific team than it is when they choose their teams afterward. Engineers hired for a specific team are eager to join their team as soon as possible, and thus, don't have much patience for a broader on-boarding. When not assigned to a team until afterward, new engineers want to learn as much as possible during on-boarding about the organization and architecture before making a decision. Hence, it is beneficial to avoid assigning teams until after the process starts.

Spotify has a much bigger team than the scope of this book—around 600 engineers at the time we interviewed Kevin Goldsmith (who was at that time VP of consumer engineering). Still, we decided to include his very interesting on-boarding story.

A Story from Kevin Goldsmith: On-boarding at Spotify

Every engineer at Spotify goes through a two week (full-time) on-boarding bootcamp. These engineers form a temporary Squad (with product owner, agile coach, and temporary partner engineer, called a "buddy") to learn the general setup and engineering approaches, such as build processes.[4] The first two days are general introductions (company, product), and then the engineer works on a product feature.

In the beginning, it was difficult to motivate product owners to spend two weeks on-boarding, but after a while, the product owners realized this amounted to getting an extra team for free. Product owners then started competing to get the new squad.

Each squad so far has shipped one feature to production.

---

4 For more information on squads, see Henrik Kniberg and Anders Ivarsson's "Scaling Agile @ Spotify with Tribes, Squads, Chapters & Guilds" (*http://bit.ly/2gSl4cR*), October 2012.

MENTOR PROGRAM

One approach that can be used either alone or in combination with other on-boarding approaches is a mentor or "buddy" program, which gives the new hire a specific person to help guide them during their early days at the company.

According to Andreea Hrab's article "Buddy System 101: New Employee Onboarding and the Benefits of the Buddy System" (*http://blog.eskill.com/buddy-system-101/*):

> A buddy is a colleague—not a manager or supervisor—who is assigned to a new hire for the first few months of employment and who acts as a guide for the day-to-day activities of the company. A buddy is someone who can be available to show the new hire around the office, go over protocols and policies, and generally help familiarize him or her with the company's inner workings and culture.

Because of this, we recommend assigning a mentor to each new employee to at least make sure they can find the coffee machine, know where people have lunch, and so on. And as mentioned earlier, it's important that mentors know the expectations of their role, are given sufficient time for it, and get rewarded when they do it well. This can also be a great first step toward leadership for a young team member, to see if they have an aptitude for helping others be more effective in their jobs.

Off-boarding

Off-boarding is about more than getting the departing employees' hardware back and closing all their accounts. Performing thorough exit interviews can provide insight into the reasons employees are leaving that might not surface otherwise. Ideally, the answers you get from the employee are unsurprising, since the manager and HR have already discussed these with the employee. If they regularly reveal completely new things, it may mean something has gone horribly wrong earlier in the process (e.g., the manager hasn't performed one-on-ones or hasn't acted on feedback the employee had given). If things are working well, there should be no surprises.

Pay attention to which departments are experiencing attrition. If certain parts of the organization lose more people than others, you should definitely take a look at the reasons. Some common sources of attrition in fast-growing startups are:

- The culture has changed (e.g., from a collaborative environment to a more competitive one).

- Employees feel there is little possibility for career advancement (see Chapters 4 and 5 for how to foster career development).

- A lack of attention to organization has led to bottlenecks, micromanagement, and a loss of autonomy.

REGRETTED VERSUS NON-REGRETTED ATTRITION

When an employee resigns, many companies will classify the resignation as one of two types: *regretted* or *non-regretted attrition*. When the attrition is regretted, it means the company would prefer that the employee remain on the team. This often triggers an attempt to "save" the employee through conversations with HR and senior leaders. These should reveal the reasons behind the resignation, which should be tracked by HR to understand any problems that need to be addressed. Make sure you consider these points:

- Did the manager listen to the person's concerns? Does the person feel treated fairly by the manager?

- Was there a disagreement over compensation or career advancement?

- Did the employee feel there was a culture problem? If so, you need to determine whether this is because the culture changed in a way the employee didn't like, or because the culture of the company was not what was promised. Especially in the latter case, you should look at what you communicate during the hiring process.

In the case of non-regretted attrition, the company is willing or eager to let the employee leave. A typical scenario is that the employee received some critical feedback or was put on a performance improvement plan (PIP) and decided to leave as a result. In this case, make sure you consider:

- Do you need to improve your hiring process? Is there a flaw in it that is keeping you from learning crucial information?

- Was the employee only a good fit during an *earlier* stage of the company? If so, this is pretty normal and not necessarily cause for concern.

Tracking these separately can help clarify whether a surge in attrition is due to solid management (e.g., "managing out" poor performers) or a management failure of some kind. But make sure that the classification isn't left solely to the manager. When someone decides to leave, there is a strong temptation to say "Well, we didn't want that person anyway." This artificially inflates the non-regretted numbers and can mask the real reason for the departure.

In all cases, it is worth doing a thorough exit interview, because often the reasons cited by the employee are not the actual reasons they are leaving. It's much easier to say, "I'm just looking for new challenges" than to say, "I think my boss doesn't like me." It may be helpful to think about exit interviews as a postmortem on the employee's experience at the company and approach them with similar rigor.

Conclusion

In this final chapter on how to scale hiring, we described how to maximize success at the end of the process, from making the offer to closing the candidate, and how to make sure employees have a successful start in their new company. We also discussed off-boarding, and how to gather information from departing employees that can help you improve your hiring process and your work environment in general. Now that you know how to grow your team in a scalable way, the next two chapters cover how to manage all these new people, ensuring that they are happy and productive as the company continues to grow.

Additional Resources

- Henry Ward's "A better offer letter" (*http://bit.ly/2gStW2b*) shows a fantastic example of an informative and honest offer letter.

- Jo Avent's "The Ones That Got Away—The Value of Finding Out Why Candidates Said No to Your Offer" (*http://bit.ly/2gSvitF*) provides solid advice for getting feedback about your hiring process from candidates who declined.

- Stefanie K. Johnson, David R. Hekman, and Elsa T. Chan's "If There's Only One Woman in Your Candidate Pool, There's Statistically No Chance She'll Be Hired" (*http://bit.ly/2gSqt3p*) is a great article about the bias in favor of preserving the status quo.

4

People Management: Getting Started

For many fast-growing companies, introducing a management role feels, at best, like a waste of time, or at worst, like the beginning of big company ills: more meetings, slower decision making, political maneuvering. You can almost hear the protests of early employees ringing in the hallway: "We're going corporate!"

But despite the potential objections, *an explicit focus on people management is vital to company success, particularly at fast-growing companies.* With proper training and a healthy culture, people managers can help teams scale by maintaining morale, ensuring alignment between work assignments and company goals, resolving disputes, and preparing the engineering team for the next phases of growth.

Consider these problematic scenarios:

- "At one point, my manager had up to 70 reports. Our feedback meetings were worse than useless. He basically cut-and-pasted my self-review with a few quotes from what my teammates had said about me..."

- "I've been at the company for six months and I've never had a one-on-one meeting with my manager. I've had a few different ones, but I'm actually not sure who my manager is right now."

- "On my first day, I was issued my laptop and badge by IT and then told to go to my manager's office. I wandered around until I found it, but she wasn't there. I waited in the hallway for two hours. Luckily, some former coworkers from my previous job found me and took me to lunch."

Any veteran of a fast-growing team can relay similar stories. Are these negative experiences just par for the course? The cost of doing business in tech? On the contrary, we believe an informed approach to scaling people management can avoid such missteps and materially improve the performance of your team and company.

In Chapters 1–3, we covered hiring, the primary lever for growth. In this and later chapters, we'll talk about the secondary effects of growth, the challenges that come from having more and more humans involved in getting the work done. We'll start with the need to manage the people that make up the team.

Understanding People Management

When new teams are formed, whether as a startup company or within a larger organization, the early days feel wonderfully efficient. Brainstorming ideas, hashing out a design, fixing problems—it all feels effortless. The hard work and long hours don't feel like a burden, because the impact of the work is clear and meaningful. The team builds a bond forged by the challenges they are tackling together and the uncertain road ahead.

If they are successful in building the right product, the team often falls victim to its own success. Overwhelmed by the demands of a flood of new customers, the already hard-working team finds that they cannot keep up. The only option to quickly scale the team's output is to grow the team. The first three chapters covered the mechanics of growing the team and how those mechanics change at different scaling points.

Remember, teams are groups of people. Because people are unique in their collection of talents and motivations, it's rare that they can self-organize into a cohesive unit that can efficiently pursue a common goal. This is the key role that people managers play.

People management is distinct from other management responsibilities:

Technical management
    Ensure the right technical decisions are being made by the team.

Project management
    Ensure projects are tracked accurately and shipped on time.

Product management
    Ensure the right product is being built for the customer.

These are important responsibilities, and at many companies the same managers may be responsible for some of these in addition to people management. But they are less critical to scaling than having a people management strategy that helps each team grow more efficiently and effectively. As my colleague Joe Xavier once said, "People management provides the structure and connective tissue to allow a group to achieve a common objective." Successful people managers achieve this by:

- Getting the right people on the team, and getting the wrong people off the team

- Ensuring the team is happy and productive by providing motivating work assignments, appropriate compensation, learning opportunities, and career guidance

- Helping the team succeed in their work by focusing on the highest-priority outcomes, resolving disputes and deadlocked decisions, and removing distractions

- Providing the team with any necessary resources, whether these are new team members that can fill a skill gap, conference room space for a brainstorming session, or a big monitor to display a project dashboard

These are the critical functions of people management. Though the specific practices involved may vary quite a bit, these functions apply whether the team is large or small, junior or veteran, composed of individual contributors or senior directors of large organizations. However, if you flip that list around, it's easy to understand how a lack of investment in people management can harm the growth of the team by:

- Adding the wrong people to the team, or allowing the wrong people to stay on the team too long before taking action

- Letting the team's morale and productivity suffer by ignoring members' work assignments, compensation, and career growth

- Providing no focus or prioritization, and allowing disputes and distractions to hurt productivity

- Starving the team of the resources they need to be successful

Those of us who have lived through periods of hyper-growth will recognize many of these problems, and can tell tales of the resulting damaging effects: burnout, team conflict, a loss of faith in leadership, confusion about the team's mission, and ultimately unwanted departures from the company. For an interesting case study in the value of people management, read Buffer's revealing retrospective (*http://bit.ly/2gStSiR*) on what happened after they eliminated managers and why they reverted eight months later.

FROM AD HOC TO FORMAL

At small companies, people management functions tend to be handled as needed by individuals in leadership positions—typically, the founders of the team. You see examples of this everywhere in the tech startup landscape, such as the common pattern of having the first dozen or so engineers report to a founder-CTO who has little or no management experience. This mode is a form of *ad hoc management*.

People management essentials

If your team is currently operating in an ad hoc management mode, there are a few essential things you should be doing, even before you think about growing the team.

- Everyone on the team should know who they report to (i.e., who their manager is). The only exception is the CEO, whose "manager" is the board of directors.

- Everyone should have a regular one-on-one meeting with their manager.

- During this one-on-one, they and their manager should discuss the fundamental aspects of their job—whether they know what's expected of them, if they have the resources to do their job, and if there is anything blocking them from making progress. Their manager should also provide feedback on how they are performing and give suggestions on how they can improve.

- Managers should understand the career aspirations of their team members, and strive to provide them with challenges and opportunities that help them move in that direction.

Without these fundamentals in place, most teams have no hope of scaling successfully. A complete tutorial on the basics of people management is outside the scope of this book, but there are numerous resources available. See "Additional Resources" on page 19 for some recommended reading for new managers.

Dealing with growth

As the team grows larger, this ad hoc mode starts to break down. A founder–CTO may find that after a week full of VC pitch meetings, partner negotiations, and architecture debates, they have no time to schedule one-on-ones, provide feedback, or resolve personnel conflicts. Or they may feel less qualified to deal with these as the team grows and people management tasks become more complex. Or a crisis may erupt: say a key employee quits due to lack of a clear career path or an unresolved conflict with another employee. Whatever the circumstances, the leaders of growing teams at some point realize they need to transition to an explicit management structure and culture, or more succinctly: formal management.

The timing and method of transition from ad hoc to formal management varies from team to team based on many factors. Despite this, there is a common path of how a company scales its people management:

Early stage
> This is when ad hoc people management starts. A team of 5 to 25 people (roughly half working on product development) forms around a handful of founders and one founder acts as the de facto people manager while the team builds its product and searches for a market and business model (Figure 4-1).

Transition stage
> During rapid growth the team finds a market and starts to grow quickly from 25 to 100. The ad hoc people management approach starts to break down. The leadership team begins to formalize management roles and transition or hire individuals into those roles (Figure 4-2).

Mature stage
> The company now has formal people management at scale. The initial management team continues to grow and evolve as the company grows from 100 to several hundred employees. An approach to multi-layer management (e.g., VPs and Directors) is put in place, as are more complex systems for performance management, career growth, and so on.

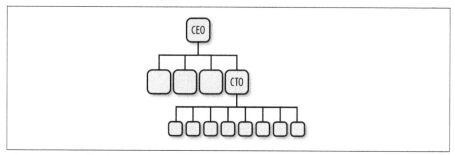

Figure 4-1. Typical early-stage reporting structure

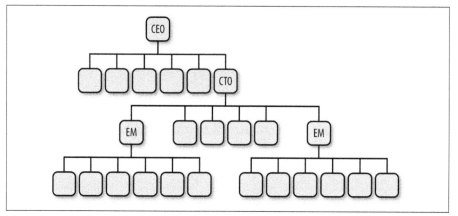

Figure 4-2. Typical reporting structure during transition stage

Note

It's important to distinguish the *reporting structure* at a company (i.e., who reports to whom) from the *organizational structure* (i.e., how individuals are organized into teams to get things done). These often overlap, but not always. *Holacracy*, for example, has a very specific organizational structure, but intentionally avoids any sort of management hierarchy.[1] And in matrix organizations, all the ICs in a particular discipline (designers, frontend engineers, backend engineers, PMs) report to a manager for that discipline, but they get distributed into cross-functional teams to tackle specific projects. We'll cover the various options in more detail in Chapter 8.

---

1 See Olivier Compagne, "Holacracy vs. Hierarchy vs. Flat Orgs," (*http://bit.ly/2hH56BG*).

WHEN TO FORMALIZE PEOPLE MANAGEMENT

As you enter the *transition stage*, it can be hard to know when the timing is right for introducing formal people management. Leaders, distracted by customer and team growth, often rely on gut and intuition, or simply wait until a crisis emerges to force the issue. But there are usually early warning signs that people management is needed. Recognizing these and taking action can help avoid a crisis.

Warning signs that people management is needed

There are a number of warning signs that suggest a move from ad hoc to formal people management is needed:

Ad hoc people managers are dropping essential duties
> Team leaders no longer have time for one-on-one meetings. They may be too busy putting out fires and doing "real work" to meet with the team. Or perhaps they spend *too much* time on one-on-one meetings. Because of urgent personnel issues, team leaders may start failing at other critical tasks like strategic planning and fundraising.

Confusion about the direction of the work and team
> Team members become bogged down in disputes about the path forward or are confused about priorities and increasingly need leaders to step in and make decisions.

Declining product quality and productivity
> Product quality is slipping—there are more bugs, customer complaints, downtime, and rollbacks. Or team leaders feel that engineering productivity is slipping and wonder whether the team is working hard enough or getting distracted by non-essential tasks.

Morale trending lower, attrition trending higher
> Team members see increasing examples of poor morale—grouchy emails, antisocial behavior, and cynical talk around the water cooler. There is a noticeable shift to later arrival times, earlier departure times, or more frequent last-minute "work from home" days. You hear rumblings from individuals that "I'm not progressing in my career" or "The work isn't interesting anymore" or "I'm feeling burned out." And employees are leaving the company at a noticeable rate.

Individually, none of these warning signs necessarily indicate a crisis. But if you're seeing several crop up at your company, it's time to act. Try to quickly diagnose the underlying causes, and in parallel start working on a more formal approach to management. "Introducing Formal People Management to a Team" on page 70 describes how to do this.

The longer you wait, the more you are probably accruing what Ben Horowitz has called *management debt*: "Like technical debt, management debt is incurred when you make an expedient, short-term management decision with an expensive, long-term consequence. Also like technical debt, the trade-off sometimes makes sense, but often does not."[2] In this case, the expedient decision is to keep doing things the way you've been doing them rather than address the warning signs by improving your management practices.

Timing the Transition

But if you're not seeing any warning signs, or if they are mild and manageable, you may be wondering when you should start the transition to formal management. There are many factors that can influence the ideal timing of this change. At first, you might just look at the size of the team. There is a body of research on how many direct reports a single manager can reasonably handle, often called *span of control*, with typical numbers quoted in the 7 to 10 range.[3] Based on this model, when the founding team grows beyond 10 people, it's time to move to a more formal management structure.

But different teams require different levels of teaching and assistance from their managers, something Drucker calls *span of management responsibility*. Some leaders are more equipped than others to perform ad hoc management tasks in parallel with their other tasks. And some team structures allow day-to-day management tasks to be distributed across multiple leaders instead of being centralized in a single people manager. So there is no simple rule for when to shift to formal people management.

There are some obvious factors to assess in planning the timing of your transition to formal management:

---

2 Ben Horowitz, "Management Debt" (*http://www.bhorowitz.com/management_debt*), January 19, 2012.
3 See Peter Drucker's *The Practice of Management* (HarperBusiness).

The founders' previous management experience
> The more they have, the longer they can get by with ad hoc management without accruing too much management debt.

Maturity of the engineering team
> This is not simply "years of experience" (although it doesn't hurt if your engineers have worked for a significant time at well-managed companies). But some engineers are simply more self-managing than others, requiring less time and input from their manager to get their job done, and less coaching on how to improve.[4]

The team's familiarity with each other
> A group that has worked together successfully in the past may need less management than a collection of individuals who are still learning about each other's strengths and idiosyncrasies.

The team's decision-making ability
> Some teams are able to act independently, while others require input from founders/leaders to approve their decisions or break ties.

Growth rate
> Teams that need to grow quickly will get the most benefit from a dedicated people manager who can drive sourcing, organize the interview process, on-board new engineers, and ensure that they have appropriate work assignments.

Importance of execution versus exploration
> If you're staring at hard deadlines and shrinking market windows, formal management can help improve predictability by reducing churn and duplicated effort. But it can also reduce exploration and serendipity as managers attempt to focus the team on the current strategic plan.

Ultimately, the ideal timing depends upon how much people management the team needs, and how well such management is getting done in the absence of an explicit manager.

---

4 See John Allspaw's "On Being a Senior Engineer" (*http://bit.ly/2gFPPPi*) and Benjamin Reitzammer's "Mature Developers" (*http://bit.ly/2gFPQCy*).

Delaying Formal Management

When is it appropriate to delay the transition to formal management? In some situations, particularly if none of the preceding warning signs are evident, waiting makes sense. But we have also seen many cases where a delay is motivated more by fear or inertia than by logic or experience. For example:

Past bad experiences with management
> Leaders who have suffered under bad managers in the past may feel that the role is more harmful than helpful. While this is understandable, seeking the advice of investors, board members, or mentors will quickly dispel this misconception.

Cultural opposition
> Sometimes a predisposition against people management is more philosophical, based on a desire to elevate the role of the individual contributor on the team. Many startups tout the virtues of their "flat org structure," which may be based on a misunderstanding of the value of good managers, fear of the cost of hiring bad managers, or a presumed inability to distinguish between the two.

These reasons, though understandable, are more likely to lead to an accumulation of management debt than to result in a novel new way of managing and scaling teams.

That said, there are sometimes valid reasons to delay, particularly when the leadership team needs to balance the cost and risk of making the transition against major company events. As this chapter should make clear, introducing formal management is not a trivial exercise. Hiring dedicated managers costs time and money, and converting individual contributors to managers will impact productivity in the near term. There are also execution costs in the time and mental focus required to make the transition, particularly from the leadership team. Financial constraints or critical events like a product launch or fundraising may be valid reasons for delaying an investment in formal management.

MANAGING PEOPLE WITHOUT MANAGERS

People management functions are crucial during growth, but it is often necessary to perform them without a dedicated manager during a team's early stage. Small teams may not have the funds necessary to hire a dedicated person. Or once they decide to do so, it may take many months to find the right person. In the meantime, team leaders may need to get creative to ensure that management functions get done and are not simply ignored.

Here are some ways to survive without a dedicated people manager:

- Establish a technical management role. Some companies give their "tech leads" responsibility for technical decisions on the team rather than rely on the team's manager.

- Formalize a Product Manager or Program/Project Manager role. Identify someone who can own the product roadmap and/or help the team break it down into milestones or sprints.

- Clearly define the development process (peer reviews, testing strategies, etc.). This allows ICs to better self-manage in these areas.

- Encourage healthy peer feedback and train the team on how to do it well. See Alexander Grosse's blog post "Peer Feedback" (*http://alexander grosse.com/peer-feedback/*) for more information.

- Invest in communication within and between teams. Chapter 11 covers a variety of ways to improve information flow without overwhelming the team with noise.

- Optimize the skill balance on the team. Sometimes the perceived need for management is actually caused by a skill gap; for example, the team keeps missing its milestones because the team members are not good at debugging or task estimation. It's also possible to move ICs around to get more self-managing units—for example, a more junior team may need to borrow someone from a more senior team to hit a particularly challenging milestone.

These approaches can help delay the costs and risks of adding formal management, when necessary. But again, if you see any of the warning signs we described in the previous section, then delaying this process is probably the wrong thing to do, especially as management debt continues to accumulate.

An Example from Alexander: The issuu Organizational Structure

At issuu, there is one VP of Engineering, 7 team leads, and 38 engineers. The teams are all delivery teams, which means that the VP of Engineering is not involved in their day-to-day work (see Chapter 7 for an explanation of delivery teams). The team lead has one-on-ones with each member of their team every other week, and then brings back any problems to the VP. A peer feedback system is in place and is used effectively. This model works well on a day-to-day basis. The biggest challenge comes during compensation review when the VP relies on performance evaluations from the team leads to adjust salary for the entire engineering staff. That is a difficult week!

Introducing Formal People Management to a Team

A surprisingly common startup tale involves a group of engineers suddenly being called into a meeting: "Hi everybody, I'd like to introduce Alice. She's your new manager, so I'll be moving all our one-on-one meetings to her calendar going forward." No matter how smart and capable Alice is, such an abrupt transition is likely to generate backlash, chatter about how the company is "going corporate," and gloomy predictions of more meetings and lots of politics.

The resulting loss of productivity can be costly, especially during a time of growth for the young team. So what can team leaders do to avoid this?

KNOW WHAT YOU WANT TO DO AND PREPARE YOUR TEAM

There are some simple steps you can take *before* making any changes to your reporting structure. To begin with, decide what sort of *management culture* you want. What are the expectations of managers? How are these different from related roles you might have, such as tech leads or product managers? What is each manager's primary focus—people development, execution, or something else? How will managers' performance be evaluated? This may sound like a lot of work to sort out, but it doesn't have to be. If you know who your first dedicated manager will be, pull them aside and ask them to read a few chapters of a book like Rothman and Derby's *Behind Closed Doors* (*https://pragprog.com/book/rdbcd/behind-closed-doors*) (Pragmatic Bookshelf). Then discuss the book over lunch. You'll pretty quickly realize what the two of you value about management, and just writing that down gives you a first cut at a management culture.

Consider defining parallel *career paths* (sometimes called career ladders), one for engineers and a separate one for managers. Many small companies don't bother establishing these until very late (e.g., Twitter didn't have them until 2011, five years after it was founded!), so why do it now? An important goal is to avoid the perception that engineers are now second-class citizens who must be "promoted" to managers in order to advance in their career. Management is a very different role requiring different talents from engineering to be successful. Not all great engineers will be great managers (and vice versa), and you want to avoid the situation where senior engineers end up feeling forced to do something they aren't motivated or suited to do. We have devoted a separate section to this topic in Chapter 5, "Defining a career path or ladder" on page 108, including references to example career ladders that other companies have published.

Find *internal candidates* who might make effective managers. You may have engineers who have been successful managers in the past who might be willing to return to the role. Otherwise, look for engineers who demonstrate the qualities you want to see in your management team (empathy, credit-sharing, mentorship, strategic thinking, etc.). Watch out for those who demonstrate warning signs such as an inability to handle conflict or stress, difficulty discussing sensitive subjects, and desire for more control or information access. And importantly, *don't confuse engineering prowess with management potential.* Tim Howes, cofounder of LoudCloud, said "Watch out for the temptation to take your top coders and make them managers...management is about people, it's not about code."[5] We have a more detailed discussion on how to identify and develop management talent in existing employees in "Developing New Managers" on page 74.

Tell your team that you're thinking about making some changes to your management structure. This is not the time for surprises. Ideally, give the team at least a month or more before you make any concrete changes, to allow anyone with concerns or with an interest in pursuing management as a career path to speak with you about it.

The overarching theme here is to *avoid surprises and an erosion of trust.* A team that understands why management is needed and is ready to take advantage of it is much more likely to maintain high productivity than a team that is confused and possibly demotivated by the change.

---

5 First Round Review, "What I Learned Scaling Engineering Teams Through Euphoria and Horror" (*http://bit.ly/2gG27al*).

COMMUNICATE AND DEPLOY THE PLAN

Introducing a new management structure can be a stressful moment, and a morale risk if handled poorly. Here are some ideas for how to ensure that this is a positive change for the team.

Be transparent and give context

Try to be as clear as possible about your *motivations and intentions* for making the change. It's really tempting to rip off the Band-aid and just show the team an org chart. But to properly digest the changes, employees need to understand why you're making those changes and understand how they will benefit.

Bad

> CEO: *Okay, folks, we're making a big change today. We've decided that we need people managers, so Ann will be taking on that role. These people will now report to Ann: Bob, Carol, Dave...*
> General reaction: *Groan!*

Better

> CEO: *Okay, folks, I've been hearing a lot of grumbling about lack of direction and career growth. I clearly haven't had enough time lately to spend with each of you in one-on-one meetings, and I don't see that changing given our upcoming fundraising. So, I've decided we need to create an Engineering Manager role, and I'm working right now on a job description and a rollout plan. If you're interested in learning more, please stop by...*
> General reaction: *Okay, we're listening.*

Keep in mind that many of us have had bad managers in the past and thus may be predisposed to think poorly of management as a role. So, take the time to fully explain the value you expect to get from having people managers and how you plan to evaluate their success.

If you took the time to define your management culture, then communicating this during the rollout will help your ICs understand the motivations for the changes you're making, as well as what to expect from their new managers. You might even pique the interest of some to consider becoming managers themselves!

Minimize fanfare for new managers

If you decide to have an existing team member take on management responsibilities, be restrained in your public praise for their transition, no matter how grateful you are (see "This is not a promotion" on page 82). In short, you don't want to risk the perception that management is the best path to greater recognition, nor do you want to make it more difficult for the person to transition back should they turn out to be unfit or uninterested in the role.

Provide ways for individual contributors to have influence

A common concern voiced during rollouts is that engineers will have less influence over the roadmap than managers, despite having a greater base of knowledge about the product and technology in use at the company. Although this is true at some companies, it does not have to be. Providing ICs with an explicit mechanism to influence the roadmap ensures that they too can contribute in a predictable and useful way.

An example: while VP of Platform Engineering at Twitter, Raffi Krikorian introduced a "Platform Steering Group," which comprised the most senior ICs in Platform Engineering. The Steering Group's charter was to solicit project proposals from anyone on the team, with a particular focus on tools and technical debt projects that would accelerate future development. They would then review the proposals and select one or more to include in the following quarter's roadmap. This acted as a bottom-up override mechanism in the planning process, helping ensure that unglamorous-but-important projects would actually get funded rather than kicked down the road.

You can also ensure that ICs have a strong voice in hiring and promotion decisions. There are various ways to do this—see "Making a Hiring Decision" on page 31 for a discussion of hiring/promotion committees, Amazon's "bar raiser" model, and other approaches. But the general point is that having managers solely responsible for hiring decisions can leave engineers feeling disempowered, and magnify resentment in cases where a new hire championed by the manager fails to perform.

Adding a new layer of management can make ICs feel like they no longer have access to senior leadership. One day, you're reporting directly to the head of your group; the next day, your one-on-one gets cancelled, and there's a new manager between you and your old boss! Counteract this via occasional *skip-level* one-on-ones, where the head of the group meets directly with ICs, bypassing any managers in between. You can also use roundtable discussions (where a selected group of ICs meets with senior leaders), attendance at planning off-sites, or participation in executive staff meetings. Try to intentionally "flatten" the org so that communication between senior leaders and the rank-and-file doesn't disappear, but is, in fact, strengthened.

Last, but perhaps most important, knowing how well the management team is performing is hugely important, and ICs can play a major role in assessing this. For detailed guidance, see "Assessing Manager Performance" on page 91.

Developing New Managers

Ask any gathering of engineering managers how many of them were trained as engineers and you'll consistently get responses in the 80%–100% range. And yet, if you ask them how many received formal management training before becoming managers, the response will be shockingly the opposite, 0%–10%. For some reason, the tech industry treats engineering management as almost entirely a "learn on the job" profession.

We recommend a more disciplined approach. Once team leaders recognize management potential in one of their ICs, they should assist them in the transition to a management role, provide them with lightweight, ongoing training, and help them grow into happy and successful managers. This can provide a strong scaling advantage, for the reasons we outlined at the beginning of the chapter.

IDENTIFYING MANAGEMENT POTENTIAL

Knowing which engineers will make great managers is a bit like knowing which professional athletes will make great professional coaches. Their background as athletes is an important requirement, but being a coach also requires so many other talents, you won't really know for sure until they try out the job. Fortunately, there are a few indicators that can help you construct an educated guess about whether a candidate will be successful in a management role.

The simplest way to evaluate management potential is the "Up-Sideways-Down" rubric (see Figure 4-3).

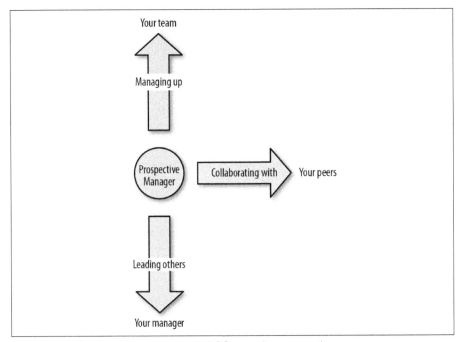

Figure 4-3. Evaluating management potential from various perspectives

Here's how Up-Sideways-Down works:

Up

Think of examples of your IC "managing up"—in other words, giving you constructive feedback, accurately representing the state of work, and alerting you of impending problems such as a schedule slip or an uncovered design flaw. Engineers typically have many opportunities to manage up during the course of a software project.

Sideways

Identify examples of how this IC has worked well with others. Have they shown that they can work well with their current and future peers, such as other people managers or technical leads? In addition to the aforementioned feedback, status reporting, and escalation of issues, they should also be an effective collaborator, sharing responsibilities when appropriate, distributing credit when credit is due, and not pointing fingers when problems arise.

Down

> Find examples of when the IC has shown leadership. You want to see that they can guide the work of other engineers, helping them learn and become more effective. Since they have not been officially managing yet, this often takes the form of mentoring an intern or helping a new hire come up to speed on the tech stack. They may have hosted a brown-bag session to teach the team about an area of expertise, or improved the team's process for getting work done. Or they may simply show a penchant for helping others who are having problems, whether those are professional or personal.

As a manager, you can also try to evaluate whether a promising IC possesses some key traits that are correlated with management success. In rough priority order:

Mentorship

> Do they happily help coworkers improve their skills and knowledge, even when it means slowing down their own work?

Communication

> Can they clearly articulate complex ideas, in both verbal and written form? Can they address difficult subjects, such as critical feedback, without mincing words or being vague?

Empathy

> Do they seem capable of understanding the feelings and perspective of others, even when they may feel differently themselves? In cases of conflict, do they first seek mutual understanding or are they focused on victory?

Organic leadership

> Does the team look to this person for guidance and direction, even without a formal leadership role? When they talk, do others listen and act?

Humility

> Can they gracefully share credit with others when appropriate? Or conversely, do they seek the limelight, even when it's not in the best interest of the team?

Strategic thinking

> Can they see beyond their current assignments to understand the bigger picture, how the work of the team fits the overall product direction and the

needs of the business? Do they push back or ask hard questions when they don't see how these fit together? Can they set aside short-term goals long enough to realize there is a larger strategic opportunity that the team should pursue?

Seeing these qualities can give you a boost of confidence about someone's ability to handle a management role.

You should also look for negative indicators that should make you wary of granting people a management role:

Handling stress

Do they lose sleep or composure when the team is on a tight deadline?

Conflict avoidance

Are they unable or unwilling to discuss difficult or controversial subjects? Do they give in quickly when others present a differing viewpoint, or can they stand up for their ideas and hash out a compromise?

Difficulty communicating

When you ask for feedback, do they have a hard time being open and honest with you? Do they prefer to talk to you first about issues with their teammates rather than addressing them directly? Have they failed to volunteer important information that you subsequently found out about via other channels?

Desire for control

Do they seem motivated by having others do their bidding? Do they often ask you to intervene in a situation to help make it go their way?

Information hoarding

Are they constantly seeking greater access to information, especially from your peers and managers? Do they withhold information from peers and reports? Do they trade in hallway rumors and gossip?

The Reluctant Manager: A Story from David

I've only had a few cases where someone came to me, unsolicited, asking to become a manager, who I felt was truly a good candidate for management. The best management candidates are often smart and perceptive enough to know that it's a hard job that they haven't been trained for, and therefore be wary of it. For these folks, it's your job to at least show them that management is a role that's worthy of consideration. Discuss the fact that they can help others be more effective through coaching and mentorship, and that their good judgment can help the team focus on the most impactful work.

My most recent experience involved a senior engineer who really enjoyed and excelled at mentoring younger engineers. She also had ideas for how to accomplish one of the big items on our roadmap. When I asked if she would manage a small team that would build and own that item, she initially balked, intimidated by her lack of understanding of the manager role. But once I promised to build a training program for her, she agreed and came up to speed very quickly. Over the next two years that we worked together, she went on to manage progressively larger teams and is now considering a second-level management role. Selecting the right ICs to convert to managers and motivating them to make the switch is an essential part of scaling your team.

Again, there is no perfect formula for predicting success as a manager, but looking at these different factors should give you a starting point and provide input for a conversation with the prospective candidate.

SURVIVING THE MANAGEMENT TRANSITION

Most first-time managers (like many first-time parents) feel woefully underprepared for their new responsibilities. And, frankly, most are. Very few receive any sort of training for the job they've been given, and often the transition is sudden and awkward for all involved. But it doesn't have to be this way.

What to expect: the first-time manager

When asking an IC to become a manager, the first step is to set their expectations. Specifically, highlight what's likely to be confusing, emotional, or challenging about the new role. It's easy to fool ourselves into thinking that ICs must know what being a manager is like, since (except for new college graduates) they have had time to observe their own manager organizing meetings, putting together career plans and roadmaps, resolving conflicts, and so on. But there are many aspects of the job that they cannot observe.

Time management and the "manager's schedule"

As has been written about in many places (most famously by Paul Graham in one of his most widely read essays (*http://bit.ly/makerssched*)), the manager's schedule and the individual contributor's schedule are completely different, for good reasons. The switch from one to the other can feel very awkward to the new manager, like "death by a thousand time slices." Remind the new manager that being highly available and interruptible is an important part of their job, that handling an interruption is actually a form of getting work done, and that when they need focus time (hopefully infrequently) there are ways to achieve this—headphones, conference rooms, or working from home.

A manager may no longer be "one of the gang"

The manager role can be a lonely one; simply wearing the manager title can leave you uninvited from informal group lunches or from that snarky chat channel that everyone seems to be enjoying. It's not inevitable, but knowing that it's likely will help the new manager handle it with less emotion.

A manager's work output is totally different

Engineers are wired to feel rewarded when they build stuff. These reward circuits take a long time to rewire after a management transition. A new manager needs to learn how to feel good about the things *their team* builds, and realize that this depends on their work as a manager: providing clear direction, helping the team develop their skills, and removing obstacles from their path. New managers often cling to writing code and weighing in on technical decisions because this rewiring process takes so long. This can distract the new manager from learning about their new job, and leave no space for engineers on the team to establish their own technical leadership. To counteract this, you should set expectations now on how much and what kind of technical work is acceptable and under what circumstances. For example, you might say "you're welcome to read your team's code, but you should only write code when all your other management work is done," which emphasizes that the needs of the team come first. For more on this, read Cate Huston's "The Hardest, Shortest Lesson in Becoming a Manager" (*http://bit.ly/2gG1Vrl*), about letting go of coding tasks, and why it's hard but the right thing to do.

Being managed as a manager

The way an IC is managed and the way a manager is managed can be very different. As a manager-of-managers, explain how you intend to provide direction, define goals, and set expectations. Also, try to be clear about where you are comfortable with autonomy and where you expect to be involved in decision making. If this is your first time managing managers, you may not be clear on these yourself, so seek some guidance from a mentor or company advisor if you need it.

Preparing the team for their new manager

We covered much of this topic in "Communicate and Deploy the Plan" on page 72. In short, be transparent about why this person is becoming a manager, how their success will be evaluated, and what changes the team should expect day to day, if any. Do this before the reporting relationships change, so any concerns can be surfaced and dealt with prior to the transition.

Lightweight management training

It would be nice to be able to say, "Sign your new managers up for this 12-week class and they'll be totally set up for success!" But it's unlikely such a class exists, nor is it reasonable for every organization to lose people for 12 weeks to get them ready for their new role. But there are simple, time-efficient things you can do to help educate a new manager on the basic parts of their new role.

The simplest approach is to pick a specific management book, blog, or article that you find particularly relevant. Ask the prospective manager to read it and then have a one-hour discussion with you when they are done. It doesn't really matter which one it is, as long as it is broad enough to cover some essential management skills (e.g., one-on-ones, providing feedback, and setting direction). The goal of your follow-up conversation is to ensure that you both have a shared understanding of the role and your expectations of it. It's not uncommon for two managers to have very different styles of management, so this is your chance to establish which aspects you want to be done a certain way, and which ones the new manager is free to define on their own. For example, you may feel strongly that managers must provide informal performance feedback to each report at least monthly, but care less about how the rest of their one-on-one meetings are structured. Not establishing these "invariants" up front can lead to friction between you and the new manager down the road.

If you have the time and motivation to do more to prepare your new manager, pick a few ideas from this menu and run with them:

Mentorship

Ask a few managers you know, either in the company or outside the company, to meet for 30–60 minutes (perhaps weekly for a month) and talk about their transition, what they wished they had known before starting the job, or the biggest challenges they've faced. If it goes well, try to make this a recurring monthly session, giving the new manager a safe space to share challenges and ask for advice.

Professional coaching

There are lots of executive coaches out there, not all of them great. But if you know a great one, or can get a referral from your network, the money you spend on this will probably be repaid many times over.

Reading group

This is a great way to foster ongoing learning in your management team, and there's no reason why a prospective manager couldn't join the discussion before their transition. Just make sure you or someone you designate is in charge of selecting the reading for each session and guiding the discussion.

Focused practice sessions

Use part of your one-on-one time to practice the skills you think will be most difficult for your new manager. For example, "Imagine that I report to you, and I've been working for several months leading a project with an important client. You've decided that my job performance isn't up to snuff and have decided to replace me as the lead with one of my peers. Take a few minutes to think about how you'd break the news to me. Then go ahead and try it." Because of your reporting relationship, some new managers may be more comfortable practicing these skills with a mentor or a trusted peer.

Shadowing

Have your new manager shadow you in all your meetings (except perhaps one-on-ones) to get a better sense of a day in the life of a manager. This is especially useful in areas where the new manager has had little or no visibility, such as recruiting and closing candidates, presenting to upper management, collaborating with other senior leaders, or meeting the legal obligations that managers have regarding harassment and hostile work environments.

Whichever of these you go with, please remember the most important thing at this stage is not adopting any specific training technique, but fostering the habit of ongoing education, which is so easy to lose track of during the confusing and busy early days as a manager.

This is not a promotion

When converting an engineer to a manager, make sure you *don't describe this as a promotion*, but rather a significant change in role and responsibilities. There are two motivations for this rule. First, you don't want engineers to think that shifting to management is the best way to get ahead, since this is not a healthy motivation for taking on such a different and challenging role. Second, describing the conversion as a promotion and/or showering the person with fanfare will make it very difficult to step back from the role if they decide it is not for them. If a new manager ends up failing or unhappy in their new role, you don't want them to have any artificial incentives to stay in that role. Better that they step aside and get some training if they want to try it again someday. Lindsay Holmwood wrote an excellent post on this subject titled "It's Not a Promotion, It's a Career Change" (*http://bit.ly/2gG1sFR*). Also see Derek Brown's post "Management Is Not a Promotion" (*http://bit.ly/2gG63I5*).

A common approach that we strongly endorse is giving an internal candidate an incrementally increasing amount of management responsibility to assess whether they would enjoy this new role or not. For example, you may have a promising potential manager who is acting technical lead for one of your teams. Before making the role change official, you could first ask the tech lead to take a larger role in career guidance for the team members by having one-on-one meetings with them, perhaps alternating with your own one-on-ones to avoid meeting overload. Then, have them take on more of the team roadmap planning and customer outreach. And then have them present the roadmap to key stakeholders. At each step, you have an opportunity to assess, provide guidance, and gather feedback on whether these responsibilities are appealing or a burden. Be sure to communicate your plans with the rest of the team so that no one is confused about the changes in management responsbilities.

PERFORMANCE ASSESSMENT AND THE GO/NO-GO DECISION

New managers, as with any other employees, should know when and how their performance will be assessed and communicated. Of course, continuous timely feedback is best, but you should also agree on a milestone for a more formal assessment. This is particularly helpful with new managers because, frankly, not everyone is cut out to be a manager, nor will everyone enjoy the new role. Without a mutually agreed-upon date on the calendar for a go/no-go decision, it's easy for months and months to pass without anyone making the difficult decision to revert.

Make sure when you pick the date, perhaps three or six months out, that you also provide the rubric that you'll be using to assess them. Will it be solely your view, or will you solicit 360-degree feedback? What aspects of the role will you be looking at? This provides some structure that the new manager can use to guide their own development and do their own self-assessment. Additional guidance on how to help managers thrive is covered in Chapter 5.

Hiring Managers Externally

When introducing formal management, most companies have a bias toward converting current ICs to management roles, and there are good reasons for such a preference. Current employees have an advantage in already understanding the product, the technology stack, and the values and culture of the company. External hires, by contrast, are often viewed with suspicion—will they be more corporate and political? Will they share the same values as the rest of us?

While these concerns are valid, hiring experienced managers externally often becomes a necessity, particularly as the company grows. At some point, you'll run out of qualified and/or interested internal candidates, and need to look elsewhere or risk accruing management debt. And there can be concrete advantages to hiring from the outside, depending on the candidate, including:

- Greater experience, particularly with less common scenarios such as firing poor performers, handling layoffs, or executing reorganizations.

- Novel techniques for management or engineering that were successful at other companies.

- Outside perspective on how the team is approaching its work. Remember that team members often become blind to the flaws in their processes once they adjust to them.

- Greater team diversity, which will, in turn, create even more diverse thinking. This includes gender, race, ethnicity, age, sexual orientation, and/or life experience.

- A new network for additional hiring and/or business relationships.

In short, a good external hire should bring enough to the table to more than make up for their lack of history and context at the company.

INTERVIEWING MANAGERS

While there may be some areas of domain knowledge that overlap with individual contributors, it's important to craft a distinct and deliberate hiring process for managers (see "Interviewing" on page 22 for a discussion on how to hire ICs). Start by being clear about what you're looking for. What are the key talents and qualities you want from your management team? Strong programming chops? Awesome at recruiting? Great at execution? Once you know what the most important qualities are, you can figure out how to source and interview for those qualities, and build a process to distinguish a good fit from a bad one. By being clear and transparent about the process, you will also clarify for the team what they should expect from the new manager.

Pre-screening

As with hiring engineers, when hiring a manager to lead your team, you should cover your most important points over the phone or video, asking questions that give you a clear yes/no signal. Avoid interviews that are just 45 minutes of chit chat. It's especially important to get an indication of values fit during the pre-screen, since this is often one of the biggest concerns about a new manager; will they radically change the culture of the team in ways I won't like? See "Hiring, Values, and Culture" on page 181 for examples of how to interview for values. Some specific qualities you might look for during your interview are listed in "Identifying Management Potential" on page 74, and Camille Fournier gives some further suggestions for how to screen for engineering manager potential in "Hiring Engineering Managers" (*http://bit.ly/2gG4VUF*).

Checking explicit and backchannel references

Checking references is an important part of the recruiting process for any role, but especially so for management candidates. Some mediocre managers have a tendency to float around because they are great at interviewing and self-promotion. You can cut through this by using your network for backchannel discussion, and by explicitly asking for references from the candidate. Some more specific tips on how to do reference checks are covered in "Reference Checks" on page 38.

Just remember to be careful with how you perform backchannel reference checks so you don't accidentally "out" someone at their current company. Ideally, start with explicit references and go to backchannel if you don't feel like you're getting enough accurate data or a complete enough perspective. You want to make sure you get a 360-degree view by talking to a mix of past supervisors, peers, and direct reports. The latter is especially important since it is so commonly left out in our standard hiring process.

Preparing ICs to interview managers

Even with the best-designed process, some members of the team will feel uncomfortable interviewing candidate managers. Most of them will have never been managers before, and therefore won't be able to discriminate between good and bad answers to questions. Furthermore, even if they know what to look for, distinguishing a top-notch answer from a ho-hum answer is often more subtle than with engineering questions.

To prepare your team for the interview process, consider holding a pre-brief meeting with everyone to discuss what qualities are most important in the manager candidate. Different teams have different needs—one team might need an experienced technical leader to guide design decisions and mentor junior ICs, while another may need help collaborating with other teams and coordinating deliverables.

Based on the manager qualities outlined earlier, discuss with the team what areas to focus on in each interview session, specifically what questions should be asked and how to distinguish good and bad answers. If you're not sure how to do this, reach out to your network for help. Your board, company advisors, and past managers should have expertise they can offer here. For example (again from Camille Fournier in "Hiring Engineering Managers" (*http://bit.ly/2gGaB1a*)):

> Q: When you bring a new team member onto your team, what kinds of things do you personally do as part of their on-boarding? Have you ever been a mentor to a new hire or intern? What was that like, what did you learn from it?
>
> A: What you are looking for: someone who is actively engaged in the work of bringing on new people, and thoughtful about making that process bet-

ter. Someone who respected the work of mentoring, who isn't just trying to shed human interactions quickly to get back to code.

Ideally, write the questions and expected answers down somewhere so that the interview process remains stable over time as new team members are hired.

Next, decide who will be on the interview panel, and how the rest of the team can meet the candidate. Panel construction is relatively straightforward—just match team members' interest and experience with the focus areas for each interview session, and do a practice run with anyone new to the process. But also recognize that almost everyone will want a chance to meet the prospective manager. It's fairly common for the interview to include a lunch session where team members not involved in the panel can get a feel for the candidate. A more formal approach is to ask the candidate to give a short talk to the entire team, perhaps just a whiteboard session, on some topic of their choice.

Doing mock interviews with the team can be a fun way to prepare and calibrate what they should look for. Offer to buy a manager friend dinner in exchange for being an interview subject for your team. You might even cue your friend to give a few bad answers to see if the team can suss them out. You probably want to sit in on the interviews so you can debrief and offer specific feedback. And of course, an in-person debrief is essential once you start doing real interviews.

Finally, if at all possible, put off making a decision until you have interviewed at least two strong candidates. This reduces stress on the team because absolute judgments are harder to make than relative judgments. Finding two strong candidates can be very difficult in tough recruiting markets, but the extra effort at this stage is far less than the effort required to remove a failing manager later on.

MAKING A HIRING DECISION

The general decision-making process for hiring is covered in Chapter 2. But when you're hiring a manager, it's even more important than with ICs to be rigorous and to bias your interview process toward saying no. A poorly performing manager can do a lot of damage, and this damage is often more subtle and harder to detect than with technical work. Teams that are eager for management help are especially vulnerable. They may have the feeling that "any manager is going to be better than no manager," which can lead to softball interviews, a hasty review process, and making an offer to a poor candidate.

Counteract this tendency by reviewing this issue with the interview team and making it clear that you want to bias toward "no" rather than "yes." As mentioned earlier, being clear about what you're looking for and the level of rigor you want to have in evaluating answers will help here.

Alternatively, if there are reasons to bring on someone you're not quite sure about, set up a timeline for an initial evaluation, perhaps 3–6 months, and make it clear to the candidate how they will be evaluated and what the possible consequences are. This could be appropriate when there is a strong advocate for the candidate (perhaps a former coworker), but others on the panel have doubts based on their interview sessions. It's important that someone, most likely the candidate's future boss, commits to this evaluation and executes on it.

Lastly, don't forget that every external hire has the potential to shift the culture of a company away from the values of its founding team, and this is especially true with managers. So, consider setting a cap on the percentage of managers that you will hire from the outside. This will encourage investment in potential leaders on-staff and help alleviate concerns with hiring from the outside in general.

ON-BOARDING MANAGERS

Because some externally hired managers have not been actively coding for some time, we strongly recommend that managers go through the standard engineering on-boarding process, if at all possible. Even for managers that haven't coded in years, participating in some way should give them context on what their engineers are expected to know, what tools they have at their disposal, and what the day-to-day workflow looks like. Some managers and/or their teams may prefer to do a coding project as a way of getting their feet wet, or even join a team as an IC for several months before taking on day-to-day management. In these cases, set expectations appropriately with the team based on the manager's familiarity with the technology stack and how far removed they are from hands-on coding. You don't want the team assuming the manager will necessarily perform as a senior-level engineer, only to have them reject them as a teammate for this reason. (Hopefully this was thoroughly covered during the interview process, but there may be some team members who weren't involved, so it's worth resetting expectations.)

Conclusion

While intelligent leaders can argue about the correct ratio of managers to ICs, or the division of labor between managers and technical leads, few would disagree that people managers play an essential role on a growing team. In this chapter, we've focused on ways to introduce people management to a small, growing team with minimal disruption. The next chapter covers how to build a people management structure that maximizes team productivity and helps the team scale effectively.

Additional Resources

Our recommended reading list for people managers:

High Output Management *by Andy Grove*
  Perhaps the most efficient education in technical management in existence. For example, a complex issue, rendered simple: "A manager's output = the output of his organization + the output of the neighboring organizations under his influence."

Peopleware *by Tom DeMarco and Timothy Lister*
  More humane than Grove, but just as insightful: "The business we're in is more sociological than technological, more dependent on workers' abilities to communicate with each other than their abilities to communicate with machines."

The Mythical Man-Month *by Frederick Brooks*
  His influence can't be understated. Get the edition with the "No Silver Bullet" essay added on.

Managing Humans *by Michael Lopp*
  A collection of bite-sized essays, as thought-provoking as they are delicious.

Leading Snowflakes *by Oren Ellenbogen*
  An excellent book focused specifically on helping engineers make the transition to engineering management.

Drive *by Daniel H. Pink*
  His motivational framework of Autonomy, Mastery, and Purpose was a major influence on the content of this book.

First, Break All the Rules *by Marcus Buckingham and Curt Coffman*
  What separates great managers from the rest? Read this book to find out.

5

People Management at Scale

In Chapter 4, you learned how to hire and/or train your first batch of managers and how to roll out a new management structure to your team. After doing this, you should be free to focus on other priorities, right?

Well, it may not surprise you that the team's continued growth will create new challenges for you and your team of managers. In this chapter, we will cover what needs to happen beyond the initial rollout, and the various ways you can supercharge your people managers to build a highly scalable team in support of your fast-growing business.

Magnifying Your Managers

Talented people managers can enhance the productivity of the entire organization. What can you do to enable and magnify their impact? And what issues are likely to crop up as you move from a handful of managers to several dozen and beyond?

IMPROVING MANAGEMENT SKILLS

If you're running a typical startup, your management team is likely to be inexperienced. They need ongoing mentorship and training to really grow into their new career. There are complex issues that take years to master, such as how to build an inclusive work environment, how to communicate difficult issues to peers and reports, and how to recruit the best new talent for the team. And someday you'll want these managers to help identify and train the next rank of new managers as their team expands in scope. So give them explicit support for growth and learning, and perhaps help them unlearn some bad habits that formed during the team's early days. Here are some suggestions for how to do this:

Provide each new manager with a mentor

It's very common for new managers to experience *impostor syndrome* as they struggle to adjust to the demands of their new role. Regular meetings with an experienced mentor provide a forum for raising difficult questions or simply validating that what the new manager is doing makes sense. Ideally, this mentor should not be in their management chain, since this can make it harder to be open about any struggles the new manager is having. If there aren't enough appropriate management mentors within the company, try tapping your external resources: the board, your investor network, friends of the company, former colleagues, and so on.

Establish a learning program for managers

This can be as simple and lightweight as a monthly book club meeting, or a more formal management training program. But making this explicit sets expectations that learning about management is an important part of the new manager's workload.

Make someone responsible for manager quality

There should be a single person on the hook for assigning mentors, coordinating reading groups, or whatever you decide to do to help your managers improve. This person should be able to answer the question "how are we making management great at this company?" and be able to back it up with data. Otherwise, you risk having your management learning activities take a back seat during crunch mode and never return.

Of course, many of these techniques can apply to managers and ICs alike. We'll cover this topic again more broadly in "Building an Environment of Continuous Learning" on page 105.

ENCOURAGING COLLABORATION AND COMMUNITY

A common failure mode for startups with 100–1,000 employees is the outbreak of "us versus them." Teams that should be working together start pointing fingers to assign blame, speaking negatively about the other team, or simply avoiding any involvement with each other. This seems to emerge naturally as the company grows beyond *Dunbar's number* (*https://en.wikipedia.org/wiki/Dunbar %27s_number*), the amount of people beyond which it's difficult to sustain meaningful personal contact. Team members can no longer keep track of everyone at the company, so they start to establish stronger ties and even tribal identities with the people they work most closely with. Short-sighted managers sometimes even encourage this pattern as a way of bonding the team together. This can be effective in the short term, but ultimately it stunts cooperation and restricts information flow, both of which are detrimental to the long-term health of the larger organization.

Leadership can combat this tendency by investing in manager-to-manager relationships and encouraging the management team to act as a peer group. Beyond typical team bonding activities, like lunches or off-site meetings, look for opportunities to encourage collaboration between managers who might not otherwise work together, such as building a training class for new hires or revising the promotion process. For example, Twitter has a fairly successful "Eng Manager Forum," which brings together small groups of managers from across engineering to discuss problems, share ideas, and collaborate on solutions. Monthly one-on-ones between peer managers, particularly those with customer–vendor relationships, can help build cooperation and avoid the conflicts that can emerge across organizational boundaries.

A management team that respects each other and knows how to work together is better equipped to handle rapid growth and resolve the inevitable challenges and conflicts that arise. For example, a reorganization might cause former peer managers to end up in a reporting relationship, which can be a very difficult transition if the former peers don't trust and respect each other. We've seen examples where managers who are unable or unwilling to work together have divided the company into competing factions, leading to wasteful duplicated efforts and political squabbling.

ASSESSING MANAGER PERFORMANCE

Regular assessment of manager performance is especially important, as a poorly performing manager can derail the productivity of an entire team. Like the interview process, accurately and regularly measuring manager performance can be much harder than measuring performance of ICs, but this is definitely not a reason to avoid doing it.

Define expectations

As with ICs, managers need to know what is expected of them. Start by asking your managers to own the long-term effect their team has on the business. Everything a manager does, from hiring to coaching to communicating and so on, is ultimately in service of the long-term health of the company. But because these effects are often indirect and the team's overall impact is hard to measure, you typically need to combine multiple second-order indicators, such as key business or operational metrics, team morale, NPS surveys from customers, and so on. Document and share these so that both your managers and their teams are aware of what's expected of them.

Continuous, timely feedback

For managers and ICs alike, feedback has more impact when it is given frequently, based on recent events. The main challenge for assessing managers is that you may need to rely on surveys of, or meetings with, their direct reports and peers, who may get annoyed if they are asked too often. So establish a regular, acceptable cadence and stick with it. "Skip-level" meetings, whether one-on-one or a group setting, can be helpful since ICs often appreciate having access to their higher-level managers.

Be wary of politics

Managers can be a competitive lot, especially in companies where competitiveness is considered a virtue. Be careful how you treat peer feedback, and don't simply rely on hearsay to form an opinion of a manager's performance. Use feedback as a motivator to take a closer look and form your own opinion. You may find that two managers simply had a difference of opinion on an issue, which is not necessarily a performance indicator.

Don't confuse performance with likeability

One of the most difficult situations to deal with is a well-liked manager who doesn't deliver on commitments. A common case is a manager who simply tells reports what they want to hear rather than challenging them to improve and holding them accountable to performance standards. Such situations reinforce the need for clear expectations tied to business goals, and not relying solely on team surveys.

HANDLING UNDERPERFORMING MANAGERS

If you've decided that a manager needs to be let go from the company, there are some special considerations given their role.

Plan, communicate, listen, adjust

Removing a manager can be incredibly disruptive to the team. This can be positive ("Whew, thank goodness!") or negative ("What? I'm quitting!") or other ("So, uh, can I go back to coding now?"). As with any disruptive and potentially controversial change, it's important to find a balance between thorough planning and quick action.

Make a plan for covering the manager's responsibilities, whether that means rolling things up to the manager's boss, or merging temporarily into a peer's team, or asking a team leader to take on the manager's role. But only consult with those who are essential to the plan's success so you can avoid rumors. Once you communicate the decision, keep your ears open for feedback from the team and adjust accordingly. You may learn things you didn't know before, and incorporating this into the plan may achieve greater buy-in from the team and minimize disruption.

Re-recruit the team

A well-liked manager can often take people with them, even with non-solicitation clauses in their employment agreement. You should consider everyone on the team a flight risk until convinced otherwise, and act accordingly. Take the time to figure out what they find most motivating, and do what you can to provide a long-term roadmap that hits those motivations. Just make sure it's something realistic and not a fictional sell job.

Happiness During Hyper-Growth

In Chapter 4, we described a key function of people management: "Ensuring the team is happy and productive by providing motivating work assignments, appropriate compensation, learning opportunities, and career guidance." The individuals and the team are more likely to be successful if they enjoy their work, their interactions with coworkers, and the work environment in general. But typical hyper-growth teams are so focused on scaling the product or the customer base that little attention is paid to the policies and practices that keep morale high. When the company is doing well, the thrill of success covers up whatever problems are lying under the surface. But the first major stumble can quickly expose these problems, potentially leading to a loss of productivity or, worst case, regretted attrition (for an explanation of regretted versus non-regretted attrition, refer back to Chapter 3).

The right ways to build team morale can shift as the team grows, in response not only to the size of the team but also to the changing context and scope of the work being done. Keeping an eye out for the warning signs listed in Chapter 4 can help you head off an emerging crisis. But to be more proactive in building morale, consider the examples discussed next and tailor them for your team and situation.

PREPARING FOR GROWTH

The moment the company shifts into rapid growth, the simplest and most effective way to prepare your team is to talk with them about what they should expect. These are all normal emotional reactions to have during hyper-growth:

- Feelings of reduced impact or loss of autonomy

- Resentment of having to shift familiar responsibilities to new hires

- Fear that new hires will stunt career growth of the existing team members by stealing opportunities

- Skepticism about new ways of doing things, or feelings that the team is "getting too corporate"

- Worry that new hires will change the culture in harmful ways (or frustration at observing that they are)

- Fear that new layers of management will lead to disempowerment and lack of access to senior leaders

These reactions will be much easier for your team to deal with if they know to expect them. Encourage patience and frequent communication, in both one-on-ones and group meetings. And remind them of the opportunities that come from growth—new challenges, new ideas, more responsibility (if desired), and more collaboration. Overall, growth can help the team have a bigger impact, but some adjustments will be necessary. Molly Graham's advice in "Give Away Your Legos and Other Commandments for Scaling Startups" (*http://bit.ly/2gSK57L*) is a great reference for this topic.

AGENCY AND EMPOWERMENT

One of the joys of working on a small team is the sheer impact a single person can have each day. Ideas turn into new features at a rapid clip and every team member can easily see how their work has moved the product forward. The feelings of ownership and impact can be incredibly energizing.

As the product and the team get larger, there is a natural tendency for these feelings to wane. Each bit of work represents a smaller and smaller piece of the overall product, and there are more and more teammates who want to weigh in on each change. Before, an engineer could just decide to add a feature based on a hallway discussion, but now there is a complex approval process to navigate for each change.

There may also be an increase in work that feels less glamorous: upgrading the revision control system, debugging flaky integration tests, refactoring a particularly ugly piece of legacy code. What was formerly an exciting place to work is now starting to feel like drudgery. Such a gloomy forecast is common, but it isn't inevitable. What can managers do to counteract this?

Build empowerment and initiative into your culture

If your company values bottom-up innovation and independent action, it's important that you make this clear in your cultural messaging. Facebook's famous "Move Fast and Break Things" motto was an intentional message to its developers that innovation and delivery speed were more important than delivering perfect bug-free code. Although it later chose to refine the motto, it kept "Move Fast" to help maintain the focus on development speed.

How Amazon Empowers Engineers: A Story from Dave

I saw a powerful example of how to enable initiative while working at A9, a subsidiary company of Amazon focused on search technology. Amazon's leadership, all the way up to Jeff Bezos, promoted the idea that anyone could run a "weblab" (Amazon's A/B testing system) on a feature or function, even if this function was owned by another team. This was encouraged as long as you communicated with the owner first about your plans to run an experiment.

During the time that I was running the Search Relevance team at A9, the Personalization team at Amazon HQ had their own ideas for how to improve the ranking of search results. With very little coordination or fanfare, they ran a sequence of experiments to test their theories out. These ultimately led to some innovative new features, generating significant increases in sales on Amazon.com.

At first, my team and I were frustrated by having another team making changes to "our feature," especially when it required extra effort to coordinate launches and fix bugs. But in the end, the numbers spoke for themselves. As shareholders of the company, we couldn't argue with the benefits to the bottom line. So we invested in better communication between the teams to make coordination easier, and the A9 team eventually integrated the Personalization team's feature into the core Amazon search infrastructure. This focus on almost-anything-goes innovation is a key part of Amazon's engineering culture to this day.

Focus failures on learning rather than punishment

Teams inevitably experience failures, and as the team grows the cost of each failure may grow as well, including more customers affected, greater revenue lost, and so on. There is a temptation for leadership to just do something, anything, to prevent further failures, and this desire needs to be carefully channeled. At one extreme, leaders may end up publicly shaming those responsible for a bug, or even terminating them. This can have a dangerous chilling effect on the rest of the team. Who will want to try out a bold, potentially game-changing idea if failure might cost them their reputation or job? Most will take a safer route. Over time, innovation gets increasingly stifled as the company grows.

A less dramatic response might be to build a tighter approval process for production changes. But how much will this process slow down releases, possibly creating a bottleneck on those who hand out approvals? How much frustration will developers have to endure, waiting for the change they made two weeks ago to finally get deployed? In the long term, such a response might harm productivity even more than the previous example.

It is obviously worth trying to understand the causes of major failures, but it's important to be careful with the process and to understand the costs of any possible remediations. Dave Zwieback does an excellent job describing the costs of blame and outlining alternative approaches in his First Round Review article "This Is How Effective Leaders Move Beyond Blame" (*http://bit.ly/2gSL6wh*).

How Risk Tolerance Changes with Team Growth: A Story from Kellan Elliott-McCrea

It's natural for the risk tolerance of your team to shift as the company grows, for multiple reasons. In the early days, your employees were, by definition, risk takers who could rely on their personal relationship with the founders. Later-stage hires will come in having been trained to expect failure to have consequences and so will self-police the amount of risk they are willing to take. This natural transition to more risk-averse employees whose relationships with the founders can't be assumed is a

major cause of "big company slowdown syndrome" unless actively managed. And being more risk averse is a rational response to increased
complexity, so tooling needs to be put in place to help manage that as
well.

Actively suppress the mechanisms of "no"

Related to the previous point, it is very common for teams to introduce increasingly formal change control processes, particularly after any large failure. A company's haggard Site Operations team, sick of being woken up in the night, might
one day demand that all production changes go through their new change control
process. Or the VP of Product may require the approval of a Product Change
Committee before any customer-facing changes are deployed. These may seem
like good ideas on the surface, and the team may accept them as just part of
growing up, but the gradual accumulation of these processes is one of the reasons companies slow down as they mature. Like a frog boiling slowly, the team
may one day realize it takes a minimum of six weeks to get a one-line change out
to production...they're cooked!

One senior engineer at a Fortune 500 company described his frustration
with how slow his team was moving:

> We've taken Scrum and added layers of gates and checkpoints to it. Of
> course, these checkpoints grew out of real screw ups—something went
> wrong in the past and we don't want to repeat it. But still, things quickly
> became bureaucratic.

It isn't practical to try to prevent all mistakes, so instead focus on improving
how you react and learn from them. It may be tempting to introduce formal gates
and checkpoints as in the preceding story, especially after a major failure, but we
recommend you first consider the possible impact to productivity and innovation.
How much time will ICs spend waiting for approvals to come through? What is
the cost of context switching to another task and back? How much will these
measures reduce their sense of autonomy? Enumerating these costs might lead
you to focus on better tools and training rather than a more stringent release process.

You should also consciously edit any accumulated bureaucracy as the team
grows. Use reorganizations as an opportunity not just to move teams around but
also to streamline how work gets done. Consider auditing the number of steps in

the development process where an engineer might be told "no" to a change, and try to reduce this or at least hold it constant. See Chapter 7 for a description of value stream mapping and how this can be applied to streamline workflows.

Praise and reward those who get things done

If you want your team to continue to show initiative and spark, make sure you publicize examples of the behavior you want. If a team goes out of their way to make a high-leverage tool better, or fixes a long-ignored "broken window" in the product, use the next all-hands meeting or company-wide email update to raise awareness of their achievement. In particular, call out the behavior or attitude you want to reinforce and not just the specific results that were realized. As your team scales, what you choose to celebrate becomes a powerful tool for reinforcing and shaping culture (addressed in detail in Chapter 9). And make sure such public praise is evenly distributed throughout the organization. There is a tendency to over-focus on visible changes in the product or revenue-generating improvements, which can leave those working on infrastructure or operations feeling left out. The folks toiling away in the boiler room need to know that their efforts matter as well.

It's also important to incorporate these behaviors into the performance feedback and promotion process (discussed in detail in "Career Development" on page 108).

Allow individuals to pursue the work that interests them

Anyone who has managed skilled professionals knows that they can have a wide range of opinions about what projects they work on. Some are happy to take whatever task comes their way, while others feel strongly that they must work on the most impactful feature, or something novel and innovative, or a particular tool that they've always wished existed.

GitHub, for example, provided engineers with the ability to self-assign projects, provided they work on the intersection of their interests and the company's problems.[1] Some companies provide less autonomy, preferring that self-directed work happen in parallel with regular assignments. Although there have been criticisms of such programs,[2] most participants we've spoken to report that

---

1 Scott Chacon, "Leading by First Principles" (*http://oreil.ly/2gFwPzg*).

2 For example, see Oren Ellenbogen's "Is GitHub's Self-Assignment of Tasks a Myth?" (*http://bit.ly/2gFzvNv*).

they were generally motivating and an overall morale boost for the participants. These programs can also be a selling point for recruiting.

Models for Encouraging Innovation

There are a number of internal innovation models that can be used as a starting point. One of the first and most well-known was Google's "20% Time" policy, which allocated 20% of an employee's time to a project chosen by the employee. Although Google has moved on from this specific practice, other companies have started similar programs:

- SoundCloud, Hacker Time—see "Stop! Hacker Time" (*http:// bit.ly/2gSHsmf*)
- Atlassian, ShipIt (*https://www.atlassian.com/company/shipit*)
- SurveyMonkey's Hackathon—see "SurveyMonkey Hackathon 2015 Edition" (*http://svy.mk/2gSQlwb*)
- Twitter's Hack Week—see "Hack Week @ Twitter" (*http://bit.ly/ 2gSL73r*)

One caveat, however, is to make sure these efforts are not just "innovation theater." Unless there is some path for projects to actually make it to production, the employees that participate may end up feeling demotivated rather than energized. At Twitter, several Hack Weeks in a row produced exciting ideas that ended up sitting on the shelf. In response to this, the engineering leadership decided that the winning Hack Week project would receive funding in the form of dedicated product management and engineering headcount, and several future winners then led to new feature launches.

When individuals are feeling bored or uninspired by their work, they may go "team shopping," looking around the company for other teams to work with. A policy for how to go about switching teams or projects, with some lightweight rules for transition time and frequency of switches, can be helpful. You want to encourage employees to find motivating work, but not at the cost of abandoned responsibilities. There are other benefits to "team shopping" beyond motivation, specifically:

- Ideas, knowledge, and techniques are more broadly shared between teams.
- The flow of engineers in and out of certain groups may provide insight into how healthy those groups are and/or how their respective managers are performing.
- Better visibility into whether there is title parity across teams—for example, does a Senior Engineer in Group A contribute as much as the Senior Engineer in Group B? (We'll discuss title parity and promotion decisions more fully in "Career Development" on page 108.)

Internal Mobility at issuu

During Alex's time at issuu, the management team wanted to encourage engineers to switch teams without causing disruption. Here is an excerpt from the policy they ended up adopting, which worked very well.

> We value the fact that sometimes engineers want to switch teams to learn all parts of our stack, work with new colleagues, and find a new challenge inside issuu. To switch teams, the following rules apply.
>
> After spending 12 months in one team, engineers have the right to choose a new team, if they wish, with the following being understood:
>
> - The new team needs to accept the new member. The team lead is asked about the transfer and then he/she discusses it with the team.
>
> - It doesn't necessarily happen immediately. It might take up to two months for the change to actually happen due to normal business activity, such as finding a replacement and/or organizing a handover.

There are other opportunities to switch teams, especially when business priorities require it. This policy only covers the case where the engineer wants to switch to a new team.

PROMOTING WORK–LIFE BALANCE

There have been many successful companies built following the classic startup model of 100-hour weeks, sleeping at the office, and late-night heroics. Those of us who have lived through such periods can tell you about the darker side of this tale: broken relationships, mental and physical health problems, and severe burnout. Although there are certainly times in any startup's life that call for the team to go into "crunch mode," the prevailing wisdom (backed up by our experience) is that helping employees maintain a balance between work and the rest of their life leads to greater productivity in the long haul, mainly through improved retention.

Here is some guidance on how to promote healthy work–life balance:

- Make sure the team can recharge on the weekend. If team members are logging significant work time on the weekends (outside of "crunch mode"), they are probably feeling pressure to deliver work, and feeling unable to do so during the workweek. It's worth your time to find out why. Also, team leaders should be careful not to send email or other messages to the team early in the weekend, since this can easily lead them to burn precious personal time researching and responding to the issue. Even if the sender doesn't require an immediate response, it can be difficult to ignore a question from the boss until Monday.

- Avoid evening meetings or team dinners. These activities can put pressure on individuals to sacrifice their social lives for the company, especially when they're scheduled last minute. Even team dinners can become a burden if scheduled too frequently. Don't force your team to make such difficult trade-offs.

- Make sure deadlines are realistic and well motivated, not arbitrary. Nothing kills morale like finding out that those 27 urgent features didn't *actually* need to be done by the end of the month. Creating a false sense of urgency in order to push the team will usually backfire and lead to a loss of trust in leadership.

- Make sure leaders set good examples. If you believe your team should have a healthy work–life balance, you need to model this for the team. Otherwise, they will feel guilty every time they arrive after you and/or leave before you, or notice you sending email at 1 a.m.

- Alex Payne has an excellent blog post (*http://bit.ly/2gSLYB9*) on why all-nighters and other "heroics" are unhealthy for your team.

As many founders have noted, startups are more a marathon than a sprint. Being able to set a healthy pace for yourself and your team will help preserve the team and give you the reserves you need when you truly need them to push to meet a critical deliverable.

BUILDING AN INCLUSIVE WORKPLACE

Retention of employees from underrepresented groups is a major problem at technology companies. Both the individuals involved and the company as a whole suffer when qualified, productive employees decide to quit. A study conducted by the Level Playing Field Institute in 2007 estimated that "unfairness costs U.S. employers $64 billion on an annual basis—a price tag nearly equivalent to the 2006 combined revenues of Google, Goldman Sachs, Starbucks and Amazon."[3] How to build a diverse team is covered in Chapter 2, but retention is an equally important component. To maintain the team you worked so hard to build, we recommend that you make inclusion a core value of the team, backing it up in both words and actions. We'll now outline some specific recommendations.

Audit your office environment

In this competitive job market, every company wants to distinguish itself by having an office that employees love. In the 90s it was bean bag chairs and Nerf guns. Today, it's more likely to be fancy coffee equipment and on-site bicycle repair. All of this is well intentioned, but taken too far it can become a source of unconscious hostility for those who don't relate to the edgy character of the office environment or are concentrating on being at work to do work. What were once standard features of Silicon Valley offices have recently been re-examined:

---

3 Corporate Leavers Survey (*http://www.lpfi.org/corporate-leavers-survey/*), Level Playing Field Institute.

Stereotypical "white male geek" office decor

Could your office be mistaken for someone's "man cave"? As discussed in "Ambient Belonging: How Stereotypical Cues Impact Gender Participation in Computer Science" (*http://bit.ly/2gSHpa2*), if you decorate your office with *Star Trek* memorabilia, posters of flashy cars, and foosball tables, you might trigger a negative effect on retention of female employees, even if they happen to like those things. Signaling that the company is designed for the comfort of a specific type of employee can trigger discomfort in those that aren't included in the stereotype, leading to higher attrition and a loss of productivity.

Drinking alcohol as a bonding activity

Many companies tout their amazingly well-stocked beer selection in their recruiting spiels. More and more cubicles feature minibars with the sort of equipment you'd expect to see in Don Draper's office on *Mad Men*. But consider: how would you feel working there if you were an alcoholic or a child of alcoholic parents? Or a devout Muslim or Mormon?

This doesn't mean you need an office devoid of character. But give that character some extra thought and be sure to consider what it might say to both employees, prospective hires, and customers alike. For example, would featuring artwork from the children or nieces and nephews of employees or scenes of local landmarks created by local artists be less appealing than the alternatives?

Beware the "null process"

Small teams are often process-phobic. They fear that introducing formal processes will stifle innovation, reduce agility, and turn the fun, free-wheeling team into a bureaucratic nightmare. But as Kate Heddleston explains in her essay "The Null Process" (*http://bit.ly/2gSjkQF*), in the absence of a formal process, employees use unspoken expectations to understand how to do their job. And since they are unspoken, members of an underrepresented group may have a difficult time distilling this information from their peers.

On-boarding is a good example. Small companies often have a very informal on-boarding process, where new hires are pointed at an outdated wiki and told to "figure things out." If they're lucky, they get a mentor to shadow for a bit. In these cases, new hires end up relying on social links to fill in the gaps in their education by chatting about them over lunch or in the hallway. New team members from underrepresented groups might have a harder time building these social connections, leaving them at a disadvantage to their peers. Better to spend the necessary time to create and maintain on-boarding docs than to demotivate a good engineer in their first few weeks on the job.

Process and documentation don't have to be heavyweight. Simple checklists can describe what is expected of a process without requiring lengthy documents or long meetings. And new hires can be asked to keep these checklists updated with whatever new information they learn during their training.

Don't focus the burden of diversity on your "diverse" team members

Companies eager to improve diversity and inclusiveness sometimes go too far in their efforts. For example, it's a common practice to ensure that interview panels for female candidates contain at least one female employee. Similarly, black employees are often encouraged to attend recruiting events at historically black colleges and universities. Although such practices are well intentioned, they can backfire if they lead to an imbalanced burden on the team members involved. A study of 1,700 professionals (*http://bit.ly/2gSQorY*) conducted by the Level Playing Field Institute showed that "the behaviors which were most likely to prompt someone to quit were: (1) being asked to attend extra recruiting or community related events because of one's race, gender, religion or sexual orientation." Summarizing a survey on the subject (*http://bit.ly/2gSIWgr*), ModelViewCulture recently wrote that "Diversity in tech work is having a profound, negative impact on advocates' happiness, mental and physical health and work–life balance, as well as their safety, relationships, careers and security." Ensure your diversity and inclusion efforts are equally distributed across interested parties, and make participation purely voluntary rather than an obligation.

Make sure everyone is heard

Google recently published findings (*http://nyti.ms/2gSRNyD*) from its analysis of team performance, dubbed Project Aristotle. What are the qualities that the most successful teams have in common? In other words, what makes great teams great? One of the key factors turned out to be the extent to which teams shared "air time" between members during meetings, or "equality in distribution of conversational turn-taking." This tendency raised the collective intelligence of the group by promoting shared ideas, but also raised morale by increasing engagement of the entire team.

Work should happen at work, during work hours

Building on the earlier section "Promoting Work–Life Balance" on page 101, a culture that praises or even subtly encourages working late nights and weekends can alienate employees with other obligations or priorities: kids, elderly parents, personal health issues, volunteering duties, and so on. Similarly, scheduling company events during off hours, even social events like a happy hour or company picnic, can leave those same employees feeling excluded. Worse yet, they may sacrifice their outside obligations to meet the expectations of the team, which all too often leads to resentment and lower morale.

Hard work is built into the culture of many companies, but this does not necessarily mean crazy hours or excessive self-sacrifice. Make your workplace safe for those who need a 9 to 5 schedule and can get their job done during those hours. Don't shower praise on the "heroes" who stay at the office past midnight every night; instead, understand why they feel the need for such long hours and take corrective action if needed. And remember that your behavior as a leader has as much influence as the words you say, if not more.

Use metrics to surface bias

In the long term, unfair treatment at work will eventually surface in measurable ways, such as:

- Regretted attrition rate (see "Off-boarding" on page 56 for a definition)
- Average compensation by level
- Promotion rate by level

Regularly reviewing these metrics and breaking them down by gender and race may reveal the presence of conscious or unconscious bias in team practices. Although there may not be enough data for statistical significance while the team is small, tracking this data early will allow you to notice trends sooner as the team grows.

BUILDING AN ENVIRONMENT OF CONTINUOUS LEARNING

An old management joke goes something like this (with apologies to CFOs everywhere):

> CFO asks: "What happens if we invest in developing our people and they leave us?"

CEO replies: "What happens if we don't and they stay?"

Those of us who join technology startups tend to be an ambitious lot. We aren't satisfied with just being good at our jobs. We want to get better and better, and to be recognized for all the ways we've improved. A scalable company needs to address both sides of this desire.

Ongoing education

Encouraging learning has multiple benefits—employees get better at their jobs, and they feel good about the investment the company is making in their careers. There are a variety of approaches to this, ranging from informal brown-bag talks by volunteers, to a highly organized Learning and Development team that develops classes and brings in outside speakers. Make sure you put your team somewhere in this range and reward those who help others learn. Here's a menu of ideas to consider:

- Encourage ongoing formal education, either online or at a nearby college, and provide a yearly budget for any class that is at all job-related. You may want to establish some rough guidelines early on—for example, online classes should never take precedence over assigned tasks or justify unscheduled work-from-home days.

- Weekly *lunch learning sessions* can be a mix of employee presentations about a topic they are passionate about, group viewing of online conference videos or tutorials, discussions about emerging technology, or outside speakers. A great option is to have senior leaders present lessons learned, oral histories of the company, or whatever they are passionate about as a way of keeping them accessible to ICs as the management hierarchy continues to get deeper. We recommend having a single individual take charge of these sessions, rather than relying on community ownership. A single owner is more likely to keep the calendar booked, and make sure that outside speakers are greeted properly and have the equipment they need for their presentation.

- *Conferences and meetups* can be a great combination of learning, networking opportunities, and fun, though they can be expensive in both time and money. Speaking at such events takes the most time, but can be a great way to improve communications skills, connect with other speakers, and build the brand of the company (see "Building an Employer Brand" on page 16). If someone is merely attending, maximize the return by asking them to write up a conference summary or give a short talk over lunch. And establish a reasonable time and money budget up front, perhaps 5 days and $2,000 per year, to set expectations and avoid having to clamp down later. More and more conferences support virtual attendance, which may be a great option for those with families or other constraints on travel.

- *Connecting with peers at similar-stage companies*, either formally or informally, can lead to an exchange of ideas and new techniques, and help build a community around shared technologies. Etsy even took the unconventional step of setting up an "Engineer Exchange" program (*http://bit.ly/2gSPVWF*) where an Etsy engineer would spend a week working for another company, and vice versa.

For more on this topic, see "Continuous Learning and Improvement" on page 186.

Mentoring

Coaching and mentoring can be particularly effective, especially for leaders who are inexperienced at their level of responsibility. In a talk about scaling LinkedIn (*http://bit.ly/2gSQoJU*), Jeff Weiner advised that "once you get to scale—you need a leadership team who will make things happen on their own. This is when you recognize the importance of mentorship, development, coaching, understanding their fears, their strength, helping them develop their weaker areas, etc. That requires time, and it requires someone who knows how to coach."

It can be hard to convince a busy team to dedicate cycles to mentoring when there are pressing deadlines and angry customers. It's important for leaders to reinforce that such investments will pay dividends in the long run, and model this in their own behavior by spending time on training and mentorship.

Team learning

There are many opportunities during the course of day-to-day developments for teams to learn from their mistakes, as well as their successes. Take advantage of these moments to help the team learn and grow, especially when the issues are explicitly tied to productivity and are customer facing: Why did our system bring the site down for five hours? What happened during that last sprint that allowed us to ship twice as many features as usual? Consider the following techniques:

Retrospectives

> Whether your team uses Agile, Scrum, Waterfall, or other methodologies for organizing work items, there are always moments when you can stop and reflect on how the work got done. What went well, and what didn't? What took longer than we thought, and what was surprisingly easy? Doing this regularly and thoughtfully is a relatively easy way for teams to improve their planning and estimation skills. For particularly important milestones, make sure any lessons learned are shared broadly, with the org or even the entire company. A recurring slot at the all-hands meeting can work for this.

Post-mortems, failure analysis

> Every team suffers mistakes and failures, and each one of these is an opportunity to learn. Make sure whatever process you use, you emphasize learning over blame assignment. Many techniques, such as "5 Whys," tend to over-focus on identifying the individual at fault, as opposed to analyzing the context that allowed the individual to make a mistake—for example, a lack of training or inadequate tools. *Beyond Blame*, by the aforementioned Dave Zwieback, explains in detail how to run an effective post-mortem. And as with retrospectives, make sure that lessons learned from failure are shared broadly, and those that are honest and thorough in their approach receive appropriate public praise.

Cross-training

> Especially as the company grows larger, more and more teams will not have visibility into what other teams are building, which hinders the sharing of novel new techniques or design ideas. Try encouraging teams to present these at a weekly lunch learning session, with a rotation to ensure every team gets covered.

CAREER DEVELOPMENT

In Chapter 4, we discussed the importance of having a separate career path for managers and ICs prior to adding formal management to the team. But what do these career paths look like?

Defining a career path or ladder

A clearly defined career path spells out what the company values in various roles, both what they should be able to do and how they should do it. Knowing what an ideal engineer or manager looks like at various stages of growth helps guide those who want to improve their skills and magnify their impact. This helps scalability because individuals can work on these improvements independently, without requiring their manager to chart the course for them (Figure 5-1).

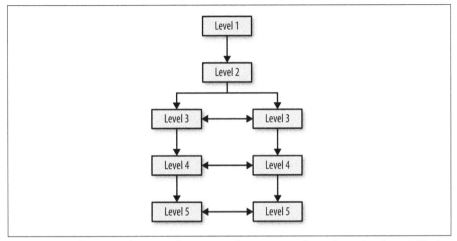

Figure 5-1. Dual career path—green for ICs, gray for managers (from Alexander Grosse's blog)

Consider the following areas in defining a career path for your team.

Number of titles or levels

Having many fine-grained levels can be motivating, since promotions will happen more frequently. But more levels also means more work, both in explaining the difference in capabilities at each level, and managing the promotion process.

Public versus private levels

Advocates for private levels tout the fact that private levels cannot be used to influence debates or decisions—everyone is publicly the same level, so a more junior engineer will be less intimidated by a principal engineer when discussing the technical merits of a proposal. The counter-argument is that, as with compensation, ICs tend to share their levels with each other anyway, and that public titles allow for some level of community policing. For example, if Henry's peers are surprised that he is a Software Engineer II instead of a Senior Software Engineer, they can raise this concern to Henry's manager and perhaps influence the next review cycle. It's not uncommon to start with private levels and move to public ones once the processes for calibration and promotion (discussed momentarily) are well established. The only downside is that it's hard to go back if the team feels that public titles aren't needed.

Slotting

The process of assigning initial titles to each member of the team is often referred to as "slotting." Is this done solely by managers, or is there some involvement by the senior ICs on the team? This is often a messy and iterative process, and the company rarely has enough historical performance data to help make decisions more objective, so the decision makers end up doing it by gut feel. Because of this, we recommend having a clear process for correcting a misassigned level (e.g., an engineer who is assigned a "Senior Engineer" title, but is actually performing at a more junior level, or vice versa). This relieves some of the burden of getting it exactly right the first time, which is nigh impossible.

Matching compensation to job levels

The common approach is to have compensation bands for each level to ensure that individuals performing at the same level have roughly the same compensation. This is important to discourage bias and avoid cases where the "squeaky wheels" end up with the highest salaries. There are companies like Radford that sell compensation data if you need help establishing your bands.

At some companies the bands are overlapping, to allow some flexibility to adjust compensation to each individual's circumstances. For example, imagine two ICs, one an entry-level engineer and one a senior engineer, who have very different feelings about equity versus cash compensation. The senior engineer may have negotiated a larger equity stake in exchange for lower salary, while the entry-level engineer may have done the opposite. In this case, the engineer may have a higher salary than the senior engineer. Some companies also subdivide each title into separate compensation levels (e.g., "Senior Engineer, level 2," with the level being kept private).

Public or private compensation

A full discussion of compensation policy is outside the scope of this book, but recently more companies are adopting a full-disclosure approach: salary and stock for every employee is published for anyone within the company to see. Although this may feel uncomfortable at first, there are definitely benefits; in particular, it builds trust between senior management and the rank and file and allows for community policing (e.g., ensuring female directors are paid as much as the median for male directors).

Rollout

Regardless of the approach you take, rolling out a career path can be a stressful and controversial step for a young team, particularly at the moment when individuals learn what their new title is. Here are some recommendations for how to minimize the disruption:

- Involve your senior ICs in the process. They will help ensure that it is grounded in reality and those involved will be able to help their fellow ICs understand the decisions that went into it.

- Communicate the career path before slotting individuals into their new job titles (if you have them). The slotting process can generate a lot of angst and controversy. It's better if the team agrees that the career path is sound before they find out where the team thinks they are on the path.

- Make sure your company values are reflected in the career path. If you believe, for example, that rapid innovation is more important than perfect solutions, find a way to describe how engineers can embody that belief. See Chapter 9 for more information about how to uncover and communicate core values.

- Keep titles private at first, to allow for managers to talk to each individual about their assigned slotting and gather feedback.

- When in doubt, it is common to slot the individual to the lower title, since it is easier to promote later than to demote. But this is also risky for morale since they may be expecting the higher level. In these cases, be very clear and specific about what they need to demonstrate to get promoted, and make sure they are set up for success (i.e., that they have a task assignment that can allow them to demonstrate qualification for the next level).

The following are some additional resources you can refer to:

- Alexander Grosse's "Creating a Career Path" (*http://bit.ly/2gSQTC5*)
- Urban Airship's tech ladder on GitHub (*http://bit.ly/2i8LiUz*)
- A different take from Rent the Runway (*http://bit.ly/2i8ND1O*)

Creating a promotion process

When is an engineer ready to be promoted to a Senior Engineer? No matter how clearly defined your career path is, at some point some person or group needs to gather the necessary data and opinions and pass judgment: "Yes, they're ready!" or "No, they aren't there yet."

These decisions are a very common source of frustration and discontent. At most companies, promotions equate to both increased recognition and compensation, so the stakes are high. The previous section covered the career ladder, and making sure this is clear and well understood is the foundation of the promotion process. Here are some steps to take to ensure that the rest of the process goes as smoothly as possible.

Use 360-degree input

A manager often only sees one side of an individual's performance. Include data from peers, direct reports (if any), and anyone else the person has had significant, meaningful interactions with. This can usually come from the most recent performance review cycle, if you have one. If not, a simple request asking "Do you think this person is performing at the Senior Engineer level?" is often enough if the definition of a senior engineer is clearly communicated.

Include diverse perspectives

Having a single individual (e.g., the VP of Engineering) make the decisions on their own will very likely increase the potential for bias in promotion decisions. This bias could be based on the individual's background, race, gender, or even the type of work they do. For example, phrases like this are not uncommon in promotion discussions: "Backend development is harder than frontend, so if Frontend Fred gets promoted, then Backend Barbara certainly should." The decision to request a promotion should initially be made jointly by the individual and their manager. But a body of coworkers with a variety of backgrounds, roles, and perspectives should at least review the decisions and possibly have the final say on which ones get approved.

Explain and own promotion decisions

The moment an IC finds out they weren't promoted is an unpleasant one, but it's even worse if they don't know why, or if the explanation is vague or muddled. The best outcome when you don't get promoted is to get clarity on exactly how you can do better, so you can focus your effort on self-improvement. Make sure to maximize the chance of this outcome by writing up the reasons for the decision as clearly as possible, using specific details and tying them to the career ladder.

Further, managers must avoid sowing seeds of dissent by failing to stand behind promotion decisions, especially rejections. It can be tempting to say something like "Well, I wanted to promote you...I can't believe the committee said no!" But this both undermines the promotion process as well as your own credibility and authority as a manager. You should of course acknowledge their disappointment, but it's much better to say something like "We put together a strong case for your promotion, but I understand and accept the reasons why it was denied. Let's review them together and talk about the path forward." If you can't honestly say that, then you need to get more information about the decision before discussing it with your IC.

Leveling new hires

"Hey, we just hired a Staff Engineer from SliceCo!"

"Fantastic! But you know, SliceCo has totally inflated titles. We should bring him in as a Senior Engineer."

"Oh, but we already negotiated a comp package based on a Staff Engineer level..."

"Well, that's a bummer, but it's OK. Nobody will know his compensation package, but if we bring him in at Staff and he doesn't cut it at that level, our Senior Engineers are going to be really angry...again..."

Figuring out what job title a new hire should get is not an easy task. Most interviews don't come anywhere near the level of rigor used during the internal promotion process. So, at best, you're making a guess based on their level at their current employer, how they performed during the interview, and how past hires with similar performance have turned out.

Companies typically take one of two approaches. One is called "slot-on-hire," where you make your best guess, assigning a level based on how well they performed in the interview. The onus is on the new hire's manager to re-slot if the person doesn't perform at that level. This is not fun. You can minimize the awkwardness by letting the candidate know this is a possibility, taking advantage of this moment to share the career path and explain the expectations for their starting level. This lets them know from Day 1 what they need to do to justify their title.

The alternative is called "slot pending." New hires do not get assigned a level (at least not publicly) for some amount of time, usually 3–6 months, allowing the team to assess their performance. The main downside is that some candidates will not accept a job without knowing their title, and it can be hard to resolve their compensation without some assumption about what level they will eventually earn. It can also be tricky to truly assess someone's level during the trial period, particularly if they are coming from a different domain and have a lot of context to absorb.

In either case, make sure these decisions are not made lightly. The impact of poor slotting on the morale of those at the same level or below can be significant, leaving you with considerable "management debt" you need to pay down.

Additional Resources

Growing Pains: Transitioning from an Entrepreneurship to a Professionally Managed Firm by Flamholtz and Randle
> Covers a wide range of topics but will be especially helpful to leaders seeking guidance on management development and organization at a scale beyond what we cover in this book.

Project Include (http://projectinclude.org)
> Publishes well-researched recommendations on how to build an inclusive workplace and how to use metrics to measure progress and success.

Conclusion

Investing in people management is one of the best ways to help your team grow effectively. Great managers know how to focus their teams on the right problems and give them the guidance and resources they need to achieve great results. But as we discussed in Chapter 4, the reporting structure does not always match the way you organize teams to work on specific projects or priorities. The next several chapters cover organization and describe some options to consider as you scale your team.

6

Scaling the Organization: Design Principles

The purpose of organization is to reduce the amount of communication and coordination necessary.

—FREDERICK BROOKS, *THE MYTHICAL MAN-MONTH*

This chapter describes how to structure an organization over time so that hiring more people results in *getting more work done*. We focus on organizations that deliver a consumer-facing product in our illustrations and examples. However, the principles we outline are valid for other technical endeavors, such as building B2B solutions.

The key to scaling organizations is to avoid *diseconomies of scale*: basically, getting less return for each hire. In extreme cases, each new hire might actually result in a reduction in overall productivity. Another focus is to connect team members as closely as possible to the success of the company. We will show how the right organization can help achieve this focus by establishing a well-defined purpose, effective communication techniques, and direct user feedback.

First, we will look at how to grow an organization. Everything we discuss is also applicable for larger and more established organizations, but we want to start by examining how small teams evolve because the decisions you make at the beginning have long-term consequences.

MOTIVATION AND ORGANIZATION

One of the core aspects of all organizational planning is *motivation*. Only if motivational triggers are set correctly will an organization blossom and be successful.

In his book *Drive: The Surprising Truth About What Motivates Us* (Riverhead Books), author Daniel H. Pink talks about the elements of *intrinsic* and *extrinsic* *motivation*. We highly recommend that team leaders read this book.

Note

As outlined in "What Are Extrinsic Motivation and Rewards?" (*http://bit.ly/2gSSDv7*) and "What Is Intrinsic Motivation?" (*http://bit.ly/2gSQYWI*), "...*extrinsic motivation* refers to behavior that is driven by external rewards such as money, fame, grades, and praise. This type of motivation arises from outside the individual, as opposed to *intrinsic motivation* [...] which refers to behavior that is driven by internal rewards. In other words, the motivation to engage in a behavior arises from within the individual because it is intrinsically rewarding." Specifics like deadlines for software development are also significant external motivators, in addition to more abstract factors like fame and praise.

Pink argues that for people to feel intrinsically motivated, they must have three things:

Autonomy

> The freedom to control how they do things and how they achieve goals. The goals might still be set by the company, but the staff are not micro-managed. They are able to make their own decisions on how to solve specific problems.

Mastery

> The ability to regularly perform tasks that challenge them and are at the same time achievable. This contributes to a sense of ongoing mastery of their work.

Purpose

> The knowledge of how their work contributes to the company's goals. This can also mean believing in the company's vision in the first place. A sense of common purpose and belief can be very motivating.

We believe that people do their best work when they are intrinsically motivated and have autonomy and a sense of purpose. Mastery is less relevant to organization, but still important for motivating team members; see "Continuous Learning and Improvement" on page 186 for more on the concept of mastery.

Planning from the Start

Organizing a business is easy when you have 5 or 10 people all sitting in the same room. Everybody works closely with one another, making an impact on the product. Engineers can touch all parts of the stack, and they're sitting next to the person responsible for product decisions. But then the company doubles in size, and the one team is getting too big; now you're thinking about breaking it into smaller teams. That's when you have to make a crucial decision: what guiding principles do you use to design the new organization? Chances are high that you'll build the third, fourth, and all the teams that follow along the same lines as that second team.

Team Size

You might have heard of Amazon's famous "two-pizza teams," which could be no larger than what two pizzas can feed. There is actual science behind this principle, and it focuses on how the number of links between people grows exponentially with team size (for more, see Chapter 10). More communication needs to happen as the team grows, which can slow down productivity. For this reason, an optimal team size is around six or seven team members, and the size shouldn't reach double digits. The minimum size depends on how many different skill sets you need within your team. For an engineering-only team, two to three people is the minimum. Of course, the minimum personnel size increases as soon you need design, product, or other functions.

Let's examine a typical scenario. If, in the beginning stages of your company, the second web engineer hired sits next to the first one, and they want to continue sitting next to each other all day, they have laid the foundation for a web engineering team. This is a natural tendency, and good for aligning certain tasks, but be aware that you have laid the groundwork for teams organized by *skill set*.

Similarly, the way you define who is a member of a team will affect the way your organization evolves. Let's say you have a group of engineers working on the customer signup experience. Does the product owner assigned to that area join the engineering team only for weekly planning meetings? Or do they work side-by-side with the engineers on a regular basis? What about other functions, like design? This is a very significant decision that can have a huge influence on how your organization evolves. For reasons we will explain later, separating the different functions of product development from each other can be quite inefficient.

Let's start by examining the steps in a classical product development workflow. The process starts when someone in management has an idea to build a certain feature. After deciding to go forward with it, a product manager is tasked with writing a specification. When the specification is done, a designer starts working on the layout. Once management has reviewed the spec and layout and had any concerns addressed, both are handed over to an engineering team, which starts implementing the feature as soon as it can be prioritized against the other items in their backlog. After the implementation has been reviewed, the feature is tested and then deployed to production. There is waiting time between each step and this can really add up—there are organizations where it takes several months (in large corporations even over a year) to get a normal feature from idea to production.

You can see how many steps and how much communication is needed to deliver a single feature—it is not rare for it to take several months (see the sidebar "Hiring at SoundCloud: A Story from Alex" on page 120 later in this chapter). Figure 6-1 illustrates the time-consuming process. Though their managers would likely deny it, we've seen quite a few companies that operate using a similar process.

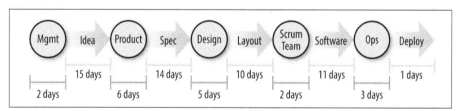

Figure 6-1. Value stream that illustrates time from idea to production

Conway's law states that "organizations which design systems...are constrained to produce designs which are copies of the communication structures of these organizations." In software engineering, this means that your system architecture will reflect your organizational structure. And the concept extends to more than just engineering. The way you set up all relevant departments has a major influence on how efficient your organization will be.

It is worth mentioning that even in the siloed approach in Figure 6-1, good communication practices and efficient tooling can mitigate the time-consuming effects of that setup. But in our experience, the best way to tackle the problem is to *remove silos*. We define a *silo* as a section of the process separated from the others in the value stream rather than integrated into one team. A silo communicates with the other teams, but mostly through tools rather than direct, daily interaction.

PROBLEMS WHILE GROWING

What actually changes when the organization grows? Brooks's law (*http://bit.ly/2g6syos*) states:

> *Communication overheads increase as the number of people increases. Due to combinatorial explosion, the number of different communication channels increases rapidly with the number of people. Everyone working on the same task needs to keep in sync, so as more people are added they spend more time trying to find out what everyone else is doing.*

Basically, the number of communication channels increases rapidly according to the number of people involved. If you organize a company by isolating teams or functions from each other, you force them to communicate through channels like email or tools beyond in-team communication, which is preferably face to face.

Figure 6-2 describes the same value stream as before, but now we have put the focus on the effort and coordination needed when functions become isolated from each other. Each backwards arrow indicates there is communication happening between the functions—each time one step of the value stream needs feedback from a previous step.

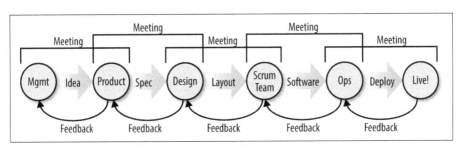

Figure 6-2. Value stream with communication overhead

Isolating functions also makes it difficult to grow all departments in balance. It's hard to have a holistic view of everyone's needs, so headcount is often distributed to the managers with the best negotiation skills. The resulting imbalance in size between teams can lead to inefficiency, requiring time and effort to correct.

Hiring at SoundCloud: A Story from Alex

During my first months at SoundCloud, the CTO wanted more frontend work done because an important release was coming up. He asked me to hire more engineers to accomplish that goal. I started recruiting, but I wanted to know why the existing team's velocity was not meeting expectations. So I went to all of the frontend teams (at that time it was Web, iPhone, and Android) and asked a very simple question: "What slows you down the most in your day-to-day work?" To my surprise, everyone gave the same answer: "We only have one designer." They went on to say that although the designer was very good, but she was completely overloaded, so new designs, design changes, and simple clarifications took forever to get done. Now that I knew design bottlenecks were actually the cause for delays, the solution to my problem was not to hire more engineers (which might have even made the problem worse with more work for the designer), but to start hiring more designers.

A certain increase in dependencies is inevitable when the company grows, since the product has to be delivered in alignment with more departments (legal, for example). Delivering a product to a few users as a no-name startup is very different from a big-name brand with a large audience. Mistakes that are excusable at a small company can severely damage a larger company's reputation. Still, it is your job as a leader to organize teams in a way that maintains high productivity. Look for these warning signs that your organization is not structured the right way:

- When you ask engineers (or other individual contributors) how they contribute to the company's success and their answer is, "I don't know," that's a sign that the goals and purpose of the teams haven't been clearly defined.

- There is a large backlog of features in the concept stage (as defined by product) and the product managers complain about not having enough capacity to implement their plans. This often indicates that product managers are not included as an integral part of the team, and therefore are detached from the team's actual capacity. The same point applies for design concepts.

- If you're seeing lots of fights about headcount distribution between departments, one of the most likely reasons is that functions are isolated from each other (UX team, engineering team, etc.).

- There are too many meetings, so "real work" doesn't get done until after hours, if at all. This is a sign that too much communication is needed to coordinate different groups, or that the communication is ineffective.

- If it feels like you're taking longer and longer to push out features, sometimes it means that the increasing scale of your company and the added complexity of being more professional has led to longer cycle times—but that's usually only one part of the problem. It can also indicate that cross-team dependencies are slowing you down.

"Organizational Design Principles" on page 122 covers how to avoid these problems.

GOALS WHILE GROWING

There isn't a single organizational model that perfectly fits every company, or even every single team inside of a company. In a way, you have to choose the lesser of many evils. In the words of George Box, "Essentially, all models are wrong, but some are useful."[1] You have to find the model that works best for you and your company at the moment.

In the previous section, we showed how things change when organizations grow. In the next section, we present possible approaches for mitigating potential problems. Here are two key goals to keep in mind while designing the organization. We want to be sure to:

- Move fast and maintain the nimbleness of a small organization. The goal of hiring more people is to get more things done, and you want to avoid diseconomies of scale.

---

1 Byron Jennings, "Essentially, all models are wrong, but some are useful" (*http://bit.ly/2g6xNo9*), Quantum Diaries.

- Connect the employees closely to the product and its success. Your employees are more motivated when they see the impact of their work—successes as well as failures.

Organizational Design Principles

Since there is no single organizational setup that works in every case, we instead recommend principles to help you build the organization that is right for your situation. We identified these principles by observing what happens when an organization grows (specifically, the increase in communication and coordination overhead) and by learning from what other successful companies have done to adapt to these demands. Some of these principles are the same or similar to the principles behind the Agile Manifesto (*http://bit.ly/2g6ybmB*).

About the Agile Manifesto

In February 2001, 17 software developers met to discuss lightweight development methods that would improve on the heavyweight Waterfall process. They published the Manifesto for Agile Software Development (*http://agilemanifesto.org*), which values "individuals and interactions over processes and tools, working software over comprehensive documentation, customer collaboration over contract negotiation, and responding to change over following a plan." If you've never read the original and only experienced Agile project management, you should. It's very short, potentially surprising, and well worth the read.

Since the Manifesto was published, many teams have implemented the principles it describes, and it's been useful and inspirational to many, including us.

We recommend the following principles when structuring your organization. They easily work alongside an established Agile framework, such as Scrum or Kanban. They are equally valid for changing an organization that already has teams, as well as for a growing organization that is thinking about creating its second team. For the purposes of this chapter, we're highlighting five key principles, and we examine the first three in depth:

Build delivery teams

We use *delivery teams* to refer to self-sufficient teams that include all the functions necessary to develop software from idea to launch. Delivery teams are covered in detail in Chapter 7.

Embrace autonomy

Allow teams to decide what actions will best achieve their assigned goals, and ensure they measure the impact.

Establish purpose and measure success

If a team is self-sufficient and has a certain degree of autonomy, it also needs to know which goals will best contribute to the success of the company.

Deliver business value constantly (continuous delivery)

This principle is taken directly from the Agile Manifesto, which states: "Our highest priority is to satisfy the customer through early and continuous delivery of valuable software." Continuous delivery enables better products and greater customer focus due to frequent feedback, higher satisfaction of team members when they see their work go live quickly, and faster speed to market, as functionality is presented to the user as soon as it reaches *minimum viable product* (MVP) status. Implementing continuous delivery also accelerates the move to delivery teams, because each team needs to be at the very least self-sufficient enough to constantly deliver features, requiring close cooperation from all parts of the value stream. For more details, see Jez Humble and David Farley's *Continuous Delivery* (Addison-Wesley).

Create a continuous learning culture

The Agile principles state: "At regular intervals, the team reflects on how to become more effective, then tunes and adjusts its behavior accordingly." Especially in fast-growing companies, there will always be areas where you can improve. It's neither bad nor unusual—you must continue to reflect and adapt. Sometimes you have to make compromises when building the organization because of its current constraints (such as open positions), but you need to constantly, step by step, work toward a better setup. And it's not just single teams that must consider how to be more effective, but the entire organization as well. What is valid on the team level is even more valid on the organizational level. In the beginning, you can do this by bringing the members of all teams into one room, such as for team retrospectives. But once you reach a certain size, retrospectives performed this way are no longer effective; it's difficult to give an exact number, but as soon as a retrospective takes longer than an hour, you might think about splitting it up. To continue doing retrospectives, try to get just one or two members from each team to participate. For more on continuous learning, see "Continuous Learning and Improvement" on page 186.

Figure 6-3 illustrates these five principles. In the center of this approach are the delivery teams, which have autonomy but are influenced by company strategy. By knowing how they contribute to the overall success of the company, the teams understand their purpose. We'll cover these principles in depth in the following sections. Finally, in order to reach their goals, the teams try to continuously deliver business value while improving their approach.

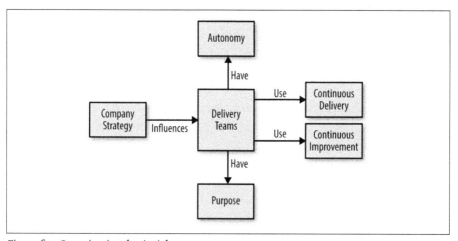

Figure 6-3. Organizational principles

A form of each of these principles has existed in other industries for some time. For example, W. Edwards Deming (a well-known American management consultant), said:

> *Break down barriers between departments. People in research, design, sales, and production must work as a team, to foresee problems in production and in use that may be encountered with the product or service.[2]*

---

2 Dr. W. Edwards Deming, *Out of the Crisis: Quality, Productivity, and Competitive Position* (http://bit.ly/2g6HJhu) (MIT Press).

This quote expresses the idea of self-sufficient teams. Another good resource is Karen Martin and Mike Osterling's book *Value Stream Mapping* (*http://bit.ly/2g6Iozu*) (McGraw-Hill), which points out that "Many organizations are structured as a series of function-based silos that bear little relationship to the customer fulfillment cycle."

Because of the specific nature of software development, some of these principles are different in other industries, especially the ability to constantly deliver value to the customer. Continuous delivery is not possible in, say, the hardware side of car manufacturing.

IMPLEMENTING THE PRINCIPLES

Take a look again at Figure 6-2, which outlines the necessary process required to deliver value when teams are separated by functional skills. This kind of process violates most of our principles:

- A product cannot be delivered by a self-sufficient team because each step of delivering that product requires a separate team. To deliver a product, a series of siloed steps have to be executed in a specific order, which increases both time to market and communication overhead.

- It is impossible to create real autonomy for any team except the management team, as all other teams are bound to the specifications they receive from the previous step.

- Having a sense of purpose becomes more difficult the further down the value stream you travel because the goals of the team are less directly connected to customer value.

- Continuous delivery is possible within certain constraints. The engineers can constantly deliver bugfixes or technical enhancements. But iterations on the product (delivering business value) will take more time as agreement from the isolated steps in the value stream will be needed.

- Continuous learning is still possible, although the process of getting all the various departments together for a retrospective becomes more complicated, as does the process of making sure all departments agree on the output of the retrospective.

The following sections cover the first three principles in greater depth.

CREATE DELIVERY TEAMS

Earlier, we defined delivery teams as self-sufficient teams that include all the functions necessary to develop software from idea to launch. This team structure brings engineers closer to the product and shortens overall development time by reducing dependencies and minimizing communication overhead. It aligns with the Agile principle that, "Business people and developers must work together daily throughout the project," but takes the concept even further by saying all people necessary to define, deliver, and (possibly) maintain the product have to be in one team.

As a rule of thumb, delivery teams are truly self-sufficient if they can deliver the vast majority (~95%) of their backlog items to production without depending on other teams. We only consider *dependencies* that require some kind of coordination with other teams and thereby slow the work down. However, note that not all dependencies are bad, and 95% is most likely a goal you might never achieve; it's an ideal to strive for, rather than a rigid standard.

Also, whenever possible, a delivery team should sit in the same office, in the same room. As the Agile principles state: "The most efficient and effective method of conveying information to and within a development team is face-to-face conversation."

Unlike more horizontally oriented teams (e.g., a frontend engineering team that relies on the backend engineering team for any backend changes), a delivery team has all the necessary skills inside their own team. For example, a team for a consumer-facing website might have engineers, designers, product managers, and support reps. The transition from functional teams to delivery teams might look something like Figure 6-4.

Chapter 7 describes in detail how to make this transition.

Cross-team projects

Regardless of the exact team setup you choose, there will always be projects that touch more than one team, such as a major infrastructure migration. This type of situation is normal, and not necessarily a reason to reorganize.

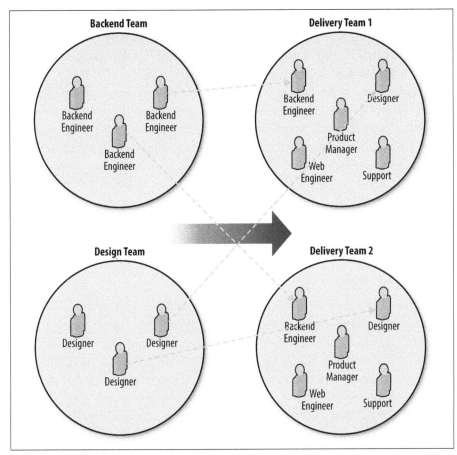

Figure 6-4. Moving from functional to delivery teams

By their very nature, these major projects violate the 95% rule, as the out-come of such a project depends on more than one team. How to organize such projects depends on the effort required, the desired schedule, and mainly on how many employees are involved. If two people from different teams end up spending the majority of their time working on that project for at least one full iteration, it might be that you need to start a dedicated temporary team (described next). Smaller projects should be coordinated by the teams themselves—meaning that the project does not warrant a change in team setup.

Here's a good example: the Android team needs a change to the backend search system that it cannot do entirely itself. The Android and Search teams both estimate three to four days' effort, so it's just a matter of agreeing on how to prioritize and coordinate the work by each team (i.e., which team will depend on the other to deliver their work first). Alternatively, one engineer from the Search team could pair with engineers from the Android team for the necessary changes and get all the work done in one pass.

You can also tackle bigger projects by creating a temporary team for that project. However, the temporary team should be structured to follow the 95% rule: put all of the people necessary for delivering 95% of that project into one room, and dedicate them to finishing that project. Some people might leave the project earlier when they are no longer needed. Others might join later, or cycle in and out as their skills are required. Try to avoid long projects that are worked on by a lot of teams, and consider creating dedicated teams for any projects longer than one month. The amount of coordination necessary and the constant fight about prioritization against the other work of the team can make those projects very tough to manage!

EMBRACE AUTONOMY

Allow teams with a well-defined purpose to set and deliver on their own priorities. Delivery teams make sure the team has the ability to do end-to-end work, and autonomy gives them the freedom to do the most important work first. This refers to the second part of this Agile principle: "Build projects around motivated individuals. Give them the environment and support they need, and trust them to get the job done."

Although autonomy is one of the three elements of intrinsic motivation, it is sometimes a difficult concept for a manager, especially when a company is growing. Autonomy in this context means that a team is free to decide what to work on (within certain constraints; more on that later). Here's why that's a good approach:

- If you believe that your job as a manager is to not be a bottleneck and single point of failure, you'll build teams in a way that you can go on vacation and work will continue without you.

- On an autonomous delivery team, disagreements with other teams are much less likely during a project, and there's less chance of finger-pointing when things go wrong (or even blaming another team for a failure). Whether the project goes well or poorly, everyone agreed on it together and was informed along the way, because they were sitting in the same room and constantly talking to each other. The ownership is clear.

- Team members are more motivated when they clearly understand the direct effect their work has on their customers. (More on this in "Establish Purpose and Measure Success" on page 132.)

- The teams working on the product often have a really good view of what needs to be done. This is especially true for the little things that sometimes have a big impact. So giving those teams autonomy often dramatically improves the product.

Team Autonomy: A Story from Alex

In one of my former companies, there was a team that got its requirements from people who were very distant from the project and just looking for the next big thing. This showed in the team's roadmap, which was filled with new features but left the team no time to improve existing ones. The team saw very clearly that it could make small adjustments to increase the engagement of the product immediately, but they didn't have the freedom to make the necessary changes.

We decided to give the team more autonomy, allowing them to spend half of their time on work they chose themselves. The team then started to make all the little improvements on existing features it always wanted to do. From these changes, there was a 200% increase in engagement. The team was extremely proud to present these results.

Where does autonomy stop?

Some teams go a little bit wild with the idea of autonomy. When team members believe "I have complete freedom to do whatever I want," there are likely to be problems. This is why we emphasize autonomy *within certain constraints* such as business priorities, organizational goals, or the team's charter. Taken too literally, autonomy can lead to a lack of alignment or conflict between teams. Teams are there for a collective purpose, and should move toward that purpose. The Netflix culture deck (*http://bit.ly/2fLrNQJ*) has some very valuable material on this topic.

Another important consideration is the maturity and experience level of the team. To trust a team with autonomy, they must have a certain level of knowledge and experience. Think about a team tasked with improving the acquisition funnel: if no one on the team has worked on this topic before and, for example, the VP of Product happens to be an expert on it, there should be a transition time during which the VP of Product is working closely with the team. The goal is that after some time, the team will be able to improve the acquisition funnel on their own.

Why not give teams complete autonomy? Consider the following points:

- What is the point of having a company at all if it consists of completely autonomous teams? Where are the economies of scale you would like to achieve?

- Imagine the company develops a big, consumer-facing product and then decides to re-brand. Is each team autonomous in their decision to participate in that re-branding?

- How do you execute company-wide strategic goals if teams are free to decide not to participate?

- How do you coordinate between teams on bigger projects, such as moving hosting providers?

Instead, find a balance between autonomy and central control. Take this proposal as a starting point: *the team has autonomy to iterate on the product they are responsible for.* Other stakeholders are welcome to give input, but it is up to the team to decide what to work on.

As we've mentioned, bigger strategic goals can sometimes override a team's autonomy. However:

- The teams should retain control of at least half of their time. This ensures that those little-but-important things—like bug fixes, feature enhancements, and removing technical debt—will eventually get done. Larger strategic initiatives, in other words, should only require half of the team's time.

- In the case that one team is the bottleneck for one of these larger strategic initiatives, then that team may need to spend all of its time on the project to unblock it. This should be the exception, not the rule!

Figure 6-5 shows this approach. A delivery team's work is partly determined by the company priorities, and partly by items the team decides to work on.

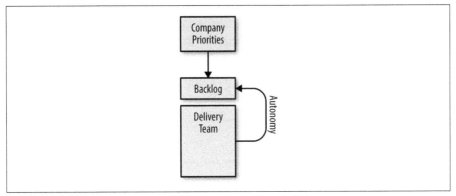

Figure 6-5. Balancing autonomy and company priorities with delivery teams

Trust

Trust issues are usually the main obstacle to empowering teams. In the words of Eric Bowman (VP of Engineering at Zalando), "There is no autonomy without trust." We have encountered quite a few organizational setups in which managers claimed their teams were autonomous, when in reality the teams were micromanaged, with endless product reviews and corrections from all parts of the company (also called "product management by committee"). It can be really hard for managers to leave teams alone. But for a specific and measurable outcome (like "increase number of page views by *x%*"), the team should have the freedom to design the solution. Besides being better for the team members' intrinsic motivation, people outside the team are much less likely to understand the team's responsibilities. Assigning a spec to a team as an outsider usually means making a lot of assumptions.

This bears repeating: *no one has a better view of a product or feature than the team who works on it every day.* If leadership can provide them with the bigger picture, they should have enough context to make the right decisions.

Managers who give their teams autonomy need to be aware of their own interactions with the team to avoid undermining that autonomy. As a leader, when you approach a team and ask why they are building features a certain way or why they did X instead of Y, be careful how you phrase your questions or they may be interpreted as an order rather than curiosity. A good book on this topic is *The Five Dysfunctions of a Team* by Patrick Lencioni (Jossey-Bass).

Strategies that can help teams and managers trust each other include:

- Visibility into the backlog and progress of the team. You can provide this visibility by sharing all work progress in a common work-tracking tool, which is accessible to everyone.

- Regularly attending demo meetings helps managers stay up-to-date on the team's progress. See Chapter 11 for more on this type of meeting.

- Participating in standup meetings and other kinds of status updates.

Managers who want to encourage autonomy need to strike a balance between staying involved and letting the team make their own decisions. Only when managers feel strongly that the team is taking a dangerous path forward should they intervene. And in this case, they should still have a discussion with the team to convince them that their suggested path is the right one.

Of course, the team's outcomes are vital as well. If a team constantly fails to deliver important features successfully, the manager will rightfully want to talk to that team to understand why. But managers also need to know which situations warrant an intervention, otherwise they will erode trust. A good rule of thumb is to let the team run with anything that can easily be rolled back or improved later, and take charge only when there is just one chance to get it right, like the launch of a high-visibility feature or a migration that could result in data loss.

It's a delicate balance. It's not easy. But it's worth it.

ESTABLISH PURPOSE AND MEASURE SUCCESS

A major reason people join companies is because they feel a sense of purpose in what the company is doing. In the early days, this purpose is quite tangible, as every employee plays a significant role in furthering the company's mission. But as the company grows and jobs become more specialized, the feeling of having a personal impact can start to fade. Maintaining a sense of purpose is a major scaling challenge.

This is one of the advantages of delivery teams, because they clarify how the members of the team contribute to the company's purpose. If, for example, the Search team deploys an improved ranking algorithm, they should immediately see that users are getting better results. In a delivery team, having a sense of purpose is easy because you see the impact of your work right away. And managers can reinforce this by communicating how the work of the team ties into the company's overall success.

Even teams that are self-sufficient and possess a certain degree of autonomy still need to know what success means. This can be expressed as team goals and/or key performance indicators (KPIs). At a high level, KPIs indicate to team members how they contribute to the success of the company and on what metrics they should focus their work. And ideally, these goals and KPIs are closely tied to the company's goals.

Metrics of success

Showing success is easiest through numbers—specifically, by tracking and measuring KPIs. Say, for example, the company has goals to increase engagement and revenue. The teams can then examine how they contribute to those goals, starting with top-level company KPIs. Probably no team will have sole ownership of a single KPI. But suppose one team works on recommendations that help drive engagement in the company's product. By then setting "engagements driven by recommendations" as a team KPI, that team clearly defines how it will contribute to the company's success. In each company, there will be work where it is more difficult to build a direct relationship to company goals, such as site availability. Here are a few guidelines when deploying KPIs.

First of all, make sure the company-level goals and KPIs are clearly defined and communicated. Then we recommend letting teams come up with their own KPIs and goals, and then reviewing them to make sure they match up to the company goals. This makes ownership clear. Regularly review those KPIs (quarterly, for example), and adjust them as priorities change. Also, keep in mind that sometimes KPIs are tied to projects, and projects end—and therefore KPIs need to be updated.

Be sure to include customer feedback as an element of establishing KPIs. Your "customer" can be internal or external. If you work in an agency and you build a website for a company, your KPIs may not be driven by you, but by your customer. In a B2B situation, the people that buy the product are not the people who use it. So, first, you have to know who your customer is. And even then, it's important to take the feedback with a grain of salt, as the most vocal customers don't usually represent your *typical* customers.

It's also important to be mindful of conflicting KPIs. Imagine one team has to drive engagement of your product, while another team is tasked with monetizing it by showing ads. These two goals might collide—for example, if too many ads end up hurting engagement. So the teams must work closely together (and receive the right support from management) in order to do their job well, or the KPIs must be changed to account for the conflict.

Be careful not to tie salary to the achievement of KPIs. If you do, resolving an issue with conflicting KPIs becomes much more difficult. And be sure to remind the team that KPIs aren't everything. You cannot define 100% of the team's work by KPIs.

Lessons Learned from Other Companies

There are a lot of frameworks and methodologies that can help you scale your organization. We believe the right strategy for small companies is to follow the five principles outlined in this chapter (along with fostering a great culture, as discussed in Chapter 9). It might still be worth your time to look at existing enterprise-size frameworks to steal an idea or two, but for companies with up to 150 engineers, you probably don't need to bother with a heavyweight enterprise approach—just learn from what other companies have done, and adapt. Here are some important lessons we've learned from a few of them:

- Yammer (*https://www.yammer.com*) realized when the company was expanding that "the marginal increase in productivity for every new engineer decreases over time because of greater overhead." To avoid this, they tried to create smaller teams that could move fast: "If those teams are in any way restricted from shipping code into production, then they're useless. They need to be free to get stuff done outside of the larger organization."[3] This is in line with our belief in self-sufficient teams.

- When Spotify (*https://www.spotify.com*) was small, it used Scrum as its Agile methodology. During growth, it realized that certain parts of Scrum didn't fit, so it decided to create its own methodology (*http://bit.ly/2gSl4cR*), which has received a fair bit of attention. At Spotify, teams are as autonomous as possible and they aggressively try to remove dependencies. Spotify calls teams "squads" and each team is responsible for what it builds and exactly how it does it. Spotify is very aware, however, that the potential downside of total autonomy is a loss of economies of scale. If each squad

---

3 Kris Gale, "Why Yammer believes the traditional engineering organizational structure is dead" (*http://bit.ly/2gW4loH*), Pando, accessed January 4, 2017.

was fully autonomous, with no communication with other squads, there would be little point in having a company.

- The core of Airbnb's (*https://www.airbnb.com*) philosophy is this: "Engineers own their own impact." To do this well, engineers at Airbnb are involved in "goal-setting, planning, and brainstorming for all projects." Also, teams are structured so that they are self-sufficient: "Teams are primarily comprised of engineers, product managers, designers, and data scientists, and some teams partner with other departments within the company."[4]

Conclusion

In this chapter, we discussed five organizational design principles: delivery teams, autonomy, purpose, continuous delivery, and continuous learning. These allow you to move fast when the organization grows, creating structure in a way that helps employees feel intrinsically motivated through autonomy and purpose. The third component of intrinsic motivation, mastery, is explained in "Continuous Learning and Improvement" on page 186.

In the next chapter, we focus more closely on how to implement the core organizational principle of delivery teams.

Additional Resources

- In "Building Self-Sufficient Teams: Autonomy Vs Automatic" (*http://bit.ly/2gVXtYL*), Tony Wilson talks about the important difference between autonomy and following repeatable tasks on auto-pilot.

- In "Blamestorming & Other Telling Signs Your Organization Is 'Siloed'" (*http://bit.ly/2gVVxM*), Marla Gottschalk gives a few more warning signs that indicate your organization is siloed.

- If you want to read more about how to perform retrospectives, see Alex's SoundCloud blog post on the subject (*http://bit.ly/2gVZXq2*).

---

4 Mike Curtis, "Engineering Culture at Airbnb" (*http://nerds.airbnb.com/engineering-culture-airbnb/*), Airbnb blog.

- To read more about Lean principles in software, Mary and Tom Poppendieck's website (*http://www.poppendieck.com*) is a great start.

Scaling the Organization: Delivery Teams

The previous chapter gave an overview of the basic organizational design principles, and introduced delivery teams as self-sufficient teams that enhance productivity by minimizing dependencies. In this chapter, we'll show you how to
identify the members of a delivery team and how to adapt your approach as your
organization scales. We look at two key questions:

- How do you organize into delivery teams in the first place?

- How do you reorganize when delivery teams get too large or need to be re-
focused?

Four Ways to Create Delivery Teams

Since organizational principles can be rather abstract, let's use a concrete example. Imagine you are building a consumer-facing application that allows sharing
of photos and updates with friends. The customer base requires apps for Android
and iOS, as well as a desktop and mobile web client. Your team is relatively
small, but will be growing quickly. How should you organize your delivery teams
to deliver this application and iterate on new features efficiently?

When organizing delivery teams, you should choose a top-level approach for
your team structure. Assess the situation and consider these four perspectives:

Platform

> Do you prefer that your delivery teams have a shared understanding of technology? That would mean that all your iOS engineers, for example, should work on the same team in order to make sure that technical alignment is high.

Features

> Do you prefer to build delivery teams that have a deep (and maybe even cross-platform) understanding of the main features?

Company

> Do you prefer to build delivery teams focused on specific business goals?

Customer

> Do you prefer to build delivery teams focused on specific customer groups?

You may be thinking, "I want all four!" which is totally understandable; all the approaches focus on important concepts. But when organizing your teams, you should emphasize one of the four approaches by choosing a specific team setup. You will likely end up with a blend of approaches anyway due to resource constraints, and there are ways to incorporate specific advantages of the other approaches by other means. For example, the shared understanding of technology central to the platform-focused approach can be achieved with other approaches by using chapters or guilds. These and other methods are described in "Economies of Scale Between Delivery Teams" on page 150.

OPTIMIZE FOR PLATFORMS

The *platform* approach organizes delivery teams according to specific user-facing platforms, such as iOS, Android, Web, and so on. The goal is to maximize iteration speed by removing dependencies on other platforms (see Figure 7-1).

Start by building one team per platform, remembering to structure them as delivery teams and include backend capabilities where needed. Then decide on the structure of the backend teams. The question here is which part of the backend is its own team and which part belongs to a general backend team (called API team in Figure 7-1). Search is a good example; depending on size of the backend team and the company's priorities, search is either a part of the general backend team or its own dedicated team, as in the illustration.

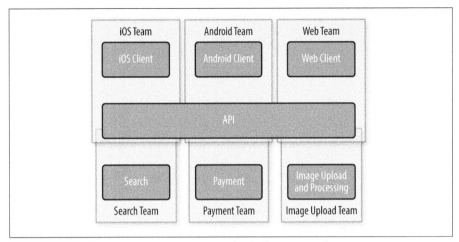

Figure 7-1. Simplified delivery team setup using the platform approach

Orienting teams based on platform may be the easiest setup of all, since it's the most intuitive method. It works best in a smaller organization (up to around 40 engineers) and it keeps people with related skill sets together, so they can pair easily and share platform-specific knowledge. It also ensures high consistency between features on a given client (as all people working on a specific client are in one team), and consistency with the platform itself (e.g., you won't end up with an Android app that looks and behaves like an iOS app).

The disadvantage to organizing by platform is that it does not scale well—there is only one team per platform. Once you've hired beyond the maximum team size (most companies stop around seven to nine), you'll need to split the team up. And now you have two teams working on the same platform, so you'll need to clearly define what each team works on. If you want to roll out a feature on all platforms at roughly the same time, you have more work to synchronize to make sure the priorities and schedules of the various teams are aligned.

OPTIMIZE FOR FEATURES

In the *feature-based* approach, you build delivery teams who can own each of the major features of your product, across all platforms. This structure can be achieved once you have the necessary number of engineers to equip each feature team with the skill sets needed for each platform. Before that point, you might still have teams dedicated to specific platforms (see Figure 7-2).

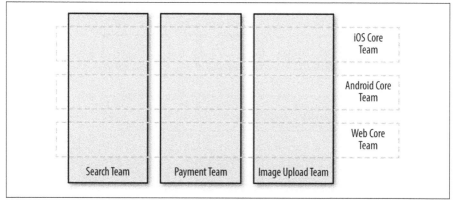

Figure 7-2. Delivery team setup using the feature approach

For our hypothetical photo-sharing app, let's say the key cross-platform features are image upload, payment, and search. So you build three feature delivery teams to focus on those areas. But you retain a "core" team per platform that does any work not handled by a dedicated feature team, and ensures the approaches of all teams are aligned.

Using a feature approach makes it easier to roll out features across all platforms at roughly the same time. It tightly couples the team's output to real user value on a granular level. From a certain scale on, it organizes teams well (once the platform teams become so big that you have to split them). Additionally, it ensures high consistency between the same feature across all platforms, giving the best user experience regardless of the platform they access the product from.

The disadvantage is that maintenance is sometimes a big problem, especially if you don't have enough engineers to staff each feature properly. If an engineer switches teams, who then fixes their bugs on their former, understaffed team? Do not underestimate the number of people needed to staff all teams correctly. We have seen companies switch to feature teams around 100 engineers. Typically, the first iteration included only web engineers on the feature teams; mobile engineers were added when engineering was much larger. The consistency of client platforms is harder to achieve, as communication and synchronization between feature teams is difficult. For example, the photo editing UI might end up looking very different from the social connection UI.

Most feature teams will need at least one engineer for each major platform. And if there's only one, losing that engineer becomes a major blow to the team's productivity until a replacement can be found. The maximum size should probably be no more than twice the minimum size and should be constrained by how many people can be effectively managed by a single person. If the company is smaller, you may not be able to have a team for every major feature.

OPTIMIZE FOR COMPANY GOALS

The *company* approach organizes delivery teams around important company goals, enabling them to pursue those goals as efficiently as possible (Figure 7-3). Every company has goals it wants to achieve, usually defined by top-level KPIs. If one of those goals is *engagement*, you build a team that works on engagement and staff it to be self-sufficient. For our photo-sharing app, the company might have defined their main goals as revenue, daily active uploaders, and daily shares, so a separate delivery team was staffed for each one. Similar to the feature team in the previous section, you will need a "core" team that takes care of all the work not directly tied to the central company KPIs. If you don't have enough employees to staff a core team, then you must find a way to accomplish non-KPI work within the company delivery teams, which can be a distraction from the team's main focus.

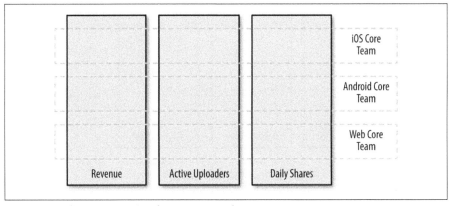

Figure 7-3. Delivery teams using the company goal setup

The advantage of the company approach is that it is very clear how teams contribute to company goals. Additionally, teams are not bound to platform-specific priorities.

The disadvantages are that the members of the core team might feel they're not contributing to the company targets. This issue comes up in the feature-based approach as well, but to a lesser degree, since the feature-organized team is closer to the team's goals. Also, the likelihood of conflicts is increased, since all teams are potentially touching the same code. It is tough to build a team that is expert-level on everything. Here, it's even tougher, as each delivery team might touch all parts of the overall stack.

This approach is also tough to scale on its own; similar to the problem with the platform approach, if you have one team per company KPI and you keep growing, you'll have to decide on a different approach for the new teams.

OPTIMIZE FOR CUSTOMERS

The goal of the *customer* approach is to develop features for one customer group with no dependencies. Here, you identify the main customer groups for your product and build delivery teams around them. In the context of the photo-sharing app, the company identifies viewers, uploaders, and curators as the main customer groups, and build teams that work toward creating value for each one. Again, this approach requires either a core team or the distribution of responsibilities between teams (see Figure 7-4).

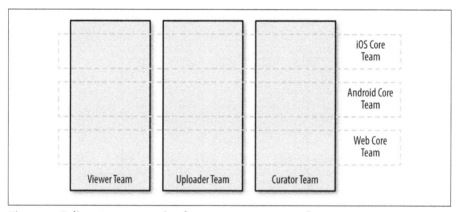

Figure 7-4. Delivery team setup using the customer group approach

The advantage of having a customer-oriented team setup is that it is clear how teams deliver value to specific customer groups, and the team can develop a very deep understanding of that customer's needs over time.

But there are a limited number of customer groups. Once you have more than nine people working on, say, the reader team, you may need to split that team and choose one of the other mentioned approaches for that (so that you use two different approaches). You also need a certain minimum number of engineers to staff each of the (in this case) six teams. Often companies start without the core teams to allow the other teams to be adequately staffed.

It is impossible to recommend one of these four approaches based solely on company size; companies are all so different, and an approach that fits perfectly for one might be a bad fit for another. Start with the one that seems like the best fit for you and read the pros and cons carefully! We've rarely seen a company where all teams were organized according to one approach; usually, you need a mix. For instance, if you're organizing your teams by feature and you have certain platforms where you haven't hired the critical mass of engineers to give every feature team capabilities in that platform, you should probably keep the platform team together until you've hired or trained enough engineers to properly staff the feature teams. You can find more details about possible transition steps in Chapter 8.

Another common pattern is to organize by feature or platform but have one or two company goal teams layered on top. Many companies have created "growth" teams, for example, to provide additional emphasis on increasing their user base without changing the focus of their existing teams.

Embrace Value Stream Mapping

The previous section presented four different approaches to team organization. *Value stream mapping* (VSM) is a tool that can help you to determine—after choosing one of the four approaches—how a specific delivery team should actually be put together. In our context, the value stream is everything involved in bringing an idea to the customer. This includes steps such as coming up with the idea, writing requirements, creating a design, implementing, testing, and deploying. Value stream mapping is a method for identifying and analyzing the steps, and detailing what kind of communication is needed between them.

Suppose, for example, that upper management decides you need to improve your search feature, so they request this from the product manager. The product manager writes a concept paper, takes it back to upper management, and asks, "Is that what you wanted?" Upper management says, "Yes." The product manager takes the concept paper to the designer and says, "Please design this." The designer builds a prototype, and then the prototype goes to engineering. Once the work is scheduled, engineering implements the specifications, and at some point in time, the new search design is delivered. This can be a very time-consuming, communication-intensive process.

Value stream mapping is a way to visualize this process. You analyze each step from end to end, which is usually a non-trivial task, and you find out that "to deliver these features, these eight functions are involved." Figure 6-2, in the previous chapter, depicts a value stream in which communication and efficiency have been emphasized.

There are some concerns about whether value stream mapping is always the right technique, as each software feature is different (compared to manufacturing the same car over and over, for instance; see Vikas Hazrati's "Does Value Stream Mapping Work for Software Development?" (*http://bit.ly/2gW4icR*)). But regardless, VSM can show the overall setup (the macro level) of your product development process. This is explained best through a real example from Phil Calcado from when he worked at SoundCloud.

Value Stream Mapping: A SoundCloud Story from Phil Calcado

When I joined SoundCloud, the most important project at the time was the complete revamp of our website. We called it "v2."

The two teams working on this project, Backend and Web, were really isolated—our offices were even in separate buildings across Berlin. Our main communication tools were issue trackers and chat apps. If you were to ask anybody from any of the teams about how our development process worked, they would describe something like this:

1. Somebody has an idea for a feature; they write a couple of paragraphs and draw some mockups. We then discuss it as a team.

2. Designers shape up the user experience.

3. We write the code.

4. After a little testing, we deploy.

But somehow there was a lot of frustration in the air. Engineers and designers complained that they were overworked, but at the same time product managers and partners complained they could never get anything done on time. This was about the time we decided to try to understand exactly what our organically grown process had become.

One of the most valuable tools I know of for doing this is the value stream map (Figure 7-5).

Through a combination of informal interviews with different engineers and gathering data from our multiple automated systems, we were able to draw a map of our actual process, as opposed to the process we thought we had.

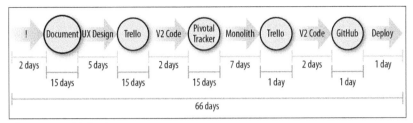

Figure 7-5. Initial value stream

The actual flow was something like this:

1. Somebody comes up with an idea for a feature. They then write a fairly lightweight spec, with some screen mockups, and store that in a document.

2. The spec stays in this document until somebody has time to actually work on it.

3. The very small design team would get the spec and design the user experience for it. This would then become a card in the issue tracking tool owned by the Web team.

4. The card would sit in that tool for a while, at least a two-week iteration, until an engineer was free to pick it up.

5. The engineer would start working on it. After converting the design into a proper browser-based experience using fake/static data, the engineer would write down what changes in the backend they would need for this experience to work. This would go into a different issue tracking tool used by the Backend team.

6. The card would sit in that tool again until somebody from the Backend team was free to look at it, often taking another two-week iteration.

7. The Backend team member would write the code, integration tests, and everything required to get the feature live. Then they would update the issue in the Web tool, letting the Web team know their part was done.

8. The updated issue would sit in the backlog for a while more, waiting for the engineer on the Web team to finish whatever they started doing while waiting for the backend work.

9. The Web team developer would then finish and test their client-side code, adjusting to whatever quirks they found in the backend implementation, and would give the green light for a deploy.

10. As deployments were risky, slow, and painful, the Backend team would wait for several features to land into the master branch before deploying it to production. This meant the feature would be sitting in source control for a couple of days, and very frequently the feature would be rolled back because of a problem in a completely unrelated part of the code.

11. At some point, the feature would finally get deployed to production.

There would be heaps of back-and-forth between those steps as people needed clarification or came up with better ideas. In total, a feature would take about two months to go live. Even worse: more than half of this period would be spent waiting (e.g., some piece of work in progress waiting to be worked on by an engineer). One obvious low-hanging fruit was to deploy daily, using the release train approach, but in our case the elephant in the room was clearly the dance between frontend and backend development. Out of the 47 days spent in engineering, only 11 days were spent on actual work. The remainder was wasted in queues and general waiting time.

We then decided to do something controversial: pair backend and frontend developers and dedicate this pair fully to a feature until it was completed. We only had 8 backend engineers to 11 frontend engineers, so the contention around this strategy was due to the perception that we needed to have the frontend developers doing as much work up-front as possible so that the backend people would spend as little time as possible on each feature. This setup was intuitive, but the process mapping showed us that it was actually very counterproductive. Even discounting the back-and-forth between front and backend developers, we still had too much waiting time before something was actually live in production!

We decided to try out the backend-frontend developer pairing approach, then extend it to others over time. Figure 7-6 shows the new flow.

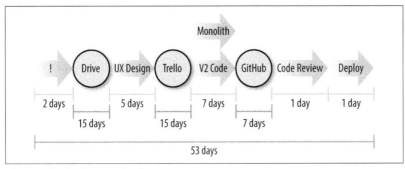

Figure 7-6. First improved value stream

Individually, each person ended up spending more time doing work per feature. This was irrelevant, though; because they were working at the same time, they were able to get the end-to-end coding done in much less time than before.

The reduction was quite a feat, and we decided to try the same approach with other steps in the process. We got designers, product managers, and frontend developers working closely with each other during the very conception of a feature, and the cycle time was reduced even more, as in Figure 7-7.

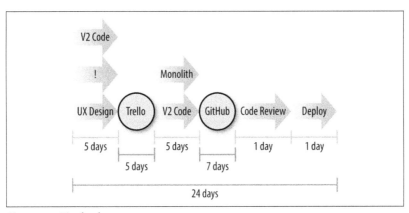

Figure 7-7. Final value stream

An additional note from Alex

Even after all the changes that Phil described, the UX/design team remained isolated from other departments and was not fully integrated with the workflow. The problems of turnaround and wasted resources still existed due to the risk of misalignment between product, design, and engineering. Therefore, the next logical step was to improve the organization by creating a delivery team per product.

This story demonstrates how to use VSM to improve an existing, suboptimal setup. In the next section, we explain how to avoid those situations in the first place.

Expanding from One Team to Two

When your company is small, there is only one team, most likely structured as a delivery team. Everybody is in the same room, working closely together. When you make decisions, they influence the company immediately. You have lots of work to do so you hire more people, but soon your single team starts getting bogged down in communication and coordination overhead. You need two teams. This section is about how to make that split.

THE ORIGINAL TEAM

Consider the team shown in Figure 7-8 as a hypothetical starting point. It includes everyone involved in the value stream of the product. Figure 7-8 describes roles, not necessarily individuals, since people can have multiple roles.

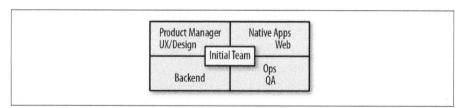

Figure 7-8. Starting delivery team

THE FIRST SPLIT

Figure 7-9 shows the ideal second team, which happens once you have all the necessary skill sets to create a perfect second team.

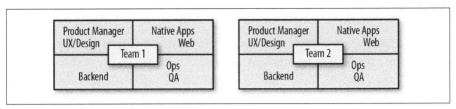

Figure 7-9. Ideal second delivery team

How often does this ideal configuration happen in reality? Unfortunately, it's quite rare. Typically, you haven't filled all the roles necessary to complete the second delivery team when the need for one begins to reveal itself. For example, let's say you only have one UX person, but you have more than one team's worth of engineers and product managers, so you have to create a second team. After that happens, the UX person has to split time between those two teams. This is an imperfect setup, but often a necessary transition step. You probably don't have all the people necessary to accomplish a complete split already hired, just waiting for a delivery team to jump into. You almost always have to make a few compromises, such as sharing a certain role between teams until another person has been hired.

So there's a transition step, which might look like Figure 7-10.

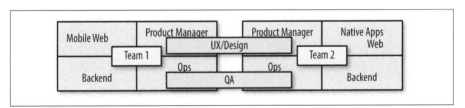

Figure 7-10. Compromise second delivery team

This situation should be temporary, not permanent. Besides the strain of extra work for that person, there's an increased risk for the company. If that overlapping-role person were to find another job, need time off for health reasons, or be absent for any reason, both teams suffer. Sharing a person between two teams means you now have the same point of failure for two teams instead of one. Wait times increase, and it takes longer to deploy new work to production.

Losing this person is especially risky because when only one person occupies a particular role there is no knowledge sharing, so a new person essentially must start from scratch in the position.

Economies of Scale Between Delivery Teams

The risk of setting up autonomous teams is that you may lose both *alignment* and *economies of scale*. Without alignment, you could have two teams working at cross purposes; for example, you might end up with two user-facing website teams implementing conflicting design/UX approaches. An important economy of scale in the context of autonomous teams is *the sharing of knowledge*. Teams within the same company are likely to encounter similar challenges, and not exchanging knowledge with each other is a missed opportunity. You can improve the situation by applying the techniques described here, but be aware that by forming delivery teams you optimize for speed and you might have to accept some duplicate work or other issues.

Spotify provides a good example of how to mitigate those risks (Figure 7-11). Spotify creates two groups, called chapters and guilds:

- *Chapters* are "your small family of people having similar skills and working within the same general competency area." A good example is that all web engineers regularly meet and discuss common challenges and approaches.

- *Guilds* are a "more organic and wide-reaching 'community of interest,' a group of people that want to share knowledge, tools, code, and practices." For instance, a guild could be made up of all team members who are interested in testing.

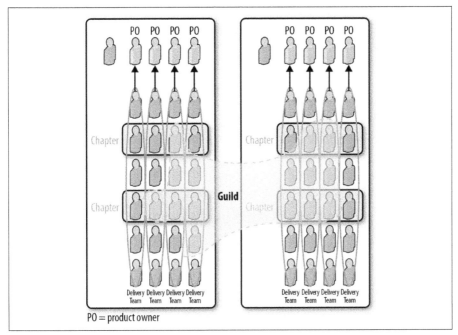

Figure 7-11. Chapters and guilds

You can take a more lightweight approach to preventing this kind of diseconomy of scale without creating a dedicated group. For example, in order to achieve a common approach in design, designers could spend one day/week working together—in the same room, if possible.

Removing Dependencies

As you move toward using delivery teams, it's important to remove dependencies to help each team work more efficiently. Here are some ways to do this with your teams.

MEASURE AVERAGE CYCLE TIME

Average cycle time within a delivery team is the average time it takes from the start of a product story to the point of shipping it to production. A lightweight method is to note the time you start working on a story and the time when the story is in production. You then enter those times into a spreadsheet. After a few iterations, calculate an average cycle time. The number itself is not that important; what *is* important is to look at how the number changes over time. If it increases (meaning it takes longer to bring stories to production), you should start looking for the reasons (dependencies, for example).

USE VALUE STREAM MAPPING IN RETROSPECTIVES

As discussed earlier, value stream mapping involves examining every step in the process of bringing the product to the customer (see "Embrace Value Stream Mapping" on page 143 for more). Luis Gonçalves—coauthor of *Getting Value Out of Agile Retrospectives* (*http://bit.ly/2gVZ8xd*) (Lulu.com)—suggests noting during the iteration all the cases where a team member was blocked or idle. This data then forms the basis for the retrospective, in which you can discuss the reasons behind the downtime and delays in more detail.

ASKING SPECIFIC QUESTIONS IN RETROSPECTIVES

Instead of an organized meeting to focus on retrospectives and day-to-day work on value stream mapping, simply visiting team retrospectives from time and time and asking questions might be enough. For each significant item of work, note which kind of coordination with people outside the delivery team was necessary. Then look at these and decide if it was acceptable to have that kind of work aligned with people outside the team (a good example would be a quick alignment with legal, as in most companies there is no need for a legal person to be part of a delivery team) or if a change in team setup is necessary. For instance, if for three retrospectives in a row reveal heavy coordination with marketing, you should consider adding someone from marketing to the delivery team.

Conclusion

In this chapter, we described how to implement delivery teams. We discussed two major aspects to this process: the approach around which to optimize the team structure, and how to split teams in order to make sure they don't have too many dependencies. Following these guidelines should enable your teams to move quickly even as the organization expands, provided you regularly examine and adapt to the challenges that come from a growing team. The next chapter combines the approaches from the people management and organization chapters in order to show you how to set up your reporting structure.

Additional Resources

- Luis Gonçalves's blog post "Using VSM (Value Stream Mapping) as Data Gathering for Retrospectives" (*http://bit.ly/2gVZ8xd*) shows a great way to utilize VSM in retrospectives and optimize the work of the team.

- Charam Atreya's blog post "The Benefit of Value Stream Mapping in Software Engineering" (*http://bit.ly/2gVZwvF*) describes how to map out your value stream using a conversation between two people as an example.

8

Scaling the Organization: Reporting Structure

Chapters 4 and 5 on scaling people management describe how to identify and train new managers, and Chapters 6 and 7 provide basic approaches for structuring teams. Now it is time to put them together to answer the question, "Who reports to whom?" The answer to this question is what we will call *reporting structure*.

Although our examples and solutions focus mainly on engineering, where we have most often seen and experienced scaling challenges, they should be equally applicable to other product development functions such as design and product management.

Initial Reporting Structure

Assume you are the newly hired VP of Engineering at a small startup, and you are directly managing roughly 20 engineers. The reporting structure might look something like Figure 8-1.

You quickly realize this structure is not sustainable. You cannot effectively do your job as the head of engineering and also provide the necessary people management to help your reports grow and succeed in their roles. It's time to change the reporting structure of the team to enable effective people management. See Chapters 4 and 5 for more details on why effective people management is important for your team's scalability.

But there are a number of options for how to structure your reporting. Let's say you've identified two of the engineers as potential engineering managers. Which engineers will report to which manager? Will it be based on domain expertise, product features, company goals...? We cover the different options in more detail later in this section.

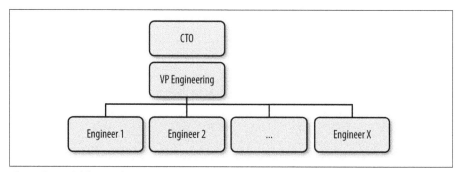

Figure 8-1. Initial reporting structure

Because there are different ways to organize the reporting structure, we've met quite a few early team leaders who did not introduce any hierarchy at this stage, sticking with a "flat" structure. This inevitably led to problems—see Chapter 4 for some examples and reasons why.

One company that didn't know how to set up its reporting structure had 70 engineers reporting to the CTO. When each engineer had a yearly review, the feedback would go something like this: "I haven't heard anything bad about you, so here's your 2% salary increase." Simply put—this is a very bad method. Sometimes people improve dramatically and then leave the company because they can get better pay on the open market. Other people don't improve at all, but still earn a salary increase, and never receive constructive feedback. Usually, you only hear about the stars and the abject failures.

The longer employees go without getting feedback on how they are doing, the more likely they are to leave. Who talks with you about your *career* at the company if your manager has 70 reports? Nobody. People start leaving, and in their exit interviews, they might say, "I don't see a career for me here." Often there could have been a career path, but nobody discussed it with them.

Even with 20 or 30 direct reports, if you do bi-weekly one-on-ones with each of them, that's roughly half of your week. That doesn't leave much time for any follow-up or other obligations.

WHAT IS A GOOD NUMBER OF REPORTS?

Just as it's a good idea to avoid an overly "wide" reporting structure, you should also avoid creating one that is overly "narrow." For example, a team of two engineers with one reporting to the other often just adds unnecessary hierarchy. But is there a sweet spot between the two extremes?

Companies adopt different target numbers of reports for managers. We are not going to make a strict recommendation here, since we believe there is no optimal number that applies in all situations. There are many factors to consider, such as:

- Experience and talent level of the manager

- Overall maturity of the individuals on the team

- Whether there is a strong leader (besides the manager) who can guide the work of others

- Whether the manager has to do day-to-day project management

- How much customer interaction is required of the manager

- Other expectations of the manager, such as contributing technical or running the company's on-boarding program

See "Warning signs that people management is needed" on page 65 for a discussion on Drucker's term *span of management responsibility*, which provides a similar perspective.

FOUR WAYS TO ORGANIZE REPORTING STRUCTURE

Assume an organization with 20 engineers has organized itself into four teams (see Figure 8-2).

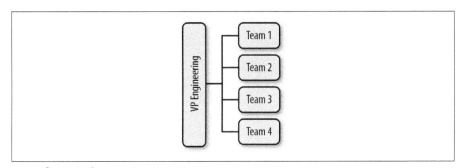

Figure 8-2. Initial team setup

We will now present four different ways to set up your reporting structure, each one optimized for a different target. Consider whether you prefer that a manager:

- Has an overview of the engineering work of a specific delivery team (see "Create Delivery Teams" on page 126 for more information about delivery teams)

- Has an overview of the complete work of a specific delivery team (engineering, design, product, etc.)

- Is an expert in the specific domain their reports work in

- Is an expert in managing people—providing feedback, giving career guidance, resolving disputes, and so on. (See "Understanding People Management" on page 60 for a detailed definition.)

Based on your preference and the needs of the team, select one of the options below to set up your reporting structure.

One engineering manager per delivery team

In this approach, all the engineers on a single team report to that team's engineering manager, while other members of the team (e.g., product owner, designer, etc.) report to managers in their respective groups (see Figure 8-3).

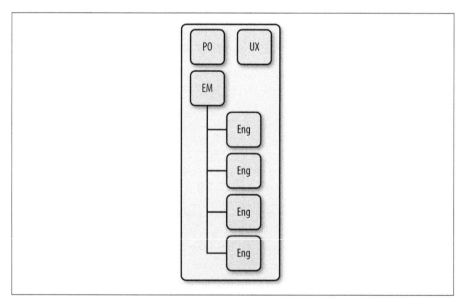

Figure 8-3. One engineering manager per team

The advantage of a setup like this is that engineering managers are very close to the work of their reports, because they are working side by side on the same team. And while the team is small and managerial tasks aren't taking up all of their time, managers can be more involved in technical work.

On the other hand, having one engineering manager per team may require finding and mentoring more managers than other approaches, since you need one for each team. Managers also might not be experts in all the technologies used, so they cannot give direct technical feedback to all their reports. Movement between the teams can be more difficult (more on this in Chapter 5) because it requires a change in reporting structure. Some managers are reluctant to let people leave their teams because their perceived importance as managers changes as a result, or because the context and relationship that the manager and report have built is lost. Others might be hesitant to take on more people because it allows less time for non-managerial work. As the managers are also intimately involved in the technical work of the team, they may have difficulty prioritizing management tasks.

One manager for the complete delivery team

In this approach, each team is like a small, self-contained company. The manager handles both product management and line management responsibilities. They are like a CEO, with everyone reporting to them (see Figure 8-4).

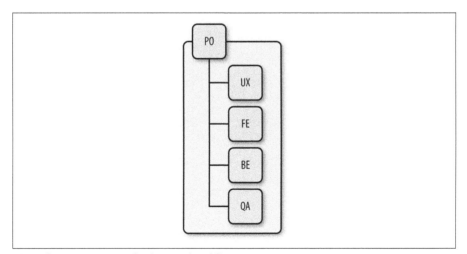

Figure 8-4. One manager for the complete delivery team

The advantage of this approach is that it makes it very clear that the team is its own small company. As a result, there are no conflicts with other managers within the team about goals and priorities.

On the other hand, the manager of this team has such a strong position that engineers or UX people may have very little impact on features; there's a danger the manager could just push ideas through, especially if the manager is also the product owner. And movement between teams is difficult for the same reason as in the previous approach: moving team members around requires a change in line management, which adds a level of complexity.

One manager per specialization

This approach is often referred to as a *matrix organization*. In a matrix organization, everyone from a specific role reports into an organization specific to that role (e.g., data scientists report to a manager in the "Data Science" group). But their day-to-day work is with a different team focused on a specific goal that requires multiple specialists (e.g., a "Setup Experience" team that needs a data scientist but also needs a product manager and several flavors of engineer). Figure 8-5 depicts this setup with two teams, but practically, you need more than two teams for this approach to work efficiently, due to the number of managers needed outside the delivery teams.

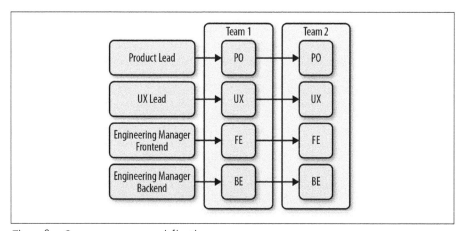

Figure 8-5. One manager per specialization

The advantage of this approach is that movement between teams is easier, as no change is needed in line management. The managers are not a member of a specific delivery team; therefore, they're not influenced by the team's constraints.

In addition, managers can give really detailed technical feedback to their reports when they are specialists in their discipline.

On the other hand, this approach only works in bigger companies, large enough to have dedicated managers who are not part of delivery teams. And since managers are not part of the team, they are not familiar with the context of the team member's work, which makes it harder to provide guidance and feedback. Additionally, it can feel more hierarchical, as there are several full-time managers whose single task is management.

People manager role

Here engineers from several delivery teams report to one *people manager*. The people manager's main job is to ensure that their reports have the information, guidance, and resources they need to be successful, not to contribute technically (see Figure 8-6). As product and UX don't have that many people yet, a people manager role for them is not feasible. For those roles, the "one manager per specialization" approach probably makes the most sense.

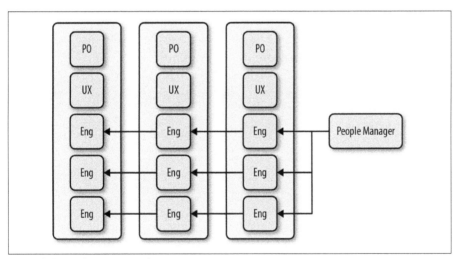

Figure 8-6. People manager role

The advantages of this approach are that movement between teams is easy, as the manager is not part of the team. While people managers may not be able to give technical feedback, they can focus on career development more and they can handle more reports than other approaches, as line management is the focus of their work.

On the other hand, a pure people management role might be less interesting to those who want to remain closely involved in the details of their team's development work. And despite the importance of people management, some view the role as "overhead" since they are not contributing directly to the product.

COMBINING MULTIPLE APPROACHES

If you look at the approaches just shown and try to map your organization to them, you will most likely realize: "None of them works 100% for the people I have." There are many reasons for that (e.g., "I want to follow the platform approach and have one engineering manager per team, but I am missing the manager for my Android team") and we haven't seen an organization that had all the necessary roles when they started introducing this layer of line management. So start with a setup that makes the most sense for you and solves your most pressing problems. For example, if your VP of Engineering has 20 reports, you might focus first on how to reduce that number (as shown in Figure 8-7).

Looking at the case of the missing manager for the Android team again, another option would be to let the Android engineers report to the manager of the iOS team. This decision depends on the willingness of the manager of the iOS team to take on more reports, but it would have the benefit that both mobile platforms have the same manager.

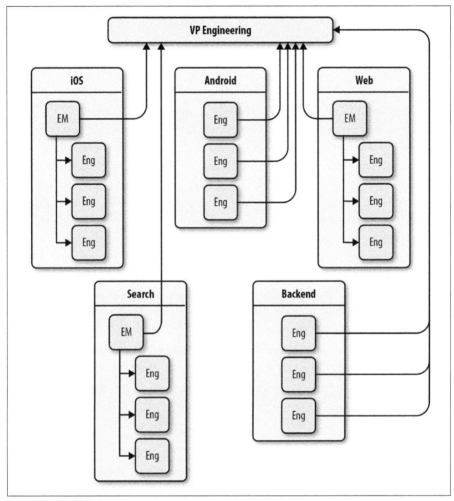

Figure 8-7. Combining multiple approaches

WHICH APPROACH IS RIGHT FOR YOU?

It is impossible to recommend a specific approach, as this choice depends heavily on the kind of people you have in your company. If you have a team of almost all individual contributors who are not interested in management tasks, you need to choose an approach that reflects that. The same applies if several people have line management experience or ambitions. Most likely you will need to change your approach during the growth of your organization, so start with the approach that feels best for you right now and adapt over time (see "Managing People Without

Managers" on page 69). We will now see how to adapt these approaches as the organization grows.

The Next Level

If you organize according to one of the approaches just described but your organization keeps growing, eventually several managers (most likely the VP of Engineering will be one of them) will have too many reports again. If you chose the "engineering manager per team" approach and your organization grows to 10 teams, it will be very tough for the VP of Engineering to do a good job handling all those engineering managers. At this point, the reporting structure of other functions within the delivery teams also might need to change. If each team has a product manager then the line manager would have 10 reports, which is likely too many.

What needs to be introduced now is another layer of management. This is often a difficult step for an organization, as this layer gets easily perceived as "overhead." But this isn't so—done properly, these second-level managers will help align their reports to common goals and provide them with the resources and context they need to achieve them.

Here the approaches to organize delivery teams from Chapter 7 come into play, as the reporting structure and organizational structure should be aligned with each other.

WHAT IT LOOKS LIKE

There are now a lot of different combinations depending on what your teams are optimized for and what approach for the reporting structure you chose in the first part of this chapter. Within this chapter we cannot show all possible combinations, so we will have to concentrate on a few. Let's assume that you started with the platform approach (discussed in "Optimize for Platforms" on page 138) and one engineering manager per team, resulting in the setup shown in Figure 8-8.

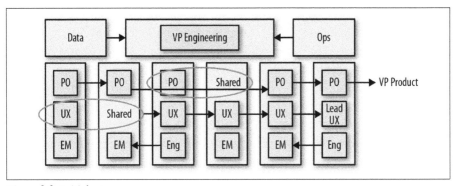

Figure 8-8. Initial setup

The VP of Engineering was completely overloaded by managing a diverse group of reports, so the organization needed to be restructured to mitigate that problem. After a lot of discussion, the company first decided to slowly change the organization to optimize for customer groups, as the platform approach did not scale for them. Single-platform teams became so big that they needed to be split. As there is more than one team per customer group, they split the single teams into feature teams.

Additionally, they decided to keep one engineering manager per team and align engineering line management with the customer group approach. The ideal structure would look like Figure 8-9.

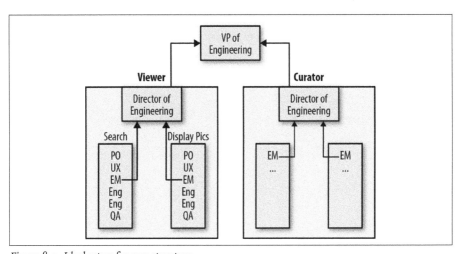

Figure 8-9. Ideal setup for new structure

This setup is also equally applicable for the reporting structure of other functions like product and design/UX. It makes sense for both functions to introduce a manager per customer group who makes sure, for example, that design/UX approaches are consistent for that customer group.

As they decided to move slowly and adapt if necessary on the way, they started with solving the most pressing scaling issues. In this case, the main issue was the high number of reports for the VP, so they started by changing their platform approach into the customer group/feature approach wherever it made sense.

Infrastructure Teams

From a certain team size on, you will need some teams that don't directly serve the external customer. These teams are usually called infrastructure teams since they focus on infrastructure automation, data collection, or similar topics. Although their customers are internal, they can be organized in a very similar way. Building them should follow the same delivery team approach and all organizational design principles apply.

Not all platform teams had enough people to distribute them to feature teams, and therefore specific teams stayed platform teams until enough engineers were hired and/or trained. Figure 8-10 shows what a temporary setup might look like. Here the Android team and another device team did not have enough engineers to move them to feature teams in a way that provided all feature teams with the capacity needed. So they were left as a platform team in the beginning.

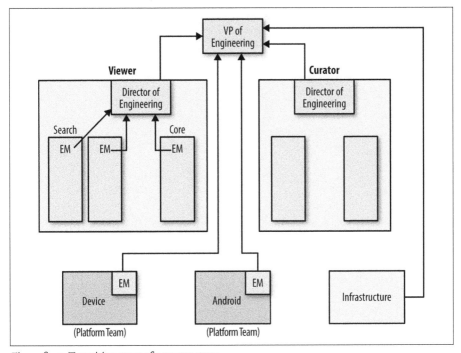

Figure 8-10. Transition stage of new structure

The next steps were then to make sure that the two remaining platform teams were integrated into the feature teams once enough engineers were hired to make this feasible.

This approach of deliberate, incremental change can be used to evolve other organizations to the delivery team model.

Conclusion

This chapter discussed one of the commonly neglected challenges of building an organization: how to build your reporting structure in harmony with your approach to organization. We discussed the first two levels of hierarchy. In the first one, you need to decide what the manager of an IC should be an expert in. Then, when your team has grown so much that another management level is necessary, try to align your reporting structure to your organizational design. A perfect structure is nearly impossible—you will have to make compromises and continuously work on improving the setup.

9

Scaling Culture

Many leaders have written and spoken about the importance of culture in building and sustaining a great team. But what specifically does the word *culture* refer to? Is it about setting up an open office layout? Or following the "no assholes" rule? Or favoring independence and risk taking over process and predictability?

What Is Culture?

The culture of your company can be any or all of those things, depending on what is important to the individuals that make up the team. For the purposes of this chapter, we define team culture as:

> *The expression of what we believe, as shown in the things we do and the way we do them.*

There are two key concepts embedded in that definition: core values and cultural practices. Let's take a closer look at each.

CORE VALUES

Deeply held beliefs, which we'll refer to as core values, are the foundation of team culture. We humans tend to hold onto our beliefs, changing them very slowly if at all. So a team's core values tend to remain fairly constant over time. Here are some examples of how companies have described their core values:

- Zappos: "Embrace and Drive Change," "Build Open and Honest Relationships with Communication" (*http://www.zappos.com/core-values*)

- Salesforce: "Equality for all," "Giving back," "Customer success" (*http://www.salesforce.com/company/*)

- Starbucks: "Creating a culture of warmth and belonging, where everyone is welcome," "Being present, connecting with transparency, dignity and respect." (*http://sbux.co/2iPQQog*)

- Instagram: "Do the simple thing first" (*http://bit.ly/2gJCg1i*)

Notice that these core values do not refer to specific behaviors or practices, but to abstract beliefs and principles.

CULTURAL PRACTICES

By contrast, the visible expressions of core values are what we tend to focus on when describing team culture. For example:

Explicit processes and practices
An engineering team that believes strongly in rigorous coding standards and cross-training might have a rule that "All our code is developed using pair programming."

Implicit behaviors
A team that values hitting commitments over achieving perfection might choose to create "war rooms" and pull all-nighters when they need to get an important feature shipped.

Persistent rituals
Examples might be a monthly dinner for new hires attended by key leaders of the company, a celebration to recognize promotions or project completions, or a recurring volunteer day for employees to donate time to local charities.

Rewards and celebrations
Teams that value creativity and innovation over predictability might give out an annual prize to the employee who showed the most initiative that year (e.g., Amazon's "Just Do It" award[1]).

We refer to these specific behaviors as *cultural practices*. Unlike core values— which change slowly, if at all—many cultural practices have to change as the team grows in order to remain effective. In this chapter, we describe how leaders

---

1 You can read more about it in John J. Sosik's *The Dream Weavers* (*http://bit.ly/2gJGK89*) (Information Age Publishing)

can adapt cultural practices in response to team growth while minimizing disruption and maintaining consistency with the team's core values.

CULTURE STATEMENTS

Lastly, we call the way a team chooses to communicate its culture and values *culture statements*. These statements can take a variety of forms, from "operating principles" to "things we know to be true," from hallway posters to training videos. We'll discuss the different forms of culture statements and show some examples later in the chapter.

VALUES VERSUS CULTURE

An excellent metaphor for explaining the differences between values and culture comes from Sonya Green and Robert Slifko of Sharepoint. Think of values as the roots of a tree (hidden, slow to change) and culture as the branches and leaves (visible, with some parts changing slowly, others more rapidly), as in Figure 9-1.

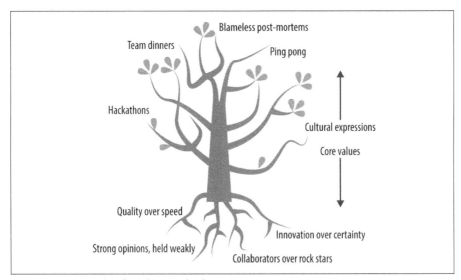

Figure 9-1. A metaphor for culture and values

When to Define Core Values and Team Culture

In the early stage of a team, before it has found product-market fit, spending significant time defining core values and culture could be a distraction. And culture is often quite dynamic in the early days, with each new employee adding something to the mix, making it hard to nail down in detail.

But given the benefits of a strong culture and the costs of resolving culture problems later on, we strongly believe that a lightweight, iterative approach is worthwhile. This could be as simple as a dinner discussion with founders and early employees, captured as a draft on the company wiki. This can serve as a seed for further discussions as the company grows, and should help surface areas of greatest agreement and disagreement. When it's time for a thorough discovery process (most likely after you've entered rapid growth and started to build out your management team, as outlined in Chapter 4), you'll have a solid starting point and some insight into where to focus your efforts.

Why Do Core Values and Team Culture Matter?

Here are some examples of how a clear understanding of your core values and the culture you want to build can materially improve your company's chances of long-term success:

Recruiting and hiring efficiency
> Companies can use the unique aspects of their culture and values in recruiting videos or blog posts to help attract the right candidates. The hiring process can also include filters to weed out candidates who have conflicting values (for more, see Chapter 1).

Independent, aligned decision making
> Shared values can help ensure that individuals make the right trade-offs when facing uncertainty or tough decisions, without requiring leadership to weigh in. Kellan Elliott-McCrea (*http://bit.ly/2gJI5vz*), former CTO of Etsy, wrote: "Culture gives us the ability to act in a loosely coupled way; it allows us to pursue a diversity of tactics. Uncertainty is the mind-killer and culture creates certainty in the face of the yawning shapeless void of possible solutions that is software engineering."

Constructive conflicts
> A shared understanding of values and culture increases understanding of decisions and actions by other groups. When conflicts arise, as they always do in fast-moving hyper-growth companies, this common ground smooths the path to resolution and channels energy in a positive direction.

Tribal identity
> A strong cultural identity allows the team to internalize what separates them from other companies. This creates a bond that can boost morale and

retention. For example, "The HP Way" at Hewlett-Packard provided a strong sense of identify that lasted for decades, helping propel the company from two guys in a garage to over 300,000 employees and 70+ years of growth. And some argue (*https://hbr.org/2011/09/how-hewlett-packard-lost-the-h*) that its recent struggles can in part be attributed to new leadership that failed to reinforce the "HP Way."

On this point, just as investing in team culture is an opportunity, ignoring it is dangerous. As Edgar Schein warns in *Organizational Culture and Leadership* (Wiley): "Culture is an abstraction, yet the forces that are created [...] from culture are powerful. If we don't understand the operation of these forces, we become victim to them."

Discovering and Describing Values and Culture

Culture often emerges organically as a team comes together. The way that founders and early employees interact and collaborate creates a de facto culture that later team members will observe and often emulate. As the team grows, subcultures may emerge if different team members feel free to define "the way we do things" for themselves.

At some point, leaders need to make this implicit culture an explicit one in order to realize the advantages discussed in the previous section. It's very difficult to create a persistent and consistent tribal identity if no one can describe what makes the tribe unique.

Although different leaders articulate and guide their team's cultures in very different ways, for the purpose of discussion we break the process down into four steps:

- Discover the team's core values and desired culture
- Describe and communicate the values in a meaningful, authentic way
- Ensure that team members act in accordance with the values and culture
- Build the values and culture into the day-to-day practices of the team

Doing all of this thoroughly can be a lot of work. But it's also possible to take an iterative approach, time-boxing the effort in the early life of a team, and expanding later as growth starts to kick in. We'll look more closely at how to do this later in this section.

WELL-DEFINED CULTURE STATEMENTS

Before diving into the process for defining values and culture, let's look at what other companies have done to communicate the things they believe and the way they do them.

Google: "Ten things we know to be true"

Google's main culture statement (*http://bit.ly/2gYqGSU*) is a list of beliefs that apply to the entire company.

1. Focus on the user and all else will follow.
2. It's best to do one thing really, really well.
3. Fast is better than slow.
4. Democracy on the web works.
5. You don't need to be at your desk to need an answer.
6. You can make money without doing evil.
7. There's always more information out there.
8. The need for information crosses all borders.
9. You can be serious without a suit.
10. Great just isn't good enough.

Carbon Five: "Our mindset"

Carbon Five's description of its company mindset shows four axes and highlights where their culture falls between each extreme (Figure 9-2).

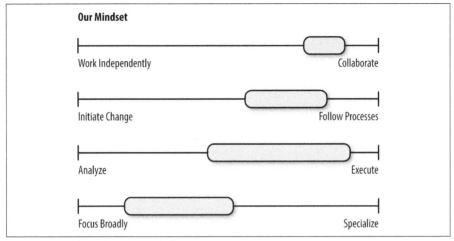

Figure 9-2. Carbon Five, "Our mindset"

Medium: "Principles to organize and manage the company"

Medium published their approach to management and organization (*http://bit.ly/2gYkomf*) in 2016 when they started to migrate away from Holacracy (*http://www.holacracy.org*):

1. Individuals can always instigate change.

2. Authority is distributed, though not evenly or permanently.

3. Ownership is accountability, not control.

4. Good decision-making implies alignment, not consensus.

5. The system is designed to be adaptable.

6. Corporate transparency, driven by technology.

There are clearly a wide range of formats that can be used as culture statements, depending on what feels right for your team.

DISCOVERING VALUES, DEFINING CULTURE

Because the benefits of having a clearly defined culture are multiplied over time, we've designed a process that is intentionally lightweight and iterative. We want even the most fast-moving, deadline-pressured team to be able to get started on this crucial task. As with all the recommendations in this book, tailor the process to your needs.

Step 1: Discover the team's core values

We like the term *discover* because core values should already be present in the members of the team. Your first focus should be understanding what they are and surfacing any areas where they may be in conflict, rather than trying to change them or impose new beliefs on the team.

Start by meeting with the founding team. It's likely they already have well-formed opinions on what the team's core values should be. Ask questions like:

- What brought us together to found this team?
- What are the qualities, behaviors, and practices of this team that we value most?
- What is our team like when we are doing our best work?
- What is the most important quality to look for in our new hires?
- What aspects of our team do you hope will still be present in five years?

If you find areas of disagreement, it's critical to acknowledge them now and bring the group together again to discuss the situation. If the key leaders of the team don't agree on what's important, you could be headed for major conflicts down the road. Better to surface that now and deal with it rather than wait for it to boil over during a time of crisis. Or perhaps there has been a miscommunication that can be corrected. Either way, it's important not to gloss over any conflict in this phase since it will surely surface later, and probably in a form that will be far more expensive to fix.

Ideally, you will see some consistency in the answers. If so, document what you've found and share it with the participants for feedback. If no major disagreements surface, move to the next step.

Step 2: Draft your team's culture statements

Next, find a way to communicate what was learned in Step 1 to the rest of the team. As shown in the previous section, culture statements can take many different forms: lists of core values, operating principles, catchy mottos, and so on. What is right for you may depend on the stage of growth you are in, the structure of the company, the personalities of the leadership team, and other factors.

Most importantly, before immortalizing your company culture with hallway posters or recruiting brochures, make sure to solicit feedback from the team. Surveys are easy and adequate for this task, though in-person discussions in groups of 6 to 10 are preferable since you can drill down to better understand any negative answers. Ask questions like:

- To what extent do you agree with these culture statements/core values/ operating principles?
- Do you find them to be authentic, motivating, and inspirational?
- Do you think your leaders and coworkers embody these in their words and actions?
- Can these be used to help you resolve conflicts or make decisions in your work?

Gathering feedback is critical, because trying to force your team to believe things they disagree with is a nearly impossible task, and a huge distraction from moving your business forward. If a culture statement doesn't align with the reality of the team, it will be rejected as corporate brainwashing and undermine the rest of the process. If you sense pushback at this stage, it's either time to go back to the drawing board or to take more significant steps to resolve the cultural conflict. Resolving conflicts is discussed in more detail in "Resolving Culture Clash" on page 195.

Step 3: Practice what you preach

For culture statements to be motivating, they need to be broadly understood and reflected in the actions of the team. If they aren't, they will be rejected as "corporate bullshit" by the team, and the effort to create them will be wasted. Most importantly, leaders must be careful that their actions match the culture and values of the team. Nothing undermines culture statements more quickly than a leader whose actions contradict them.

For example, imagine a company that preaches "trust, but verify" as a way of encouraging autonomy while retaining accountability. An executive who requires that all candidate offers be approved by the CFO is acting in direct contradiction to this idea, saying with their actions, "I don't trust you to make appropriate compensation packages for our new hires." Such behavior may then be modeled by lower-level managers, who want to ensure offers coming from their team will not be rejected by the CFO. Pretty soon, managers at every level are undermining this aspect of the desired culture.

There may be times when team leaders want or need to change the culture of the team, reasons for which are described in "Evolving Team Culture" on page

191. But these changes must be undertaken intentionally, and preferably accompanied by broad internal communication that motivates the change, as well as a corresponding change to the culture statements.

Step 4: Build culture and values into the environment

Fast-growing companies are full of distractions: customer demands, late-night bug fixes, training new hires, and so on. Unless leaders make the time and effort to knit culture statements into the work environment and ensure that they are consistent with each other, the culture might change in unforeseen and possibly undesired ways.

Reinforcing Core Values at Twitter: A Story from David

During my time there, Twitter had an on-boarding class that explained its core values and the rationale behind each one. At the end of the class, each new employee was asked to pick the one core value that resonated with them the most. They then received a skin for their laptop imprinted with that core value. The skin for each value had a distinctive color, so it was easy to recognize which one a person had chosen. This led to informal conversations between team members about why they had made that choice.

Such a simple technique, but so powerful. Employees were reminded of the company's core values on a daily basis, without any heavy-handed messaging from leadership or corny hallway posters. And it created a very personal connection between employees and their chosen value. It also provided feedback to the onboarding team about which values resonated most with new hires based on which laptop skins were chosen most frequently.

Other areas where values and culture should be integrated:

- The *feedback and promotion processes* should reinforce core values and culture by asking questions like "To what extent does this person embody our core values/company culture in their daily work? Which aspects do they demonstrate most? Which ones could they demonstrate more?" And in the spirit of 360-degree feedback, employees should also have the opportunity to comment on how well the leadership team, and the company in general, is demonstrating the core values in their words and actions.

- Instances of *culturally destructive behavior* should be taken seriously. Individuals who behave in ways that contradict the core values of the team need to modify their behavior or be removed from the team. The famous "no assholes" rule is a form of this. This can be difficult with individuals that otherwise perform well, but as Joe Stump wrote in his First Round Review article (*http://bit.ly/2gYw2o0*), "A lot of people say don't fire great engineers—but they're wrong. It only takes one asshole to destroy an entire team."

- Leaders should regularly *celebrate successful demonstrations of core values.* For example, if company culture values rigorous attention to quality over ability to ship quickly, then project teams that demonstrate this trade-off should be praised publicly when they ship quality features. (Side note: Amazon has consistently held to a culture of frugality, preferring to spend money on customer experience rather than on employee perks. Company lore held that early employees would make their desks out of a door and some 4x4s purchased at a local hardware store rather than spend hundreds of dollars on fancy office equipment. To commemorate this practice, Amazon instituted the "Door Desk award," given out annually to the employee who most appropriately demonstrated frugality in their work. For more about the history (and the irony) of the door desk, read Glenn Fleishman's blog post (*http://bit.ly/2gYjdDc*).)

More examples of how to reinforce values and culture, particularly as the team grows, are discussed in "Scaling Challenges for Culture" on page 180.

Best practices for crafting useful culture statements

Based on our own experience and numerous examples from successful and failed companies, we have some suggestions for crafting meaningful and useful culture statements.

Focus on trade-offs A surface-level investigation into values might reveal tropes like "Focus on the customer" or "Innovate, don't stagnate." But these concepts are like "mom and apple pie"—almost no one would disagree with them, so what do they mean in practice? Go deeper by finding out what, if anything, the team is willing to sacrifice to pursue these goals. Should innovation come at the expense of the stability of the current product? Facebook's motto, "Move fast and break things," made it clear that rapid iteration was more important than stability for Facebook at the time, a trade-off that not every team would make.

Be unique Google's "You can be serious without a suit" is novel and memorable, but it probably wasn't the first phrasing they came up with. It's worth iterating to find an expression that's new but still fits the team.

Think "excavation," not "advocacy" You're trying to find the values that are already shared by the team, not trying to transplant what's already there with what you wish was there. Interviews with a broad cross-section of the team can help ensure that the value statements actually become a useful tool and not something to be mocked.

Be both realistic and aspirational Ryan King, an engineer and manager at Twitter, told us that the group who led the core values definition process at Twitter felt that their mission was to uncover values that were both authentic and aspirational. He recommended asking the question "What is our team like when we are at our best?"

Scaling Challenges for Culture

> *The enemy of cultural cohesion is super-fast headcount growth. Companies that grow faster than doubling their headcount annually tend to have serious cultural drift, even if they do a great job of on-boarding new employees and training them.*
>
> **—BEN HOROWITZ, "HOW TO RUIN YOUR COMPANY WITH**
> **ONE BAD PROCESS" (***HTTP://BIT.LY/2GYK2ME***)**

Rapid growth is the enemy of team culture. Even if you have spent the time to identify and articulate your team's core values and culture, growing quickly will challenge your ability to retain that culture, for a variety of reasons. Table 9-1 breaks down some common scaling challenges and proposes solutions that we'll describe in the following sections.

Table 9-1. *Scaling challenges for culture, with possible solutions*

Scaling challenge	Possible solutions
Diverging values: hiring new team members that don't share core values, which leads to conflict.	*Hiring:* interview for "values fit"
Culture ignorance: newer team members don't understand core values or culture. *Culture divergence:* entire teams adopt their own ways of doing things that don't mesh well with each other.	*On-boarding:* train new members on value and culture. *Leadership:* reinforce culture through words and actions. *Leadership:* assess and correct cultural divergence.
Culture stagnation: failure to adapt cultural practices to team growth.	*Leadership:* pay attention to warning signs, adapt cultural practices as needed.
Culture clash: failure to address conflicting values or culture.	*Leadership:* address any such culture clashes quickly and decisively.

Let's look at each of the proposed solutions in more detail.

HIRING, VALUES, AND CULTURE

Never in the history of my career has my ability to drink beer made me better at solving a business problem.

—CASEY WEST, "REDEFINING CULTURE FIT" (*HTTP://BIT.LY/2GLUKXS*)

Interviewing for values is difficult but important, especially when the company is growing fast. Once values start to diverge, team members lose the common ground upon which cultural practices are based, which can lead to productivity-killing culture clashes. But how does a team interview for values?

In our experience, the common "culture fit" interview (which has often been referred to as the "beer test"—that is, whether you would want to have a beer with the candidate) does a poor job of surfacing values. There are several things wrong with such a test:

- Drinking beer is not a valid test of the candidate's value to the team, nor is it something that all candidates feel comfortable doing, for health, religious, or safety reasons.

- One's desire to hang out with a candidate after work is also not a valid test of value to the team.

- Such an unstructured and "gut feel" evaluation is likely to harm diversity, as interviewers may subconsciously favor candidates that have familiar surface-level behaviors or similar backgrounds.

Far more important is whether the candidate is truly qualified to do the job, of course. But almost equally so is whether their values are compatible with the team's.

Some examples of how to interview for values fit are listed in Table 9-2.

Table 9-2. Interview questions for "values fit"

Desired core values	Interview questions	What to look for
Open communication, critical thinking	"What should we do to improve our interview process/product/ business?"	A strong candidate should be able to offer up a critique and ideas for improvement without sounding overly cautious or harsh.
Empathy, emotional intelligence	"Tell me about a professional conflict you had at your previous job. How was it resolved?"	Candidates with strong EQ can explain the conflict from the perspective of their antagonist, not just their own. Be concerned if you only hear "I" and "me" in the answer, or if their only solution was to escalate to an authority figure.
Curiosity, continuous learning	"What skills are you most interested in learning?" or "What is the most interesting problem you've wrestled with?"	Difficulty answering this can indicate a lack of the desired core values.
Collaboration	"Help me work through this specific problem..."	Those comfortable working with others should be able to demonstrate it in practice. Pick a problem big enough that it can be subdivided. Assess the candidate's ability to see these divisions, work with you to decide how to tackle them, and collaborate in putting together a solution.

ON-BOARDING AND CULTURE

When your company is growing fast, it can be hard to spend the time and effort needed to properly train new team members on why the team's core values and culture matter. But this obviously leaves them vulnerable to moving the culture in different directions based on their own preferences and past experience, and makes it even more difficult for them to interview for values fit once they start interviewing other prospective new hires.

We recommend treating values and culture as a first-class part of onboarding. Find someone on the team who is especially passionate about this, help them design a "Team Values and Culture" session, and make sure every new hire attends it. And lastly, survey new hires afterward to understand how well the values resonate with them. This will obviously help you improve the session, if needed, but can also be an indicator of whether values fit is being properly assessed in the hiring process. If new hires don't find the values meaningful, you may be headed for culture conflicts down the road.

LEADERSHIP AND CULTURE

The dynamic processes of culture creation and management are the essence of leadership and make you realize that leadership and culture are two sides of the same coin.

—EDGAR SCHEIN, *ORGANIZATIONAL CULTURE AND LEADERSHIP* (WILEY)

As with many aspects of a team, leaders wield a tremendous amount of influence on team culture. This is true no matter what is written on the posters on the wall or repeated over and over again at all-hands meetings. As Ron Westrum wrote in his seminal paper, "A Typology of Organisational Cultures" (*http://bit.ly/2gYsAmh*):

The underlying idea is that leaders, by their preoccupations, shape a unit's culture. Through their symbolic actions, as well as rewards and punishments, leaders communicate what they feel is important. These preferences then become the preoccupation of the organisation's workforce, because rewards, punishments, and resources follow the leader's preferences. Those who align with the preferences will be rewarded, and those who do not will be set aside. Most long time organisation members instinctively know how to read the signs of the times and those who do not soon get expensive lessons.

Ensure values are reflected in words and actions

Leaders must model the behavior they want to see from the team. This can be used in positive ways—for example, to bolster areas where the team culture seems weak or dispersed, or to shift culture in a new direction (described further in "Culture shift" on page 196). Conversely, any leadership behavior that conflicts with team values must be addressed and corrected quickly before employees start to perceive culture statements as hollow and useless.

Screen new leaders for values fit

Because of their outsized influence, it is especially important that any new leaders brought into the company are closely screened for values fit. Not only will these leaders act as models for team behavior, they will likely help set the hiring standards for their organization. If they bring in new employees with differing values or build a culture that diverges from the rest of the company, you are likely on a path to culture conflict.

Adapt cultural practices to team growth

Rapid growth can make obsolete even the most treasured cultural practices. What works for a team of 10 might suddenly break down at 50 or 100.

For example, a team that values openness and transparency might decide that hiring huddles should be open to anyone on the team, not just the interview panel. But once the team has grown to dozens of members, this policy can cause the huddles to get bogged down in lengthy debates, leading to slower decisions and a lower offer acceptance rate.

Or imagine a company that values breadth of knowledge over depth. They may adopt an on-boarding process in which each new employee does a one-week rotation with each team. Once there are more than five teams to rotate through, this practice becomes impractical.

Growing rapidly makes it harder to adapt such practices in a timely fashion. Fast-growing teams may find that their practices are always one step behind, leading to lost productivity and lower morale. Because of this, leaders need to pay attention to the warning signs listed later in this section.

More details on how to change the culture of a team to account for growth are described in "Evolving Team Culture" on page 191.

Assess and correct cultural divergence

During hyper-growth, entire new divisions of the company may be born and staffed within a few short months. In such cases, it isn't uncommon for the new groups to end up doing things their own way. Sometimes these culture differences can be harmless, other times toxic. It can be hard for leaders, upon noticing the changes, to determine whether such variations are healthy or likely to lead to culture clashes down the road.

Since the latter can be so expensive to correct, it's important to recognize culture divergence early, do the work needed to assess the source, and if needed, bring the culture in line with the rest of the team. For a more detailed discussion on resolving cultural differences, see "Resolving Culture Clash" on page 195.

WARNINGS SIGNS FOR SCALING CULTURE

How do you know if your culture is scaling with the growth of the team? Keep your eyes and ears open for the warning signs in Table 9-3 and react appropriately.

Table 9-3. Warning signs of culture issues

Warning sign	Possible cause(s)
Factions forming: certain teams don't seem to work well with others, teams blame others for failures.	Not hiring for values; allowing teams to diverge cultures.
Transfers between teams don't work out. Person who transfers feels uncomfortable with new team's processes or culture. New team doesn't feel that the transfer is strong enough to "cut it," or that they do things the wrong way.	Culture and values between the two teams may have diverged, perhaps due to not hiring for values at the leadership level.
Noticeable shift in tone of internal communications, perhaps snarky questions at all-hands meetings or bitter debates in group chat.	Culture is out of sync with core values; leaders not acting in sync with core values; leaders not correcting culturally destructive behavior; culture not adapting to growth.
Veteran employees have lower morale, higher attrition.	Culture has changed too quickly, or not in accordance with core values.
Newer employees have lower morale, higher attrition.	Not filtering for values in the hiring process; poor on-boarding program; toxic work environment.

Not every instance of these warning signs indicates a widespread culture problem. Some could simply be a single employee affecting their coworkers, perhaps due to factors outside of the work environment like a relationship problem or a sick relative. But they each warrant investigation in case there might be deeper dysfunction causing these symptoms to appear.

Building a Culture That Scales

Much has been written about what makes for a "good" team culture. But this designation begs the question: are some cultures truly *better* than others—more effective, more scalable? After all, culture is highly context-dependent; each team is different, with particular values and priorities. What makes a culture "good" is in large part the breadth and depth with which it reflects those values and priorities.

However, from our experience, research, and interviews, it's clear that some cultures are inherently more effective than others, particularly when you're trying to scale a team. Let's look at the aspects that set those cultures apart and how they contribute to team success.

CONTINUOUS LEARNING AND IMPROVEMENT

One of the hallmarks of top-performing individuals and teams is a strong motivation for self-improvement. This speaks to the "Mastery" element of Daniel Pink's motivational framework that we introduced in Chapter 6, *Scaling the Organization: Design Principles*. Encouraging your team to work on learning new job skills and giving them the time to do so not only improves their morale but increases their effectiveness as well. And building a culture that emphasizes learning can make teams more resilient to common scaling challenges like finger pointing and politics. For example, one of the reasons blameless postmortems are effective is that they emphasize learning over calling out a particular person or team that might have been at fault.

Teams that emphasize cooperative learning can also better leverage the knowledge and talents of the entire team, both old-timers and new, thus turning rapid growth from a challenge into a strength. When each new person is able to share their unique knowledge with their coworkers, they can provide a productivity boost beyond just the work they are able to do themselves.

Consider whether the following techniques can help build a learning culture for your team:

Conference attendance
> Give team members a yearly conference budget, provided they share what they learn with the group.

Ongoing education
> Most companies have a university or community college nearby, and even if not, there are many resources for remote learning. Companies can provide a money and time budget for individuals to take work-related classes.

Internal "brown bag" sessions
Create a forum where team members can present on any subject they are interested in.

"War stories"/"tribal knowledge"
Old-timers often have a trove of interesting tales to tell about the early days of the company, how they survived the tough times, and why things turned out the way they did. Creating a forum for this can help avoid veterans feeling marginalized by newcomers, a common problem during hyper-growth.

External speakers
There are many experts who can help educate the team on topics related to their work.

Performance feedback and promotions
Include teaching and mentorship as key elements of the feedback and promotion process.

Building a learning culture not only motivates the team individually by tapping into their desire for Mastery, but improves the team as a whole by ensuring that knowledge and best practices are widely shared. This is one of the best ways we've seen to bend the productivity curve upward during periods of rapid growth. More on this topic can be found in "Building an Environment of Continuous Learning" on page 105.

TRUST AND SAFETY

The concept of *psychological safety* has become popular lately, due in part to Google's "Project Aristotle," an internal research study on what aspects of teams are most correlated with overall team performance. A *New York Times* article (*http://nyti.ms/2hMLhqQ*) about the study wrote that "Google's data indicated that psychological safety, more than anything else, was critical to making a team work."

First introduced in a research paper by Amy Edmundson (*http://bit.ly/2hMHauL*), psychological safety is defined as "as a shared belief that the team is safe for interpersonal risk taking," or, more simply, "a sense of confidence that the team will not embarrass, reject, or punish someone for speaking up." This confidence comes from team members trusting one another, learning through words and actions that it is safe to voice opinions without fear of retribution.

We believe that emphasizing these concepts in culture statements is a key component to realizing psychological safety in the workplace. And because violations of trust can take so much time and effort to repair, we strongly recommend training new managers in how to foster psychological safety before they take on a management role.

Violations of trust must also be dealt with swiftly and decisively. For example, managers who unfairly punish team members for voicing concerns should be removed from their position and possibly from the company. Doing nothing can have a very high cost. As Ben Horowitz writes in "CEOs Should Tell It Like It Is" (*http://bit.ly/2gM9nBq*): "If you investigate companies which have failed, you will find many employees who knew about the fatal issues long before those issues killed the company. If the employees knew about the deadly problems, why didn't they say something? Too often the answer is that the company culture discouraged the spread of bad news, so the knowledge lay dormant until it was too late to act."

Trust and psychological safety create an environment where even difficult ideas can be freely exchanged. If your team can express their concerns and ideas, you won't miss out on possible problems or innovations that your people might otherwise keep to themselves. Be sure to never repeat the old adage, "Don't bring me problems—bring me solutions!" Such an attitude means the most difficult problems will never surface, the exact opposite of what the company needs.

The Ursa Oil Platform: How Psychological Safety Can Improve Physical Safety

The NPR podcast *Invisibilia* did an excellent piece (*http://n.pr/2gM6j8i*) about the Ursa Oil Platform that illustrates the importance of trust and psychological safety. Ursa was at the time the biggest oil platform ever built. The culture of the men who worked on oil platforms was based on traditionally male norms: "If you make a mistake, hide it. If you don't know something, pretend that you do. And...never appear weak. If, for some God forsaken reason, you feel an emotion rising, swallow hard." Injuries were part of the job, and often gruesome: "It wasn't unusual...to see people die."

But the man in charge of running Ursa, Rick Fox, "had this nagging dissatisfaction that things could be different and better." Rick hired Claire Nuer, who ran a consulting group called Learning as Leadership, to help change the culture of the workers at Ursa. They put the workers through a series of workshops designed to help them open up to each other and feel comfortable sharing doubts, failures, and concerns: "Because it's scary what you're doing. And it's normal to be scared. And if you just don't tell people you're scared, you're not going to create safety together." And what was the result? Robin Ely of Harvard Business School studied the culture change at Ursa and concluded, "These changes that they instituted resulted in an 84 percent decline in the company's accident rate. And in that same period, the company's level of productivity in terms of number of barrels and efficiency and reliability exceeded the industry's previous benchmark... Part of safety in an environment like that is being able to admit mistakes and being open to learning."

DIVERSITY AND INCLUSION

To grow effectively, teams need to do two things very well:

- Locate the most qualified candidates for the roles they need to fill

- Provide those they hire with a supportive and engaging work environment

If done well, these goals will achieve growth while also building a more diverse team. Teams that can source and retain great talent regardless of their background or physical characteristics have many competitive advantages:

- Broader hiring networks, since a more diverse staff will have a greater breadth of connections

- Reduced loss of institutional knowledge due to lower attrition

- Increased psychological safety (discussed earlier in "Trust and Safety" on page 187)

- Increased creativity in solving problems

- More complete understanding of different customer groups

Many leaders, unfortunately, undermine these goals. There are various ways that this can happen. They may source candidates from a narrow channel, for example, only from "top universities" or places where the founders studied or previously worked. This requires less effort in the short run than a more broad-based recruiting effort, but is likely to lead to a less diverse team. And there are many ways that bias can influence an unsophisticated hiring process. Numerous studies show that access to names and faces during resume screening and inter-

viewing tends to discriminate against underrepresented groups. Some companies are moving toward blind interview (*http://bit.ly/2gM3dBl*) techniques as a
result. Refer back to "Hiring, Values, and Culture" on page 181 for a discussion
of the "beer test" and better ways to screen for values fit.

Companies can also hinder growth and inclusion by failing to build a diverse
leadership team. There is a growing body of research showing that mentorship of
an employee from an underrepresented group is most effective when it comes
from someone of the same background.[2] Because of this, a homogeneous leadership team may have difficulty fostering the careers of emerging leaders from outside the dominant group. Another danger zone is a failure to support team
members equally in their career growth. For instance, women are less likely, on
average, to ask for a promotion than men. Managers need to be aware of this tendency so that when a man asks for a promotion, they will pause to consider
whether there is an equal or better-qualified woman for the job who just hasn't
asked for it yet.[3]

And finally, one of the worst things a company can do to undermine diversity goals is to fail to build an inclusive work environment or, worse yet, to ignore
signs of a hostile work environment, such as high attrition for employees from
underrepresented groups. (See "Building an Inclusive Workplace" on page 102.)
Carefully conducted and analyzed employee happiness surveys and exit interviews are one way to surface such problems. It's also worth starting to gather
attrition data early while the team is small, so trends can be observed and investi-
gated, and most importantly, addressed swiftly.

These tendencies are at least partially to blame for the lack of diversity in the
tech industry. This failure alone is a reason to build a culture that values diversity
and inclusion. But doing so can also help the business for the reasons mentioned
before: expanding the pool of qualified candidates, increasing retention, boosting
creativity and innovation, and expanding the team's understanding of different
target customers.

Chapters 1 through 3 cover some ways to potentially reduce bias in the
recruiting process, and Chapter 5 has a section on building an inclusive work

---

2 Herminia Ibarra, Nancy M. Carter, and Christine Silva, "Why Men Still Get More Promotions Than Women"
(*http://bit.ly/2gMabq0*), *Harvard Business Review*, September 2010.

3 Linda Babcock, Sara Laschever, Michele Gelfand, and Deborah Small, "Nice Girls Don't Ask" (*http://
bit.ly/2gM8uZP*), *Harvard Business Review*, October 2003.

environment. Combining these best practices and building them into your culture should help your team scale more effectively.

Evolving Team Culture

This ability to perceive the limitations of one's own culture and to evolve the culture adaptively is the essence and ultimate challenge of leadership.

—EDGAR SCHEIN, *ORGANIZATIONAL CULTURE AND LEADERSHIP* (WILEY)

Leaders have two key responsibilities when it comes to team culture:

- Reinforcing the core values and culture that currently exist
- Recognizing the need for cultural change and implementing it

Most of our discussion so far has been about the former. But when does it make sense to change the team's culture? And what tools do leaders have to shape team culture as the team grows and the business evolves?

REASONS FOR CULTURE CHANGE

We covered why team leaders may need to change their team's culture in response to growth in "Leadership and Culture" on page 183, but let's look at all the possible reasons for culture change:

- Evolving cultural practices to adapt to team growth
- Adjusting the culture to better fit with core values
- Improving the culture to make the team more effective
- Adapting the culture to changing business needs

Let's look at each one in more detail.

Adapting to team growth

As discussed earlier in this chapter, a cultural practice that works for 15 people doesn't always work for 50 or 150. Leaders need to recognize or anticipate these failure points and help encourage a change in the way things are done.

Adjusting to fit core values

Sometimes the actual day-to-day practices of the team don't fit with the core values of the team. For example, the team may firmly believe in "getting it right":

that a quality product is more important than shipping on time. But due to financial or customer pressure, the team has fallen into a mode of hitting their ship dates whether the product is ready or not. Or a team that prides itself on openness and transparency may overreact to a damaging press leak and decide to restrict the information it gives out in company meetings.

Large disconnects between the core values and the cultural practices of the team will over time start to manifest in various ways: a mistrust of management, disbelief in the usefulness of core values and culture statements, and ultimately, lower morale and productivity. It's important that leaders recognize such disconnects and take action to correct them.

A more subtle disconnect can occur when a core value for the company as a whole doesn't fit with the practices required by a specific discipline. For example, a company with a value of "surprise and delight" may find that the operations team, who generally hate surprises, don't resonate with this core value. In such cases, the core value may need to be adapted, or the operations management team may need to create org-specific culture statements that explain why the disconnect is appropriate and acceptable.

Improving the culture

Sometimes culture change is warranted independent of core values fit. In the previous section, "Building a Culture That Scales" on page 185, we argued that certain elements of team culture may be especially valuable to a fast-growing team. So, for example, if your team doesn't currently emphasize continuous learning and improvement, you might decide that this should be introduced into the team culture. We'll explain how to do this in the next section.

Adapting to business needs

Back in 2010, Facebook was struggling to replicate its success on the desktop to mobile platforms. As SC Moatti describes in her First Round Review article (*http://bit.ly/2hRDTxH*), "Facebook had to dramatically alter its mindset to become a great mobile company":

> *As a free web service, the cost of a mistake for the company had traditionally been rather low. So low that "move fast and break things" was a motto that made sense for a long time. Whenever something went wrong, a few engineers would team up to fix it—no harm, no foul. But this isn't how mobile operates... If the cost of an error on web is 1X, the cost of a similar error on mobile is 10X.*

We will discuss how Facebook went about implementing culture change in the next section.

Recognizing the need for a cultural change like this is no easy feat. As Edgar Schein put it in the quote at the beginning of this section, it is the "ultimate challenge of leadership." Leaders must constantly challenge their teams to meet the needs of the business they are building, and never accept "that's just the way we do things" as a complete answer. Changing the way things are done is par for the course at fast-growing companies, and it is often possible to make changes that meet the evolving needs of the business while remaining consistent with core values.

IMPLEMENTING CULTURAL CHANGE

Regardless of the reason or the approach, there are always some risks involved in changing a team's culture. Done poorly, the change can disrupt productivity and cause team members who don't agree with the change to leave. Here we discuss ways to ease the transition and maximize the chance that it will be accepted and embraced by the team.

Motivate the change

As with any significant change, cultural or otherwise, the first step is to prepare the team by explaining the motivation for the change, the "why" behind the "what." In the absence of a clear, well-communicated rationale for the desired change, employees may fill the information vacuum with incorrect motivations, such as "this is just leadership posturing" or "they're trying to get rid of our startup spirit!" Explaining the desired outcomes enables the whole team to participate in achieving them, perhaps helping in ways that team leaders haven't even considered.

Leadership must walk the walk

We discussed this earlier in "Leadership and Culture" on page 183, but want to reiterate it here because it's nearly impossible to shape a team's culture without both buy-in and follow-through from the leaders of the team.

To effect change, team leaders must be able to motivate the change to their reports as well as model the new behavior they want to see. The classic counterexample is a new CEO who comes in and decides to impose a culture change by fiat. Perhaps they liked the way things worked at their previous company ("Having a hiring committee is the only way to go!"), or they heard a compelling anecdote from a colleague ("I hear work-from-home days kill productivity, so let's get rid of those"). Either way, without the support of the executive staff, team managers, and key IC leaders in the company, such a change is likely to fail and possibly even backfire, resulting in a loss of faith in company leadership.

Watch for warning signs

Culture change can be difficult to weather, particularly for veteran employees who helped build the original culture. Use the warning signs listed earlier to identify cases where the change is not being received well and make a plan for how to react.

Case study in culture change: Facebook's shift to mobile

In the previous section, we talked about Facebook's need for culture change in order to more effectively pursue the mobile market. This required a concerted effort by leadership to explain and reinforce the change:

- Mark Zuckerberg's first move was to publicly retire the word "hack" (*http://bit.ly/2gMbW6C*) as Facebook's rallying cry. Although this was intended to be motivating for developers, "hack" had a connotation of quick-and-dirty solutions, which clashed with the more formal development model needed for mobile clients. Unlike web applications, which can be fixed on the fly, native mobile apps require a testing and approval cycle, meaning bugs take more time to fix and are thus more painful to customers and the company brand.

- Next, they reorganized the engineering team and product planning processes to put more emphasis on mobile. In the past, new features would be tested on the web client first and then rolled out to the mobile clients if successful, so Facebook adopted a "Mobile first" mantra and approach to try to reverse this. They also changed their org structure to focus on the product rather than the client—that is, all the developers for the various Facebook Messenger clients reported to one team rather than being separated into web, iOS, and Android client teams.

- A new culture statement was introduced to boost developers' attention to quality. In a 2012 article in AllThingsD (*http://bit.ly/2gbLnXd*), Mike Isaac wrote: "Perhaps the most drastic change is philosophical. Product managers want teams to *'own their code,'* to put more intention and responsibility behind any changes they make."

- Lastly, they moved away from their most public and pervasive culture statement, "Move fast and break things," turning to a more mobile-compatible slogan, "Move fast with stable infra" (meaning "infrastructure"). Zuckerberg took a significant chunk of their 10th anniversary F8 conference to explain the motivations for the shift: "What we realized over time is that it wasn't helping us to move faster because we had to slow down to fix these bugs and it wasn't improving our speed."[4]

The effort paid off—today, more than 90% of Facebook users access the service via mobile devices, and mobile ad revenue represents 82% of total ad revenue for the company.[5] The message here is that cultural change often requires leaders to make grand gestures, public announcements, and repeated internal messaging to shift the team's mindset from the old way to the new way.

RESOLVING CULTURE CLASH

For reasons described in "Scaling Challenges for Culture" on page 180, hyper-growth teams can suffer from disagreements over values or culture. Sometimes these variations are natural and harmless. The team building native mobile apps is likely to place greater value on rigorous coding and release processes than the team that builds a cloud-hosted web application. The relative difficulty of fixing bugs in the different products naturally leads to a different approach and even attracts developers whose values differ in that regard.

But other times, culture differences may reflect deeper, potentially incompatible divides in core values, or the relevant practices may simply be incompatible with each other within the same organization. It's important that leaders diagnose the root cause of the conflict before attempting a resolution. Let's review some common cases and discuss possible remedies for each.

Culture drift

The most common case is also the simplest. When leaders don't take steps to communicate and reinforce company culture, different groups within the company may develop their own culture organically. Sometimes these differences are harmless—who cares if the data science team always has lunch together, but the

---

4 Samantha Murphy, "Facebook Changes Its 'Move Fast and Break Things' Motto" (*http://on.mash.to/ 2gCBGlc*), Mashable, April 30, 2014.

5 Deepa Seetharaman, "Facebook Revenue Soars on Ad Growth" (*http://on.wsj.com/2hMlaPx*), *Wall Street Journal*, April 28, 2016.

mobile team tends to eat at their desk while working? Or they may reflect the personality differences between two subject matter areas, such as between finance and sales, or similarly, between two divisions of a larger organization—Instagram is part of Facebook, but it has a different approach to product planning. In such cases, it's often best to allow such variation to continue rather than to force consistency.

But other times, culture differences may lead to conflict. Imagine an applications team that builds new features incrementally, using weekly sprints to iterate toward the final solution. They need a new API from an infrastructure team that requires a detailed design doc and a rigorous sign-off process with their lead developer before they begin coding. Such development models don't mesh well, and you can bet at least one side will end up frustrated.

If the teams can't resolve such issues themselves, leaders need to get involved. The right way to resolve each situation depends on too many contextual details to lay out a general approach. But one key step is to find common ground between the factions, and point out that their viewpoints stem from differing contexts. Most likely, everyone involved shares similar values and wants to do what's right for the business. Establishing this first will help the rest of the process go smoother.

Culture shift

As discussed in "Evolving Team Culture" on page 191, there are times when leaders feel compelled to change the company culture in some way. A common scenario as companies mature is a shift from an innovation-focused, entrepreneurial startup to an execution-focused, professionally run business. This shift may require a migration toward formal processes and control mechanisms that can cause old-timers who are accustomed to a more informal and intuitive approach to bristle.

Such cases often necessitate some amount of attrition—team members attached to the old way of doing things may be unable or unwilling to adapt. It's important for leaders to identify whether such culture shifts actually represent a change in underlying core values, and if so, do the work necessary to identify the new core values that they believe will better fit the business. Mechanisms based on the old core values, such as hiring filters and performance standards, will need to be updated. Internal communication explaining the shift and the reasons behind it is essential.

Culture mergers

Company acquisitions or acqui-hires frequently encounter some level of culture clash. The companies involved are most often at different stages of growth, and therefore one tends to have more formalized and less entrepreneurial practices. And it's very natural for distinct teams, made up of unique individuals, to have different values and cultural practices.

A complete guidebook to merging the cultures of two separate companies is beyond the scope of this book. But here are a few guiding principles:

Ensure that leaders can find common ground
> The leaders of the teams should try to identify a significant number of shared core values that can be highlighted during the merger process. If they can't, that is a sign that culture conflict is likely.

Consider running the acquired company as a separate independent unit
> When Facebook acquired Instagram back in 2012, it could have folded the Instagram engineering team into its own, but chose instead to allow it to operate fairly autonomously. In so doing, they avoided a culture clash between Instagram's more deliberate, design-oriented development style and Facebook's "move fast" approach.

Encourage mobility between the acquired and acquiring companies
> Twitter's acquisitions of Vine and Periscope benefited both from allowing them a fair bit of autonomy, and also allowing Twitter employees to transfer to both companies, and vice versa. This mobility can help avoid the "us versus them" mentality that can creep in following acquisitions.

Measuring Culture: Information Flow

Is it possible to measure the effectiveness of a particular team's culture? Compelling research points to information flow within an organization as an important indicator.

In "A Typology of Organisational Cultures" (*http://bit.ly/2gbLPEN*), Ron Westrum writes:

> *Because information flow is both influential and also indicative of other aspects of culture, it can be used to predict how organisations or parts of them will behave when signs of trouble arise. From case studies and some*

systematic research it appears that information culture is indeed associ-
ated with error reporting and with performance.

His research was aimed at safety industries like healthcare and aircraft
design, but the problem of handling and learning from failure is a familiar one
for technology companies. Site outages, security flaws, and buggy clients are all
forms of failure that healthy information flow could help prevent or at least
understand. Similarly, information about new opportunities (which can be
threatening to entrenched leaders focused on retaining power) is critical to helping companies evolve and stay ahead of competitors.

Westrum breaks down organizations using the typology shown in Table 9-4.

Table 9-4. How organizations process information

Pathological	Bureaucratic	Generative
Power-oriented	Rule-oriented	Performance-oriented
Low cooperation	Modest cooperation	High cooperation
Messengers shot	Messengers neglected	Messengers trained
Responsibilities shirked	Narrow responsibilities	Risks are shared
Bridging discouraged	Bridging tolerated	Bridging encouraged
Failure→scapegoating	Failure→justice	Failure→inquiry
Novelty crushed	Novelty→problems	Novelty implemented

He cites (*http://bit.ly/2gbLPEN*) numerous case studies showing how generative organizations outperform pathological ones. Here's a striking comparison
from 1999, when a hospital discovered recurring misdiagnoses:

Two of its pathologists had made 20 wrong prostate biopsy diagnoses...A
urologist had discovered the problem when one of his patients was diag-
nosed with prostate cancer yet had had a negative biopsy. After a second
similar example, suspicions were raised about biopsy standards. The hos-
pital then carried out an internal audit of 279 prostate biopsies...which
showed 20 of them to be in error. Rather than attempting to cover up the
situation, or downplay it...the hospital reported the biopsy problems to
state authorities, sent regular updates to its staff, and wrote 88,000 let-
ters to hospital patients explaining the situation. The response was very
positive from the regulators and the public: "Throughout this process,
there was no measurable negative impact on the hospital's workload or
financial performance...Our openness reaffirmed our reputation for

putting our patients first. Our patients were much more accepting of the inevitability of human error than we were, and they were impressed that we were doing something about it. Our experience suggests that putting patients first is also a good business strategy when addressing errors."[6]

Obviously, we all want to work in a generative organization, not a pathological one. But how do you know where your team stands? Is a lack of information flow putting your customers at risk, or is your organization able to respond effectively, as the hospital in this example did when it realized patients' lives were at risk?

The DevOps Enterprise Forum has proposed (*http://bit.ly/2fVyQty*) a set of statements based on Westrum's data that attempts to measure the health of information flow on a team. Respondents answer using a Likert scale where "strongly disagree" = 1 and "strongly agree" = 7:

- On my team, information is actively sought.

- On my team, failures are learning opportunities, and messengers of them are not punished.

- On my team, responsibilities are shared.

- On my team, cross-functional collaboration is encouraged and rewarded.

- On my team, failure causes enquiry.

- On my team, new ideas are welcomed.

The accuracy and effectiveness of such metrics and what actions should be taken based on a specific score on this survey have yet to be proven out. But regular sampling and watching for trends in the scores is likely to be useful in understanding how a team's cultural health is changing over time.

Summarizing Yang Jisheng's *Tombstone: The Great Chinese Famine, 1958–1962*, Ron Westrum provides another motivating (and tragic) example of the need for information flow in an organization in "The Study of Information Flow: A Personal Journey (*http://bit.ly/2gPfJPn*)":

---

6 DA Pietro, LJ Shyavitz, RA Smith, et al., "Detecting and Reporting Medical Errors: Why the Dilemma?", *BMJ* 2000; 320:794–6.

During the "Great Leap Forward" in China, a famine was raging, but information about it was incorrect. If local leaders came forward, they would be accused of being "right deviationists" or food hoarders, and would suffer brutal punishments or death. Lower level leaders, eager to appear proper communists, lied about the harvest results, with the outcome that little about the reality appeared on the surface. In addition the party cadres often had food when the peasants did not, decreasing their motivation to raise the issue. In the end, 38 million people would die during the famine. It would be years before the truth was generally known.

Conclusion

Building a strong team culture is a true test of leadership. Beyond the business benefits outlined in this chapter, leaders should invest in this area if only to ensure that they continue to love coming to work every day. As Ben Horowitz put it in "The Hard Thing About Hard Things":

After you and your people go through the inhuman amount of work that it will take to build a successful company, it will be an epic tragedy if your company culture is such that even you don't want to work there.

The work required to define core values and evolve a team culture based on those values is a small price to pay to build a company that employees love working for and want to be a part of for years to come.

10

Scaling Communication: The Complexity of Scale and Distance

If communication seems to succeed in the intended way, there's a misunderstanding.

—WIIO'S LAWS

Certain complaints are frequently overheard in fast-growing teams:

"I have no idea what is going on anymore"
> When the company was small, information spread easily. But as the company grows and the organization becomes more complex, employees start to feel that they are missing out on important news.

"I'm spending all of my time in meetings"
> As you hire more people you'll need more synchronization, which typically leads to more meetings. Some of these are necessary, but the more the meeting load interferes with product development, the less you will gain from each person you hire.

"I can't keep up with all the email"
> Getting through your email and catching up on group chat channels used to take just 10 minutes in the morning, but now it takes 30 minutes, multiple times per day.

When a team first comes together, communication is effortless. There are only a handful of people on the team, all sitting in one room, and talking openly and freely about everything. These discussions are all interesting and easy to digest because, frankly, there's not that much of it, and it all feels important while the team is struggling to figure out its product and business model.

But that's just the beginning of the story. This idyllic environment starts to break down as the team grows, so you need to adapt.

What Breaks When You Grow?

At some point, the growing team enters a stage when all employees still *expect* to know everything, but there is too much information to keep up with. They want to stay informed, but they also complain about getting too much email, and that most of it goes to the whole organization. Eventually you reach the point where no one can know everything.

When this happens, it's important to reduce the distractions of internal communication so your team can focus. You have to make sure all the important things get through—and hopefully *only* the important things. If you receive 2,000 emails, and only 10 of them are important, it's difficult to sort out your priorities. Kurt Schrader elaborates on this issue: "At most startups once you get to 15 or so employees you enter a period of time where everyone still wants to know what's going on everywhere, but the amount of information about what's happening slowly starts to exceed what any one person can know. This period can last quite some time."[1] We will discuss how to improve this situation later in this chapter.

Incomplete Communication: A Story from Alex

I worked at a company that had quite a few offices around the globe, all of which needed constant alignment. In a meeting attended by half of the employees, the CEO mentioned that the company needed to save money, and there would be a stop on travel for the next few months. The CEO did not do any follow-up communication and therefore a lot of people were still making plans, aligning with their families, and creating

---

1 Kurt Schrader, "Scaling Communication at a Growing Startup" (*http://bit.ly/2gYNvpy*), October 21, 2013.

meeting agendas with employees in other offices. Many didn't find out about the travel stop until after booking their tickets!

One way or another, this story has probably happened in every growing company. The missed information might be different, but the pattern is the same. The result is that employees perceive the organization as unprofessional.

Effective communication doesn't just happen. You can't just check it off your to-do list and assume it's working. As discussed in Chapter 9, information flow is vital to the health and scalability of organizations. But communication gets more complicated as your organization grows, as explained by Tim Howes' article "What I Learned Scaling Engineering Teams Through Euphoria and Horror" (*http://bit.ly/2gG27al*): "At 10 people, team communication is interactive. Grow to 50 or 100 people, though, and this changes drastically. [...] Communication is no longer interactive; it's one-to-many [...] Clarity often needs a helping hand from repetition." In the example discussed in "Incomplete Communication: A Story from Alex" on page 202, if the CEO had repeated the message from the meeting by sending out an email, nobody would have been confused or surprised.

There are sometimes surprising outcomes when leaders don't communicate effectively. In "Examples of Organization Communication Breakdown" (*http://bit.ly/2gMf3LE*), Karen S. Johnson describes that "It may seem paradoxical, but if organizational leaders don't communicate effectively to employees, it can lead to more communication—just the wrong kind [...] Absence of accurate information allows inaccurate information to circulate, fueling rumors and subsequent fear."

A study (*http://bit.ly/2gMfqpv*) conducted by the Project Management Institute concluded that bad communication is a primary cause for the failure of one-third of all projects. Good communication, on the other hand, drives performance. According to a report (*http://bit.ly/2gMiX7q*) from Towers Watson, "organizations that are highly effective in both their communication and change management practices are more than twice as likely to significantly outperform their peers as organizations that are not highly effective in either of these areas."

A Nearly Failed Project: A Story from Alex

Once, I was working with a real estate portal. They had a big contract out, and they gave the contract agency written specs for the product they wanted built. The agency said, "Yeah, we'll see you later, in six or nine months." After I was hired, I asked if the company had seen the product or knew how far along the agency had gotten. They said no. They were waiting for the agency to give an update. I said I'd contact the agency to suggest they do a demo for us. The contractor got a bit panicked. Two weeks later, we got the first demo.

The product looked terrible, and needed different functionality than what had been built. The agency's understanding of the product had changed completely over time due to the lack of communication between the agency and the real estate portal.

Everything changed after that. We started doing product demos regularly. This led to much better alignment on the functionality we needed.

The Complexity of Scale and Distance

Communication channels grow exponentially with the size of the team. In *The Mythical Man-Month* (Addison-Wesley), Fred Brooks describes this dilemma: "If each part of the task must be separately coordinated with each other part, the effort increases as $n(n-1)/2$." Using the group intercommunication formula $n(n-1)/2$, the number of communication channels for a five-person team would be $(5 \times (5-1))/2 = 10$, which seems manageable. But when you increase the team size to 12, you suddenly have 66 communication channels! Figure 10-1 shows what the equation looks like in reality.

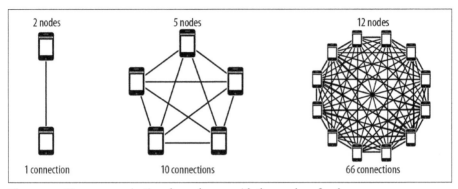

Figure 10-1. How communication channels grow with the number of nodes

Distance is also a significant contributing factor in the complexity of communication. Because of physical separation, the team can no longer rely on direct, face-to-face communication and must use less efficient and effective channels. There's a difference between having eight employees sitting in one room, and having four people sit in two rooms each. And it gets more difficult if the two rooms are on different floors or in different buildings. At one company, we had roughly 65 people spread across three offices in a single city. Although the offices were separated by just a five-minute walk, we really *felt* that distance and had many communication problems. Most significant was that teams in different offices stopped talking to one another as the lack of informal, face-to-face communication degraded their ability to collaborate. Additionally, information flow from the management team's office to the other offices was poor, as most of the communication was done in person without any written follow-up.

There are ways to mitigate the effects of physical separation. At one company, we had a single kitchen for 400 people (it was a *huge* kitchen). But since most everyone congregated there, it facilitated a great deal of informal interaction between colleagues who otherwise might not see each other.

The increasing complexity of communications can lead to dramatic increases in communication tools, in-person meetings, and the volume of email or other messaging types. Let's look at each of these in more detail.

TOOLS EXPLOSION

As communication gets tougher and employees start complaining about the lack of information, teams often adopt new communication tools to deal with the problem. It's very common to see individual delivery teams adopting different tools, which soon leads to a *tools explosion*. The company can end up with three or four different project management tools that don't work together. Or you might discover that the marketing department has a wiki, engineering has a separate wiki, and sales has yet another wiki, and then you have a jungle that needs to be tamed. It's important to keep track of the communication tools people are using to keep in touch. Ideally, you want to be able to test a few different approaches, but at the very least, you should be aware when different groups are testing tools so you can consider whether it makes sense to consolidate.

MEETING EXPLOSION

The next communication crisis is an exlosion of meetings. Certain meetings are necessary to make decisions and coordinate the activities of fast-growing teams, such as post-interview hiring syncs. But many meetings are neither useful nor efficient, wasting the time of the attendees. And teams tend to build up a surplus of unnecessary meetings that can be often be canceled without making communication worse.

The quote from *The Mythical Man-Month* cited earlier describes the explosion of communication channels, but this only happens on an exponential level if everyone needs to communicate with everyone else. The organizational setup you choose heavily influences how much communication is necessary. Here, the principles described in the chapters on scaling the organization (Chapters 6 through 8) once again come into play. In Chapter 7, we discussed *value streams*, as shown in Figure 10-2.

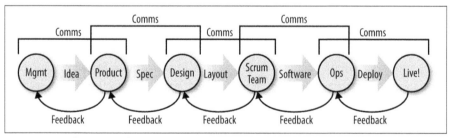

Figure 10-2. Value stream focused on communication

Between each of the steps in the value stream, people must interact with one another, usually through meetings and email. All that back-and-forth causes delays, as each meeting or email increases time-to-production. In the end, it can easily take months to launch a new feature.

The solution to this problem is to put the whole value stream into a single delivery team (see Chapter 7). This can reduce or even eliminate the need for written communication and meetings, relying on in-team (and hopefully in-person) communication instead. This setup is illustrated in Figure 10-3.

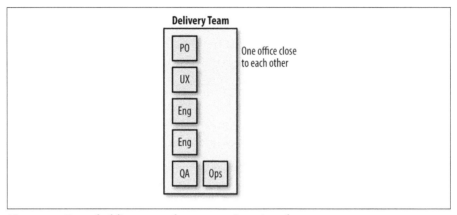

Figure 10-3. Example delivery team that can own its entire value stream

Best practices for meetings

As you grow, meetings can start to dominate your team's available work hours. Very few of us in technology startups were trained in how to run an effective meeting, so many of them are inefficient and waste the attendees' time. Follow these suggestions to minimize the growth in meetings and maximize the value the team gets from them:

- All meetings must have an owner, who provides a stated purpose or an agenda. If a meeting doesn't have one of these and you cannot immediately come up with one, cancel the meeting.

- Distribute all relevant documents before the meeting so participants can prepare and meeting time doesn't have to be used to bring everybody up to speed. Or, make it clear that the beginning of the meeting is allocated for document review, so attendees know how they need to prepare.

- Make sure that all points on the agenda are prepared. This is usually the task of the meeting owner.

- If the purpose of the meeting is not to inform people but to make decisions, restrict the number of attendees to only the most essential stakeholders; otherwise, it may be difficult to reach a decision.

- If you need to make a decision urgently, don't wait for the scheduled meeting. Assemble the right stakeholders and make the decision as soon as possible. Use someone's desk, the hallway, or a conference call if you need to.

- Be sure to review the action items from the last meeting. Not only does it remind participants what happened last time, but it also holds attendees accountable.[2]

- You don't have to use the entire scheduled time. If you have nothing left on the agenda to discuss before the scheduled time is over, end the meeting early! Try to avoid saying, "Well, since we're all here, let's talk about...".

- Avoid slides when possible, but if they are needed, streamline them and keep information focused. Slides are a useful tool for conference talks, but not so much for small, interactive meetings. We've rarely seen a good discussion originate from someone presenting a slide set—even one in which a lot of time was invested. Here's a quote from Steve Jobs, explaining why he wouldn't let people hide behind PowerPoint: "I hate the way people use slide presentations instead of thinking. [...] People would confront a problem by creating a presentation. I wanted them to engage, to hash things out at the table, rather than show a bunch of slides. People who know what they're talking about don't need PowerPoint."[3] In one company we know, a member of the management team hired an extra slide designer to make their monthly slides as pretty as possible (and needless to say, the actual content suffered).

- Declare one or two days a week as meeting-free days. Except for in-team meetings, no other meetings are allowed. This practice enables everybody to have uninterrupted time to focus on their core work.

- Decide whether meetings are laptops-open or laptops-closed and try to stick with it. We recommend the latter, as an open laptop distracts the owner and signals to others that they don't really need to pay attention.

---

2 Sean Blanda, "How to Run Your Meetings Like Apple and Google" (*http://bit.ly/2gMmOBx*), 99U.

3 Drake Baer, "3 Ways Steve Jobs Made Meetings Insanely Productive—And Often Terrifying" (*http://read.bi/2gMpJKe*), *Business Insider*, August 28, 2015.

Similarly with phones and tablets—ask attendees to step outside if they need to do something on their device.

Meetings and growth

Not all meetings that work well in the beginning of a business will scale as the company grows. For example, status meetings are efficient and effective when the team is small. The status update for the whole company is short and easy; the CEO says something, the marketing people say something, the designers say something, and everybody finds everything interesting. It's nice to be in the same room, talking to one another, and often informal chats lead to other discussions.

Once you have 30 people in the room, though, it starts to become a very *long* meeting. Attendees might only be interested in, at best, *half* of what's discussed. At that point, it's time to break it out into multiple meetings, and then eventually break it out again, if needed. For more, see "Status meetings" on page 225.

When to cancel meetings

Meetings often outlive their usefulness. Sometimes the format can be changed to make it useful again, but other times, canceling the meeting is the right move. There are certain indicators that a meeting can be canceled; the most obvious is when people complain about why they need to show up, and just stop attending. Other times, they still show up, but hide behind their laptop throughout. You can stop such a practice by simply issuing a policy that nobody uses their laptop during the meeting, but there's usually more behind this behavior than just bad style. Look for meetings that your people describe as "a good time to get your email done." Another indication that a meeting needs to be canceled is that it's supposed to be a decision-making meeting, but no decisions are made. In the case of status meetings, if no follow-ups or useful discussions originate from it, you can either cancel the meeting or replace it with a status email.

Meetings often live well beyond their useful lifetime simply through inertia. But they are so expensive in time and disruption that leaders should always be on the lookout for unnecessary meetings and cancel them. Here are some warning signs of meetings that probably need to be canceled:

- Attendees complain about the meeting in one-on-ones or hallway chats.

- Invited attendees stop showing up, or show up inconsistently, or send a more junior person in their place.

- Attendees use their laptops, phones, or other devices during the meeting. You might hear "that's a good time to get through your email."

- No decisions are being made in decision-making meetings. This could also mean the meeting owner needs some training.

- There are no follow-ups from status meetings or useful discussions originating from them. These meetings can often be replaced with an email.

In general, it's important to measure the cost of meetings against their benefit, and take action accordingly. An interesting thought exercise is to calculate the hourly cost of everyone in a meeting to decide whether the value of the meeting is worth the expense.

EMAIL EXPLOSION

Email handled well reduces meetings. And meetings handled well reduces emails...[4]

—AMY GALLO

So your team is growing, you are getting more and more emails, and they're taking up too much of your time.[5] A lot of people blame the tool for this phenomenon, but that's rarely the source of the problem. We have some basic guidelines for sending emails and dealing with your inbox. But first, let's look at the possible underlying reasons for email overload.

Unclear decision making

One reason for excessive email is that employees need help making decisions. "Email overload is only a symptom of a larger issue: a lack of clear and effective protocols. If your organization has ambiguous decision-making processes and people don't get what they need from their colleagues, they'll flood the system with email and meeting requests."[6]

A trivial but common example of this issue is an unclear purchasing process. In the absence of clear directives, employees won't purchase things to make their

---

4 Amy Gallo, "Stop Email Overload" (*http://bit.ly/2gMqHXa*), *Harvard Business Review*, February 21, 2012.

5 We call this section "Email Explosion," but most of the points we make here apply to other forms of written electronic communication, such as chat, instant messaging, and so on.

6 Amy Gallo, "Stop Email Overload" (*http://bit.ly/2gMqHXa*), *Harvard Business Review*, February 21, 2012.

lives easier, such as software that makes them more productive. Instead, employees may send emails to several people "to be on the safe side" before making a purchase. Repetitive emails like these start to add up.

Poor organization

If you haven't formed delivery teams (see Chapter 7) and people must interact with one another between each step in the value stream, you will receive and send a lot more emails. It is preferable to have in-team personal communication inside a delivery team. Remember to seat all team members together so you can minimize communication overhead.

Using the wrong channels

Email is not the best channel for some types of information. But companies that decide email is the root of all evil and move all communication to a chat app, for instance, tend to see the same problems in a slightly different way. The chat app may foster openness in some areas, but as soon as somebody comes back from a two-week vacation and tries to catch up with all the important news, they will find themselves missing email.

Mismatched Expectations: A Story from Alex

At a former job, we acquired a small company in a different country. As a result of the acquisition, the employees of the small company went from having a single email per day to 30 emails per day. They all thought they were expected to read and reply to emails immediately, and so it completely disrupted their workday. After they were assured that it was fine to read emails only twice a day, their productivity returned.

Problems also occur when the sender's expectations of a channel don't match the recipient's. Who hasn't experienced a colleague coming by their desk to say, "I sent you an email five minutes ago; why haven't you answered?" It's not reasonable to expect someone to read every email immediately, and the sender needs to change their communication channel or their expectations. As your team grows larger, you may want to create guidelines about which channels should be used for what types of communication and what the expected response times should be. See the next section for an example.

Messaging guidelines

Clearly defining messaging guidelines can help ensure the right information flows through the right communication channels, based on the goals of the sender and the nature of the message and the audience. The following guidelines describe one possible way of choosing methods of written communication. Before we get to the guidelines, though, let's start by classifying messages in two ways: expected response time and the lifetime of the message.

Most messages have one of three expected response times:

Immediate (synchronous)
> Something urgent that recipients should read and react to as soon as possible—a site outage alert, for example.

Within a few business hours
> Responses are expected, but are not urgent—perhaps a discussion where the recipient's opinion is important.

At your convenience
> No reaction is expected, but is possible. There is an expectation that the message is being read, though, typically within a business week.

You also need to think about how long a message is supposed to *live*; in other words, how long the message will remain relevant after it is sent. We break down message lifetime into three categories:

Ephemeral
> Messages that are not important once they have been read. A good example would be: "Hi, I am late for our lunch appointment."

Searchable
> Messages that might be important later, such as a discussion about how to solve a specific support ticket.

Highly visible
> Messages that should be easily accessible by anyone for a long time. An important change in purchase policy is a good example.

And lastly, let's review the typical communication channels in use at most companies:

Email

> An *asynchronous* form of communication, in which people usually take more time to respond and therefore the responses often are more thoughtful than in synchronous tools (such as chat). You can easily search your own messages, but group communication is only searchable for others if organized within an email group. A typical expected reaction time to email is a few business hours to a business day.

Chat app

> A mostly *synchronous* form of communication. We assume the app has a group chat function and that you can search the history. With public chatrooms, you can create a more open form of communication; for example, a designer can look at what the engineering team has been discussing. Fast response time is usually expected in this channel; if employees have mobile notifications turned on, the expected reaction time to a direct message can be measured in single-digit minutes.

Mobile phone text messages or phone calls

> These are ordinary texts or phone calls to your mobile device, often used when the communication is urgent.

Company intranet/wiki

> This is a site where important content is stored so it can be accessed easily. You cannot really define a reaction time for this communication channel, but you can expect employees to look here when they are searching for an answer to a question, or for reference material on a particular topic.

This all leads to Table 10-1, where a channel is recommended based on the urgency and lifetime of a message.

Table 10-1. Channel recommendations

Lifetime/ urgency	Ephemeral	Searchable	Highly visible
Immediately	One to one: text/call One to many: text/ chat Example: "The meeting was moved to room *X* on short notice"	Chat Example: First report of a site outage	Multi-channel (chat and wiki) Example: Announcement of acquiring another company

Lifetime/ urgency	Ephemeral	Searchable	Highly visible
Within a few business hours	Chat Example: "The meeting this afternoon is moved to the lunch room" (at least a few hours before the start of the meeting)	Chat/email Example: Announcing the launch of a product feature	Wiki and email Example: Announcement of new purchase policy effective immediately (assuming purchases are happening frequently)
At your convenience	N/A	Email/wiki Example: The results of a post-mortem on a site outage.	Wiki Example: Update to our holiday calendar— doesn't happen frequently, no need for an email

Use this as an example and adapt it to your company. Companies with offices in different time zones will at least need to adjust response times based on how far apart their offices are.

General email guidelines

Besides the right organizational setup and careful consideration of which channel to use for certain kinds of communication, there are also general email guidelines that will help you both manage your own inbox and minimize the amount of emails that your organization has to deal with.

- "Respond quickly and clearly to those who need your attention or input— this will reduce the amount of email you receive."[7] Otherwise, you might receive reminders or the same message on a different channel.

- Apply some proven techniques for managing your inbox. A technique like *inbox zero* can be very helpful (see "Additional Resources" on page 215 for more details).

- Leaders should model good email behavior. For example, if you send emails at night or on weekends, employees will do the same thing. If you use emojis or strong language, expect to see the same from your team.

---

7 Amy Gallo, "Stop Email Overload" (*http://bit.ly/2gMqHXa*), *Harvard Business Review*, February 21, 2012.

These examples could be good or bad depending on your team's culture. Just remember that the team will use your behavior as a model.

- Your behavior can also strongly influence how much email you receive. As Amy Gallo put it: "Don't send one-word emails and reply to everyone on a thread—the more email you send, the more you will receive."[8]

Conclusion

In this chapter, we described how communication becomes more complex as an organization grows, and how that complexity is influenced by the organizational setup you choose. We focused on three aspects of communication: tools, meetings, and email. We gave you some guidelines on how to make meetings more efficient and send fewer emails.

In the next chapter, we will help you design efficient communication by defining the information employees need to know and making choices about communication channels in order to keep employees well informed.

Additional Resources

- Jake Gibson's "Why Having an 'Open-Door' Policy Is Imperative for a Scaling Company" (*http://bit.ly/2gMqMKn*) explains how communication develops while scaling and makes the great point that "uneven information distribution kills morale."

- Tamara Snyder's "Seven Key Studies on the Business Impact of Employee Engagement" (*http://bit.ly/2gMt2RU*) provides some great data about how good communication and change management drives high performance and employee engagement.

- In "The 5 Most Common Mistakes in Internal Communications" (*http://bit.ly/2gMxQqp*), Glen Chambers gives a great summary of an internal communication strategy.

- In "Email Transparency" (*http://bit.ly/2gMvpUC*), Greg Brockman describes how and why Stripe made all emails available to everybody.

---

8 Ibid.

- Drake Baer's "3 Ways Steve Jobs Made Meetings Insanely Productive—And Often Terrifying" (*http://read.bi/2gMvec9*) shows the three most important meeting techniques from Steve Jobs.

- In "Internal Communication Guidelines & Norms" (*http://bit.ly/2gMxfow*), Arno du Toit gives good advice about internal communication guidelines.

- Merlin Mann's "Inbox Zero" (*http://www.43folders.com/izero*) shows how to reach inbox zero.

- Mic Wright's "Forget 'Inbox Zero': Your Empty Email Account Means Nothing" (*http://bit.ly/2gMrjvV*) is a great article about the actual intention of inbox zero, and suggests that you avoid "living in your inbox," where your inbox is not only email, but also other communication channels.

Scaling Communication: Communicating at Scale

One of the core challenges of a growing team is ensuring that everyone has the information they need without overwhelming them. Well-designed communication can achieve this by, as Caryn Marooney puts it (*http://bit.ly/2gMtPlQ*), "Tuning out the noise so your team can hear the signal." This is the mission of good internal communication.

Too Much Information: A Story from Alex

I worked at a company where we kept all information open by default. Every company document, for example, was put into Google Docs and shared. Everyone in the company received notifications for the documents, and would promptly review any changes. On the one hand, this setup was great, because you might end up seeing an interesting discussion between an intern and the CEO. On the other hand, some people spent their whole week in Google Docs looking at information mostly irrelevant to their work. This example illustrates the main problem of scaling communication: you want people to know everything they need to know, but still be able to focus on the jobs they were hired to do.

Communication Design

There are three steps to a good communication design: define what employees need to know, select the appropriate communication channels, and finally, implement the strategy.

STEP 1: DEFINE WHAT EMPLOYEES NEED TO KNOW

There is some information that every employee needs to know. Then there's information that every *designer* needs to have, and information every *engineer* needs to have. Being aware of these different target audiences lets you focus your communication on the right audience without distracting the rest of the company. What you need to communicate depends on who you need to communicate it to.

Here we give a few examples, looking at two possible audiences: all employees, and all members of a specific department.

All employees

The mission, vision, and strategy of the company are examples of core, long-term information that everyone in the company needs to know. We recommend presenting such fundamental company knowledge during the on-boarding process. These important messages bear repeating at some interval, but it's helpful to assume a baseline of familiarity so that they don't need to be repeated in every all-hands meeting. This lets you use all-hands meetings to build on that knowledge with updates and additions, such as important news, organizational changes, or product updates. (More details on running an effective all-hands meeting are included in "Design effective meetings" on page 222.)

All members of a specific department

Individual teams or departments, on the other hand, need to know long-term information targeted specifically to them and their responsibilities. A few examples of what should be covered during on-boarding include:

- High-level architecture (for engineering), UX/design guidelines (for Design/UX)
- The team's work methodology (like Agile or Scrum in engineering)
- Team structure and organization
- Existing standards (like coding standards for engineering)

In a department all-hands meeting, for example, teams can be updated on topics like changes to existing standards or product design, new hires, and architecture updates.

STEP 2: SELECT THE COMMUNICATION CHANNEL

There are so many different communication channels, all with their own pros and cons, as well as different reaches and levels of immediacy—synchronous, asynchronous, one-to-one, one-to-many, and so on. It's important to choose the right channel for the information you need to deliver. To make sure we're all on the same page, here's a quick definition of the communication channels we are referring to.

- *One-to-many* meetings include all-hands, town halls, and other types of group meetings described later in this chapter. These meetings let you spread information from one person to many people at once in a live setting. These can be time-consuming to prepare and costly because so many people attend, but they are good for when you want to let people ask follow-up questions. (That said, some people will be more likely to ask questions in one-on-ones, described next.)

- *One-on-ones* are mostly meant for managers to listen to concerns from ICs and provide guidance and feedback. They are a great way to review an all-hands meeting and validate its quality. You can discuss the most important points mentioned at the meeting to find out if you communicated them poorly. For more information, see "Pragmatic Advice on 1on1s" (*http://bit.ly/2gMAZ9o*).

- *Email* is best for delivering asynchronous information to one or more people, and for leaving a written record that can be referred back to later on (see "Messaging guidelines" on page 212).

- A *wiki* or *intranet* is useful for making information available to many people at once (whether passively or actively) in a non-urgent fashion, and good for posting multiple pieces of related information in a single place for future reference. If you choose to use a wiki, realize that there is a common failure mode where pages get added but not updated as things change. Over time, the team encounters these out-of-date pages and starts to distrust the information in the wiki. It takes some additional investment, such as a dedicated maintainer who updates or removes out-of-date pages, to combat this and make a wiki truly useful. Have a look at usage statistics such as page views and created documents in order to make sure the wiki is being used.

- For visualizing information, *dashboards* are often the right tool. Instead of setting a meeting to tell people, "Oh, we now have five million users," you can just put up a graph. By graphing information, you make it continuously available, and people can review it when they're interested. That said, nobody *needs* to look at it, which can be a disadvantage. If you want to communicate something everybody needs to know within a short time, putting it on a screen somewhere is not the right way to go. But for certain long-term information, like business metrics, dashboards can be very useful.

Incomplete Communication: A Story from Alex

Not paying attention to the right medium for the message can lead to poor information flow. At one of my former companies, we announced that a few teams would be moving to a new office soon. Three days later, I asked one of the people affected by the change for his thoughts. He replied, "A new office?" He hadn't attended the all-hands meeting, and since we hadn't spread that information any other way, he'd had no opportunity to learn about the new office.

When multiple channels are needed

Somebody is always traveling or on vacation. If you rely on employees to tell one another everything, some employees will end up uninformed about important things. We recommend giving employees the possibility to either watch a recording, or read a written summary of such a meeting later on. Important information—the kind everybody needs to know—needs to be communicated in multiple ways. This doesn't necessarily require a lot of work. A short summary of the important information can suffice. For example: "By the way, on May 1st, we're moving to a new office. The address is XYZ. If you need, please contact the person responsible for the move for further details." You don't need to write a book.

For important information, keep a record of meetings and if possible, write a summary email covering the most significant points. Depending on the content, this email should be sent to all attendees, a wider audience including all stakeholders, or a meeting notes mailing list. Alternatively, you can share the slides from the all-hands meeting, as long as they sufficiently explain the information (since slide decks often contain images rather than information). But a video recording is often more useful to anyone who missed the meeting.

STEP 3: IMPLEMENT YOUR STRATEGY

This section contains some best practices for implementing a communications strategy. This list is by no means exhaustive, but it will help get you started.

Repeat yourself

As the leader of a fast-growing startup, you have new employees coming in constantly. You have to assume that everyone you're communicating with has a different level of knowledge about the company. As a result, simply *repeating yourself* is important and effective.

On-boarding should create a baseline of knowledge about the most important aspects of the company. But new hires get so much information during their first few weeks at a company, it's inevitable they'll forget some of it. So if something is truly important, you have to say it again, and then again.

It can be awkward to say something that you assume everyone already knows. But as long as you don't belabor the topic, repeating important information reassures those that already know it that nothing has changed. And again, it helps ensure that new hires are on the same page as everyone else. The downside of not repeating important information can be severe. For example, someone who is frustrated about their compensation may end up finding a higher-paying job because they missed the one meeting where upcoming compensation adjustments were discussed.

Communication training

Because large group meetings are so expensive, it's important to train your presenters. Consider enlisting the help of a speaking coach, or having frequent presenters attend speaking classes. And as your company grows, it becomes increasingly important to do a run-through before any large meetings and to have dedicated staff for handling details like video recording and microphones. It can be painful to calculate the amount of time wasted while hundreds of employees wait for you to debug problems with the video projector.

Consider offering communication training to all employees. Explaining something to an audience with a different background (e.g., engineers explaining their work to salespeople) is a common and important task for many employees.

If they are unable to explain domain-specific concepts to a lay audience, they may end up wasting a lot of people's time.

An increasingly popular option is to provide improvisation or "improv" classes for employees. These can help the attendees be more comfortable speaking in front of a group and reacting to questions from the audience or even just participating in a meeting. See the *Forbes* article "Why Improv Training Is Great Business Training" (*http://bit.ly/2gzhksU*) for more information.

Keep channels current

As previously mentioned, it's important to keep your wikis and dashboards up to date. Once you've read a wiki page and tried to apply what you learned, only to realize that it was out of date, you're much less likely to trust what's in the wiki the next time.

One solution is to have an employee dedicated to internal communications who is responsible for tending to them. For reference, SoundCloud put one employee full-time on internal communications when it reached 250 employees.

Design effective meetings

In the words of David Noel, "Organizing one meeting is easy; a series is hard." It's not difficult to set up a new meeting, and usually, the first in a series is successful. Attendees come together, excited by the subject matter, and relevant topics are discussed. But after a few meetings in the series, the momentum fades and agendas start to get thrown together at the last minute. Soon, people stop showing up and the meeting becomes useless. In the following section, we give some advice on the most important kinds of meetings and how they should be run. There are two kinds that every company should have: *all-hands* and *demos*. Other types of meetings that may be useful include *cameos, town halls, fireside chats,* and *status meetings.*

All-hands meetings *All-hands meetings* are for making important announcements to the whole company (or a large department) and for answering questions. Sending email about important changes and news is usually not good enough, as employees don't have the opportunity to ask questions and listen to questions asked by other employees. Agendas for these meetings are usually defined by management, except for the Q&A portion.

Because a whole company or department is assembled, the all-hands meeting requires significant preparation (an agenda, guest speakers if needed, a follow-up email, etc.). A good all-hands meeting can be very motivating, while a disorganized one can be bad for morale. Hold all-hands meetings every two to four weeks in the beginning in order to ensure steady, regular communication, and consider having some sort of social hour before or afterward. For more information on all-hands meetings, have a look at "Additional Resources" on page 236.

Company demos *Demos* are meetings in which teams present their recent achievements. As the company grows, employees can have a hard time keeping up with what the other teams or departments are working on. Viewing a short presentation every few weeks helps a lot. Usually, delivery teams present the results of their last iteration. Other teams should present, too—who hasn't heard the comment from engineers that they have no idea what the marketing department is working on?

Company demos give each team an opportunity to showcase their work to the whole company and get a high-five (or some constructive feedback) for their work. It's also the easiest way for attendees to keep up to date with product development.

Here are some suggestions for holding great demos:

- Schedule this kind of meeting at the end of each iteration.

- Give each team a timeslot during the meeting and limit each presentation to three to five minutes, depending on the meeting's length.

- In each time slot, a team demos their work from the last iteration, ideally revolving the presenting team members to give everyone an opportunity to represent the group.

- Tell everybody that slides are the exception, and that either working software or graphs should be presented instead since these focus more on achievements than on plans.

- Each team should also quickly mention the focus of their work for the upcoming iteration.

- Provide guidance to individual contributors on how to present their work to an audience that includes nontechnical people. See "Communication training" on page 221.

Cameos Let's say the product management team has a meeting every week in which they talk about priorities. One day, somebody who is not usually part of that meeting attends, and just sits and listens to the entire meeting. This kind of visit is called a *cameo*.

As an example, we worked at one company that held regular engineering leadership meetings. We invited one engineer to each meeting, and asked that engineer to write a summary of the meeting and send it to the other engineers. Sensitive topics like individual performance issues were scheduled for the end of the meeting, so the cameo attendee could leave early without missing any other topics.

A similar approach is to invite "guest speakers." In this case, someone from a related team attends the meeting to talk about their team's current and future plans and answer questions. This practice can help build understanding and better working relationships between related teams.

Cameos not only create more transparency, but have the surprising side effect of making meetings more effective. When you know somebody outside the team is listening, you tend to do a better job of organizing the meeting.

Cameos in Real Life: A Story from Alex

As a result of inviting people to do cameos in the company I worked for, the engineers' leadership meeting felt less mysterious to the members of the rest of the team. They got summaries, and were able to participate themselves. Leadership also improved, as we tried harder to have constructive meetings and make a good impression. Finally, setting up cameos promoted cross-disciplinary respect for people not ordinarily inside the same delivery team.

Town halls A *town hall* is similar to an all-hands meeting—you invite the whole company—but the agenda is set by employees rather than management. This is typically done by having people ask questions and offer input in advance of the meeting. A senior leader or an internal communications person then compiles the questions and feedback, inviting the appropriate people to answer the questions that have been asked.

In "This Company Retains 95% of Its Employees—Here's Its Secret" (*http://bit.ly/2gzoGwr*), Joel Grossmann explains that he "often administers anonymous surveys, sent to the entire company, soliciting questions people want management to answer. Those questions are tackled at monthly meetings, which also include an open Q&A." After your first one, Grossman suggests sending out another company-wide survey to learn what the team thought and what could have gone better.

A major benefit to this kind of meeting is that staff get to drive the conversation and ask questions they may not normally get to ask. It's a bottom-up version of an all-hands meeting.

One note: if you allow people to remain anonymous when asking their questions beforehand, you will get tougher questions. This can be valuable, but whether you do this or not depends on the company culture; some companies like it, some don't. We recommend allowing anonymous questions but also encouraging people to add their names so that the appropriate person can follow up with them and ensure their question was answered.

Fireside chats with founders/leaders *Fireside chats* are intimate, interview-style conversations with one or more of the founders or company executives. A moderator typically asks some prepared questions as well as taking some from the audience. These meetings are entirely optional, but can be beneficial for people who, because the company has grown, don't necessarily have regular access to the founders. It's an opportunity to get to know the person and the history of the company better (*Why did you start this company? What were your ideas? What did you need to change?*). It's not for must-have information, but rather for more contextual, big-picture topics.

Status meetings *Status meetings* ofallow a group of people to share short updates with each other. In "Meetings That Don't Suck" (*http://bit.ly/2gzveeA*), Ken Norton argues to get rid of these meetings because "the vast majority of updates are only relevant to one or two people in the room, and everyone else painfully waits for their turn." While we don't think that every status meeting is useless, consider getting rid of a status meeting if the following holds true:

- There are no valuable follow-ups from the meeting (e.g., meeting participants don't informally discover a topic they need to discuss)
- The group is getting so big that the meeting takes more than 15 minutes
- Updates are only valuable for one person, usually the manager

If any of these points are true but you still think the information communicated in the meeting is valuable, consider using email to distribute the information instead. If the meeting takes too long, break it up into smaller, more focused meetings.

The Evolution of the Engineering Status Meeting: A Story from Duana Stanley at SoundCloud

When SoundCloud was around 15 engineers, we had a weekly engineering meeting in which every engineer gave a short update about their work. We liked to do it in person, as it was much easier for people to have a follow-up after. Then we grew to around 25 engineers, and the meeting took more and more time, and the single updates became less and less interesting for everybody. To cope with the issue, we changed the meeting so only one representative of each team gave an update. This strategy worked for a while, but after more growth (we then had around 8–10 teams) the context switching and level of detail was hard to follow.

Then I suggested we make it an email. There was fear that it would be too much administrative hassle for someone to compile updates, but we solved that easily with Google forms. Then once we had the email, we just stopped the meeting. It meant anyone else in the organization could read it too. And then it started to be more product-oriented than engineering-oriented as a lot of people outside engineering started reading it and giving feedback. At that time the emails looked like:

Team 1
> Achieved A
> Busy with B
> Problems with C and D
> Will do E and F next
> Other details like Mike will join the team soon, Andrea and Tiffany are on vacation

Team 2
> ...

Eventually, the email got really long and too detail-oriented once we had more than 12 teams in the organization. So we introduced an executive summary, which highlighted only the one most important thing from each team and moved all the details to the end of the email.

Over time we found that almost nobody was reading the details; now, all we do is email-collated executive summaries, with links to backlogs.

There were a few things that had to be sorted out while we were instituting the new summaries. First, we had to take the time to come to an organization-wide agreement on when the summary would go out, which was complicated since each team ran their planning meeting on a slightly different day. We also found it was useful to allow extra time for people to just miss the submission deadline (e.g., asking for the summaries a day early). Once we figured out these strategies, our executive summary email saved us a lot of time.

The following story shows a different approach Raffi Krikorian first used at Twitter and how he used that experience to create a different kind of status update at Uber.

The Evolution of the Status Update: A Story from Raffi Krikorian

When I was running Platform Engineering at Twitter, we had a weekly newsletter called "The Good/Bad/Ugly," which at first was very well received. The team, my peers, and my boss all appreciated the detail about what was working and the honesty about what wasn't.

The process of getting the newsletter together required that all managers (or team leads) send me something by Sunday night that I would go through and edit down to the right level of detail. For a while, up to about a dozen teams, this worked well. But beyond that, things broke down. Because of the volume of information and the need for back-and-forth clarification with the managers and leads, Sunday morning became Monday morning, which then became a threat of not including updates from the late teams, or just delaying the whole thing.

I eventually realized the updates were at the wrong level, that they served almost no purpose for the people who were reading it except for infotainment. There was very little actionable information. All it provided was fodder for people to poke and ask "Why are you doing it that way?" (thereby reducing team independence and autonomy), or to yell at the "bads" and the "uglies," which therefore demotivated people to actually write what was going on. Ultimately, the incentives for talking about something being bad or ugly broke down, so we got a whitewashed story.

Finally, what was also missing was a narrative, which is what people really wanted. For a while, I included a weekly memo on what we were doing at a high level, but that too fell over because I fell into the same trap of Sunday night becoming Monday morning becoming Monday evening becoming "Sigh, I guess it's OK to skip this week." I contend the weekly memo actually provided a lot of value, especially in the early days, but, sadly, it just was too hard to do as we scaled up.

Based on these learnings, here is what we do at the Uber Advanced Technology Center (ATC):

- Our head Technical Project Manager puts together a beginning-of-sprint plan, a mid-sprint report, and end-of-sprint report.

- 85% of what is on that plan is metrics based—not "build the following," but rather "make deploys to car be under 5 minutes."

- The majority of the plan is focused on things that actually matter to other teams. For the ATC, we are highly intertwined teams that depend on one another to do things. So, we publish metrics that other teams can see and depend upon, so we can reason about the system as it evolves.

- The mid-sprint report talks about how we are doing against the metrics we claimed, and the end-of-sprint report talks about what we actually achieved, with maybe a bullet or two if we missed a metric.

- We have an engineering communications person who actually puts together the top-level narrative that gets sent at the end of each sprint—here is what the autonomy map (where the cars can drive) looks like, here are the big milestones each of the big departments hit, here is a cool story from the field, and so on.

Focusing on metrics really pushes people to just build a dashboard for any important metric. Then, reporting on that metric is trivial and doesn't require any additional effort to get into the sprint report, which is a huge plus. And having an engineering communications person who is willing to personally focus on getting the narrative together seems to get the incentives right. They don't need to beg people to send updates; they *want* to send updates about the cool stuff, because it then gets *published*.

I'm super-fortunate to have that engineering communications person, but for a 300+ person team, it seems to have paid off.

Meeting feedback

Because of the time required, it's important to check that meetings are working as expected. There are a few ways to do this, but in general, leaders should verify that important information is reaching their reports.

One approach is to ask follow-up questions in one-on-ones. Just be careful to frame your intentions as verifying whether your communications strategy is working rather than testing the individual's recall.

You can also use surveys. David Noel and his team send out a simple survey to all employees to get their thoughts on the material and format following every major info meeting.[1] The survey asks just three questions:

- Was the recent all-hands valuable?

- What did you like best?

- What can we improve?

By tracking the responses, the organizer should be able to monitor the value of the meeting over time, and understand what's working and what's not for the audience.

Keep an eye on the effectiveness of meetings, and confirm that your messages are getting through. You want to make sure the time everyone invests in these meetings is worth it.

OTHER FORMS OF COMMUNICATION

So far we've focused mostly on *top-down communication*, or how management can inform employees of important news and decisions. But there are other kinds of communication in a company, and another direction in which information should flow. As Fred Brooks states in *The Mythical Man-Month*: "The com-

---

1 "How SoundCloud Keeps Communication Flowing Across 4 Offices in 4 Time Zones" (*http://bit.ly/2gzgzQB*), First Round Review.

munication structure in an organization is a network, not a tree, so all kinds of special organization mechanisms ('dotted lines') have to be devised to overcome the communication deficiencies of the tree-structured organization." In the following sections, we demonstrate how to set up a *network* of communication by making sure information flows from the employees to management, and providing ways for employees to learn from one another and exchange information.

Bottom-up feedback

Bottom-up communication is very important because it allows management to know how the employees are doing—what they have learned, what important feedback they can give, how decisions have worked out in practice. Here are some possibilities for how management can receive that kind of information:

- Many companies send out quarterly surveys to their employees asking for feedback. Most of these surveys have multiple questions with numeric-style answers (for example, Net Promoter Scores (NPS) (*https://www.netpromoter.com/know/*)) and a few text fields for qualitative feedback. For such surveys to be effective, someone must be responsible for digesting all the feedback, acting on it, and making it visible to the organization in some way. The anonymity of responses must also be assured so that participants will be encouraged to participate honestly.

- Upper management (C level, VP level) can have regular skip-level one-on-ones with employees from various groups to find out what is on their mind.

- The town hall meetings discussed earlier are actually a form of bottom-up communication in that management gets direct input on what open questions employees have.

Peer-to-peer

In this context, peer-to-peer communication is about teams and individuals learning from one another. Shared knowledge helps build a pool of experience that works to everyone's advantage. On top of that, it creates connections between team members. We've described some techniques for doing this in other chapters, particularly in "Economies of Scale Between Delivery Teams" on page 150, which describes how teams can learn from and align with one another by building chapters and guilds.

Additionally, "Team learning" on page 107 describes techniques like retrospectives, post-mortems, and cross-training, all of which make it easier for teams to learn from one another.

MULTIPLE OFFICES

Communication can be challenging when your team is distributed across several offices, and even more so when there are substantial time zone differences (e.g., one team in Europe and another in California). Habits that may have worked well when everyone was in the same office stop working when people are separated. Although this is a complex topic with many different scenarios, in this section, we'll focus on the common case of opening a second office a significant distance from the first.

The first and maybe most important advice to follow is, "one team, one office," meaning you should strive to keep individual teams within the same physical office. As soon as you split teams between offices, communication overhead increases dramatically. A top priority is to invest in high-quality and reliable video conferencing infrastructure. These meetings should be easy, seamless, and respectful of everyone's time. We have seen many meetings start with attendees spending the first 10 minutes trying to figure out how the system actually works. Then, after the meeting finally starts, the audio quality is bad enough that half of the attendees can't follow anything. Don't let that happen. Make somebody responsible for ensuring that video conferencing is effective, and don't hesitate to invest in connection speed, room acoustics, and software. Establish basic video conferencing etiquette, such as explicitly asking remote offices for questions, and enforcing a rule of never starting the discussion until the dialed-in parties are on the line and have a good connection. A lot of pre-meeting chatter actually contains valuable information.

Try to "share the pain" of time zone differences. If one meeting is in early west coast US time so that Europe can attend during their normal work hours, schedule the next one for late Europe time so that the US office can attend during their normal work hours.

Although a big part of the daily work can easily be done remotely, there is no replacement for meeting in person from time to time. After you meet someone in person—say, by having a meal with them—it is much easier to understand and relate to that person when working remotely. So, invest in travel. If people in remote offices never meet one another, it is very tough to feel united as one company. From the Lighthouse blog (*http://bit.ly/2gzqZiZ*): "You'll build more rapport in a few days of teamwork in person than months of remote efforts."

When opening a remote office, be aware of established in-person communication practices, such as the habit of making decisions at the coffee machine, or using whiteboards that can't be seen over video conferences. When people can meet freely in the main office, remote attendees tend to get treated as second-class citizens. To deal with this kind of ingrained behavior, some companies demand that all meetings are video conference–only, meaning *no one* meets in person, and everybody has to dial in. This way, everybody experiences the reality of the video conference. This can be difficult to enforce, but is effective in our experience.

Finally, expend extra effort to include remote teams in celebrations and cultural touchpoints. This could mean flying them in, or organizing the same events in the other offices.

Communicating Change

Every minute you save communicating change you will have to pay back (at least) twice later.

—JUERGEN ALLGAYER

Leaders in high-growth environments tend to be so busy that they think, "I really don't have enough time to invest in this very important change, so let's just do it and see what happens."

What usually happens next? Employees feel left out or disrespected, and you end up spending way more time communicating your reasons for the shift than you'd hoped. Then people start complaining that the culture has changed, and attrition rises.

Here, we present a five-step approach to introducing a change.

1. Choose an appropriate change

2. Plan the change

3. Test it with a small group

4. Share it

5. Implement the first version

To illustrate these ideas, we will tell the story of how one company implemented peer feedback.

STEP 1: CHOOSE AN APPROPRIATE CHANGE

A common scenario: a team leader reads a blog post or talks to someone from a company five times the size of their own about an organizational change, and becomes convinced they need to introduce the *same* change. They often find out, however, that a change that solves a problem in one situation does not always solve a problem in another. It can, to the contrary, *create* problems.

A real-world example would be a company that decides to integrate their mobile team engineers into delivery teams too early. If there aren't enough of them to adequately staff each team, the mobile engineers will end up switching teams on a weekly basis. This will not only make the engineers unhappy, but will make feature maintenance nearly impossible. Rather than solving problems, such a change would create chaos.

As outlined in "6 Things To Expect When Your Company Hits 100 People" (*http://bit.ly/2gzqUMr*): "Don't make a change just because it worked well for Google or Facebook. Do what's right for your company." The change needs to fit the team's core values. Talk to the relevant stakeholders to make sure that an intended change will really help deal with a problem you are having right now.

If a change won't solve a problem you're having *right now*, don't introduce it.

Case Study: Peer Feedback, Step 1

This case study illustrates how a peer feedback program might be introduced, based closely on our experience at previous employers. Each step contains the piece of the story that matches that step.

The engineering team at ScaleCo was growing quickly. The manager of that team had over 20 direct reports. A lot was getting done, but giving meaningful feedback to each engineer had become nearly impossible. The manager decided that this was a real and present problem that needed to be solved.

After some consideration, the manager decided that peer feedback would help.

STEP 2: PLAN THE CHANGE

Once you've decided what you want to change, work out the details in a working group that represents all the relevant stakeholders.

Start by explaining your motivations for making a change, and what sort of change you're thinking about. Then, make it clear that you are looking for people to help plan and execute it. Besides pulling stakeholders together, this creates a general awareness that a change may happen soon, which helps prepare the rest of the company.

Try not to invite more than 6–7 people, but make sure the group includes stakeholders who will be affected by the change and, if applicable, any departments that must be included (e.g., Human Resources, for changes related to people management). Also try to find one or two employees who have experience with the new approach at a previous company or better yet, have even previously *introduced* it at another company.

Prepare for the meeting by reviewing possible approaches and creating a summary of pros and cons for the group. Come prepared! Form an opinion, but don't force it on the group. Remember, the point here is to include everybody.

Research the approaches that other companies have taken (reach out to your network, for example) or that members of your planning group have experienced and discuss whether or not one of these could be the basis for your change. Consider which of these approaches best fits the culture of your company. When you've found one, don't be afraid to adapt it to create an even better fit. Again, a change that worked for someone else may not work for you, but you can probably modify it so that it does.

Be very conscious about how sophisticated the first approach should be. The concept of a minimum viable product applies to organizational changes just as it does to products; find something lightweight that solves the biggest problem, and then continue to iterate on it.

Once you have a proposal everyone in the group agrees on, continue to the next step.

Case Study: Peer Feedback, Step 2

To form a meaningful working group, the manager chose representatives from both Human Resources and Engineering. In total, the team included six people, two of which had previously worked in companies that used peer feedback.

After aligning on a very basic approach, they split it into two groups. Both groups worked in parallel on the details of the change strategy. When both teams were finished, they compared the two approaches, which turned out to be similar in many ways.

After settling on a combined approach, the two people who had worked with peer feedback in the past proposed some changes, which then became the basis for the proposed solution.

STEP 3: TEST IT WITH A SMALL GROUP

This step is often overlooked, but it's very important that you test the change with a small group before rolling it out more broadly. If you're planning a change to the structure of feature teams, for example, choose a single team to test the new setup.

Controversial changes, such as those involving job levels or performance feedback, might elicit strong reactions from some team members. Reach out to these "opinion leaders" first to make sure they are comfortable with the change. Not only will they feel included, but their feedback comes early enough that it can be integrated easily. And once you get them on board, they often become advocates for the rest of the team, which can only help you long term.

Case Study: Peer Feedback, Step 3

Next, we chose three people to do a round of peer feedback. One of them was involved in the group that designed the feedback approach. The other two were not.

When they were done, we gathered input from all three people, as well as input from the people who'd received peer feedback during the test. We used this information to make a few small changes to our planned implementation.

Because the changes were quite small, we were able to finish things up in one round of testing.

STEP 4: SHARE IT

Next, write up a RFC (Request for Comments) and invite everyone who will be affected by the change to comment on it.

Google Docs is a great way to facilitate this, as it enables everyone to read and comment on the RFC so that you can get feedback before a change goes live.

If you've planned the change well enough and have already earned the buy-in of your most resistant team members, it's unlikely you'll need to make any major changes. Since everyone has had the opportunity to comment and ask questions, they will feel included and more likely to embrace the change.

Case Study: Peer Feedback, Step 4

Soon, we sent out the RFC. Most of the questions we were then asked were about how the peer feedback would influence salary decisions. Once we'd addressed those questions, there were no other concerns.

STEP 5: IMPLEMENT THE FIRST VERSION

The implementation details will depend on the nature of the change, but you'll at least want to formally announce that it is happening. For large changes with broad impact, consider announcing the rollout during an all-hands meeting.

Since everyone should have already read the RFC by the time you hold the meeting, a simple announcement should be enough.

Just remember: most likely, you are not done yet. A lot of problems appear only after you've fully implemented a change. Now is the time to start tracking the outcomes, gathering feedback, and making adjustments.

Case Study: Peer Feedback, Step 5

Finally, we made a short announcement at an engineering all-hands meeting that the first peer feedback cycle would start soon. As we expected, there were no concerns. Everyone had already been told about the upcoming change and there had been several informal discussions with our "opinion leaders."

However, when we actually conducted the first round of peer feedback, we discovered a few problems. Some people received so many feedback requests that their work was severely impacted, and others received feedback that was meaningless or vague. In response to these issues, we started allowing employees to reject feedback requests, and we organized training sessions about how to give better and more meaningful feedback.

MOVING FORWARD

As you can see, implementing an organizational change is much like implementing any kind of strategy: identify a need, decide on a possible solution, plan it, test it, roll it out, and gather feedback for the next iteration. Stick to this approach and you'll have much smoother transitions from now on.

Conclusion

In this chapter, we focused on communicating with employees efficiently by defining what they need to know, choosing the best communication channel, and implementing an appropriate communications strategy. We also talked about the right way to plan and communicate the many inevitable changes your company will encounter as it grows.

Additional Resources

- Jake Gibson's "Why Having an 'Open-Door' Policy Is Imperative for a Scaling Company" (*http://bit.ly/2gMqMKn*) explains how communication develops while scaling and makes the great point that "uneven information distribution kills morale."

- In "The 5 Most Common Mistakes in Internal Communications" (*http://bit.ly/2gMxQqp*), Glen Chambers gives a great summary of an internal communication strategy.

- In "Ask the CTO: Achieving Friction-Free Status Updates" (*http://oreil.ly/2gzt4LL*), Camille Fournier explains well how to get status updates without "tapping engineers on the shoulder."

- Marcy Swenson's "All Hands Meetings" (*http://bit.ly/2gzrpFW*) gives great advice about how an all-hands meeting changes when a company scales to more than 10–15 employees.

- Juraj Holub's "8 Tips for Organizing a Killer All-Hands Meeting" (*http://bit.ly/2gzmiWw*) offers tips on how to organize a great all-hands meeting.

- Erica Spelman's "All Hands Meeting—What It Is and Why You (May) Want One" (*http://bit.ly/2gzpZeR*) explains why Zappos has all-hands meetings.

- In "Internal Communication Guidelines & Norms" (*http://bit.ly/2gMxfow*), Arno du Toit explains the importance of internal communication guidelines and what they should include.

Scaling Your Team

So far we've examined five critical areas for effectively scaling teams: hiring, people management, organization, culture, and communication. We covered the major challenges each area will face during rapid growth, and provided best practices that we hope you can apply, regardless of your team's growth rate.

Building Blocks of a Scalable Team

In this final chapter, we revisit these practices, highlighting the ones that are most critical in preparing for growth and those that are significantly easier to address while the team is small. We call these practices *scaling essentials*. Each one references the relevant chapter and section where you can get more detail. Since some recommendations can take a long time to implement (such as recruiting qualified people managers or clearly articulating the team's core values), getting a head start on them could be a competitive advantage.

Next, we've gathered together the *warning signs* from previous chapters that leaders should watch out for. We suggest regularly checking for these warning signs as your organization grows, so you can take action before simmering problems boil over into a crisis. A regular slot in a leadership meeting, perhaps 10 minutes once a month, should allow you and your team to recognize these warning signs and react appropriately.

And last, we present an example of how you might apply these scaling essentials and warning signs to your specific team in the form of an actual *scaling plan*. A scaling plan is conceptually related to a product plan or technology roadmap, which chart the expected changes to a specific product or technology over time. But a scaling plan is focused on the team itself, outlining the changes that are needed now and those expected in the future that will allow it to operate at full capacity. Just as a product plan is unique to each product, a scaling plan is unique to each team's situation.

Whether you decide to build a comprehensive scaling plan or to more surgically apply specific ideas, we hope we've provided some guidance that will help you and your team succeed.

Why You Need a Scaling Plan

Since this is likely the first time you've heard the term *scaling plan*, you may be wondering whether it's worth your time to create one. Although scaling plans are a new concept, we base this recommendation on our experience with and observations of numerous companies.

During the early days of a team, everyone is focused on finding product-market fit. Team leaders spend as much time as they can trying to understand customer needs, how their product might fill those needs, and whether this will lead to a sustainable business. An obsessive focus on building the right product is exactly what leaders should be doing at this stage.

But once the team finds product-market fit and starts to shift into growth mode, we have observed that leaders fail to shift their focus from building the right product to building the right team. After all, it is the team that will ultimately build the product, not the team leaders. Our hope is that creating a scaling plan will facilitate this mental shift. And regularly reviewing this plan provides a backstop that will catch emerging scaling problems before they become crises.

In our opinion, failing to make this mental shift from product to team is the source of many scaling crises in hyper-growth teams.

Scaling Essentials

Table 12-1 breaks down the essential practices critical to team growth, and references where to find more information in this book.

Table 12-1. Essential best practices for scaling teams

Dimension	Essential	See also
Hiring	In order to hire employees who are a great fit, particularly those critical early hires, introduce two things. First, choose a founder or early employee who is passionate about hiring to be part of every hiring decision. (We refer to this person as your "bar raiser" later.) Second, conduct a hiring sync after each interview to allow interviewers to learn from one another and align expectations.	"Bar Raisers" on page 35 and "How to Gather and Discuss Feedback" on page 36
	Make sure everyone is aware of the most important facts about the company by creating a lightweight program to on-board new employees that includes basic lessons about the company, product, roadmap, and organization.	"Improvised On-Boarding" on page 51
People management	Each team member should have a specific manager, even if it's the CEO or CTO, and have a regular one-on-one meeting with them.	"People management essentials" on page 62
	Anyone managing people should have some form of management training. Start by having them read a book about management and meet with a mentor on a regular basis.	"Lightweight management training" on page 80
	Decide when you will move to formal people management, such as when the team reaches 15 engineers, or once the CTO is unable to keep up with one-on-ones. Identify internal candidates for this role and/or plan your approach to external recruiting.	"When to Formalize People Management" on page 65

Dimension	Essential	See also
Organization	Implement the five organizational design principles. Keep it lightweight: • Take a look at delivery teams. If they seem like a good fit, start planning how to transition • Make sure each team member understands how they contribute to the success of the company • Give teams some level of autonomy • Make sure they can deliver continuously • Make sure retrospectives are set up at both the team level and the cross-team level	Chapter 6, *Scaling the Organization: Design Principles*
	Make a plan for how and when to move to delivery teams, if you haven't already.	"Expanding from One Team to Two" on page 148, "Create Delivery Teams" on page 126, and "Planning from the Start" on page 117
Culture	Run a lightweight core values exercise. For example, discuss values and culture with the founding team, and write down the areas of greatest importance and agreement. Discuss any points of disagreement. Document and share the findings with the team.	"Discovering values, defining culture" on page 175
	Incorporate some sort of values screen into the hiring process.	"Hiring, Values, and Culture" on page 181
Communication	Set up a regular all-hands meeting and demo sessions to ensure that employees can see what other teams are working on.	Chapter 11, which details the different types of meetings

Warning Signs: Early Stage

Table 12-2 highlights issues to watch for as your product development team grows to roughly 50 people.

Table 12-2. Warning signs of early-stage scaling problems

Dimension	Warning sign	Recommended actions
Hiring	Recruiting process is disorganized: interviewers aren't sure what questions to ask, candidates wait several days to hear back, etc.	Assign one employee to be responsible for the recruiting process and organize a training for all employees involved in interviewing. Hire a part-time recruiting coordinator to help with communication and scheduling.
	Early employees feel the talent level is dropping and some recent hires are not working out.	Review whether your bar raisers are really calibrated to the expectations of the company, and whether they feel empowered to say "No" to candidates.
	There are questions in all-hands (or other meetings) about very basic things that everyone should know.	Review your on-boarding program to see if it teaches new employees the information they need. Also, check if every new employee really visits those lessons; there is a tendency to deep-dive into the day-to-day work right away. Additionally, make sure that you repeat important things from time to time: for example, explain the company strategy every few all-hands.
	The people involved in scheduling interviews, booking flights, and so on are overwhelmed by these tasks and do not have time for the tasks they were actually hired to do.	Hire a recruitment coordinator. See "When to hire an internal recruiter" on page 14 for details.
	Your bar raiser is getting overloaded with interview tasks due to the amount of hiring you're doing.	Define a decision-making process that works without relying on a single bar raiser. "Making a Hiring Decision" on page 31 gives some different approaches; we recommend following the approach outlined in "Choosing a Process That Works for You" on page 35, which combines bar raisers with a hiring sync.
	Your new employees don't get enough insight into what the other teams are doing.	Expand the improvised on-boarding you created before by moving to a team rotation (see "Team Rotation" on page 52).

Dimension	Warning sign	Recommended actions
People management	One-on-one meetings are frequently canceled or rescheduled, or are not very helpful.	Your people manager(s) may be overloaded or poorly trained. Consider moving from ad hoc to formal management, or hiring more managers, or otherwise reducing their workload. See "Introducing Formal People Management to a Team" on page 70.
	Complaints that performance problems aren't being addressed.	Your people managers may be overloaded or poorly trained in managing performance. Consider hiring/converting more people managers and training your existing ones in setting and evaluating goals. You should also look into hiring practices if the issues are mostly from recent hires. See "Developing New Managers" on page 74, "Hiring Managers Externally" on page 83, and "Magnifying Your Managers" on page 89.
Organization	Employees don't know how they contribute to the success of the company.	For each team, clearly define how they contribute to the success of the company. Read "Establish Purpose and Measure Success" on page 132 for more details.
	It feels like it takes longer and longer to ship features even though the company is growing.	Use value stream mapping in team retrospectives to understand where time is being spent. See "Removing Dependencies" on page 151.
Communication	Employees complain that they have too many meetings.	Read "Meeting Explosion" on page 206 to find out possible reasons. If most of the meetings people complain about are interviews, try to involve more people in interviews to balance the load. Think about introducing meeting-free days.
	Employees complain that they receive too much email.	Think about applying some of the best practices for email outlined in "Email Explosion" on page 210. Check "Messaging guidelines" on page 212 to see if applying a policy might help.
Culture	Veteran team members complain that "the new employee is a real jerk!" New hires resign after only a few weeks at the company.	You may need to do a better job filtering for values in the hiring process. See "Hiring, Values, and Culture" on page 181. New hires might need a better on-boarding experience. See Chapter 3.

Warning Signs: Later Stage

The warning signs in Table 12-3 focus on larger teams, with roughly 50–150 employees working on product development.

Table 12-3. Warning signs of later-stage scaling problems

Dimension	Warning sign	Recommended actions
Hiring	The employees doing screening calls complain that it takes too much of their time.	A well-calibrated recruiter, who does most of the screening work, can help here (see "The First Recruiter" on page 14).
	Employees feel the interviews they are doing are not worth their time, as the quality of candidates is not high enough.	This usually means the calibration between recruiter and hiring manager isn't working (see "Calibration between hiring manager and recruiter" on page 13). Or the screening calls may not be good enough, resulting in too many candidates getting invited for interviews.
	Feedback from candidates about the hiring process is negative.	Negative feedback can come from candidates who went through essentially the same interview multiple times, encountered unprepared interviewers, or waded through general disorganization (see "Interview Structure" on page 27).
	You don't have enough quality CVs in the top of the funnel.	Hire a recruiter to do sourcing, and try to boost your outreach in general. Start building your employer brand (see "Building an Employer Brand" on page 16).
	A lot of candidates reject their offers.	Review whether your compensation is at market levels. Look into whether you're making offers the right way. See "Full-Cycle Recruiting: A Story from Erik Engstrom" on page 43.
	New employees take a long time to understand the company, its strategy, architecture, and so on. Some leave because of the confusion.	See "On-boarding and Culture" on page 182 to improve here. Also make sure you have exit interviews to find out why people are leaving.

Dimension	Warning sign	Recommended actions
	Your team is too homogenous and you're struggling to hire new employees from more diverse backgrounds.	Look at your hiring and retention data to try to locate the source of the problem. See Chapters 1 through 3, for advice on hiring for diversity. And examine whether your workplace is inclusive of those from other backgrounds, so that you can retain the people you hire. See "Diversity and Inclusion" on page 189.
People management	Team members are bogged down in disputes about the path forward or confusion about priorities and increasingly need leaders to step in and make decisions to unblock progress.	Make sure that company priorities are being communicated effectively and consistently from executives and people managers to ICs. Training management on effective comms strategies might help. Chapters 2 and 10 may be relevant.
	Product quality is slipping: there are more bugs, customer complaints, downtime, and rollbacks.	Inadequate people management could lead to poor training, sloppy development practices, or poor release/rollback planning. Investigate whether your managers are overloaded or ineffective. See "Assessing Manager Performance" on page 91.
	Team leaders feel engineering productivity is slipping, and wonder whether the team is working hard enough or if they are distracted by nonessential tasks.	This could be organizational, but could also be due to poor upward communication and/or lack of focus and oversight by people managers. See "Magnifying Your Managers" on page 89.
	Teams are engaging in finger pointing—for example: "We couldn't hit our milestone because Team X failed to adequately support us."	Investigate why the teams in question aren't collaborating effectively. Could be a culture mismatch, conflicting team-level goals, or a personality clash between the managers or their bosses. Also, make it clear that this is not an acceptable excuse—managers need to find ways to mitigate risks so they can meet their goals. See "Encouraging Collaboration and Community" on page 90.

Dimension	Warning sign	Recommended actions
	You see increasing evidence of poor morale—grouchy emails, antisocial behavior, and cynical talk around the water cooler. There may be a noticeable shift to later arrival times, earlier departures, and more frequent last-minute "work from home" days. You hear comments such as, "I'm not progressing in my career," "The work isn't interesting anymore," or "I'm burned out." Employees are leaving the company at a noticeable rate.	Many possible causes, but consider these actions: • Ask your line managers to spend extra time on this in their next one-on-ones and provide a summary. • Host some skip-level meetings, perhaps round-table discussions. Allow ICs to have a safe space to vent. • Ask HR if they have noticed any trends. • Closely review exit interviews of departed employees. • Review "Happiness During Hyper-Growth" on page 93 for ideas.
Organization	There are a lot of new feature ideas blocked due to a lack of staffing, and the product managers complain about not having the capacity to implement their plans.	Likely a sign the product managers are not included as an integral part of the team, and therefore are detached from the team's actual capacity. The same point applies for design concepts. See "Create Delivery Teams" on page 126.
	You're seeing lots of fights about headcount distribution between departments that are involved in the product.	The cause might be that the concept of delivery teams is not well understood or supported by all departments. Or there could simply be a lack of investment in growing the teams due to financial constraints.
	There are too many meetings, so "real work" doesn't get done until after hours, if at all.	This is a sign of excessive and/or ineffective communication between groups or departments. Make sure you have created delivery teams that can really deliver 95% of their backlog to production without dependencies.
	Engineering complains the designs they are getting from designers are creating too much work and the actual functionality could be achieved in a simpler way.	Design is not really integrated in delivery teams. This can happen when designers are formally part of a delivery team, but are not sitting with the team or are assigned other work to do.

Dimension	Warning sign	Recommended actions
	You ask team members how actual users perceive the delivered features, and they don't know.	There are two different reasons for this issue: either customer support is too isolated from the teams and the team doesn't get the customer feedback, or teams did instrument their features enough but are missing data.
	Certain functions (designers, for example) are overworked.	Most likely there are hiring imbalances between the different functions in delivery teams; for instance, one designer might be shared between different teams. Try to put more effort into recruiting to balance teams out.
	Teams are duplicating work or solving the same problems again and again.	There's no coordination set up to exchange information between delivery teams. See "Economies of Scale Between Delivery Teams" on page 150.
Culture	Certain teams don't seem to work well with others, and teams blame others for failures. Factions are forming.	You're not hiring for values, and may be allowing teams to diverge cultures. See "Hiring, Values, and Culture" on page 181 and "Resolving Culture Clash" on page 195.
	People who transfer between teams feel uncomfortable with the new team's processes. The new team doesn't feel that the transfer is strong enough to cut it, or think they do things the wrong way.	Culture and values between teams may have diverged, perhaps due to not hiring for values at the leadership level. See "Leadership and Culture" on page 183.
	There's been a noticeable shift in tone of internal communications, perhaps snarky questions at all-hands meetings, or bitter debates in group chat.	Your culture is out of sync with your core values; perhaps the leaders are not acting in accordance with core values, or your culture is not adapting to growth. See "Evolving Team Culture" on page 191.

Dimension	Warning sign	Recommended actions
	The morale of veteran employees is trending lower, and their attrition is trending higher.	The culture has changed too quickly, or not in accordance with core values. See "Evolving Team Culture" on page 191. This could also be a lack of strong people management, or a result of not preparing employees for the changes that come with growth. See "Preparing for Growth" on page 94.
	The morale of new employees is trending lower, and their attrition is trending higher.	Spend more time filtering for values in the hiring process; you may also have a poor on-boarding program, or even a toxic work environment. See "Building an Inclusive Workplace" on page 102.
Communication	Certain meetings are seeing lower and lower attendance.	This is a clear indicator the meeting is becoming less relevant for attendees. Check if the meeting actually makes sense at this stage of the company. See "Best practices for meetings" on page 207.
	Employees feel there are two classes of employees: the informed and the uninformed.	You can deduce this from your one-on-ones and surveys; it's a clear sign that you have reduced the "noise" too much, and employees are not informed well enough. Review the content of the all-hands meetings to see if you need to add things here. Also, check if certain important information is only communicated person-to-person.
	Your remote workers don't feel included.	As soon as you make the decision to have remote workers, a lot of things change. See "Multiple Offices" on page 231 for more.

An Example Scaling Plan

As mentioned before, a *scaling plan* is like a product plan that focuses on the team rather than the product. It should cover the changes that are needed now and those expected in the future. And it should include the warning signs that the leadership team feels are most relevant.

COMPANY A

Here we present an actual scaling plan that we prepared for a company we'll refer to as Company A, which was building a B2C product and had 65 employees in two offices (one in Europe and one in the US) at the time.

Initially, we spent the first several weeks looking at the five dimensions. After looking at all the warning signs and scaling essentials, we compiled the following status report:

Hiring

- **Good:** Hiring sync with people not afraid to say "no."
- **Good:** The CEO interviewed every candidate.
- **Good:** A pretty well-organized on-boarding program; for engineers, they used the team rotation approach.
- **Missing:** No real in-house recruiting role, as the company was growing only by roughly one employee per month.

People management

- **Missing:** Didn't have regular one-on-ones for engineers; performance reviews were organized by HR.
- **Missing:** No management training was available.
- **Good:** Overall the team was pretty diverse.
- **Missing:** No conference budgets, no hackdays.

Organization

- There were quite a few departments that existed as a silo (product, design, QA, operations), so they weren't organized as delivery teams.
- The teams were organized toward customer groups, but they didn't have a clear understanding of how they contribute to the company's success.
- There was no autonomy for teams, as all the work was dictated by a roadmap created by management.

- They used continuous delivery with some hiccups, as operations was a separate team and performed deploys for most of the engineering team.

- They used continuous improvement on a team level (retrospectives after each iteration).

Culture

- They never defined their values.

- There was no explicit screen for values in the interviews, but new employees fit in well.

- But culture felt good (people were on the same page regarding how they do things and what is important).

Communication

- The company had monthly all-hands meetings.

- Communication between the offices in Europe and the United States had severe problems, mostly due to the time difference.

- There was no demo session, which made the communication problems between the EU and US offices worse, as there was very little insight into each other's work.

- Meetings were mostly run well, and they didn't take too much time from the employees.

Scaling Plan for Company A

After all the findings were compiled, the next step was to order them by priority and identify solutions. We could not handle all the items at once, so we started with the ones we thought would impact the company the most. As a result, we mostly focused on organizational improvements (Table 12-4).

Table 12-4. Concrete scaling plan for Company A

Issue	Solution	Timeframe	See also	Follow up
Teams are not delivery teams, since several functions existed as silos	Start the move to delivery teams by first announcing that this would be the future way of working. Then start integrating the different silos. Some are easy (removing the QA silo by just adding the QA engineers to the delivery teams); some are more complicated —mostly because numbers don't match. There are five teams, but only two (overloaded) product managers. So we need to make some compromises while we hire the missing roles.	Now	"Create Delivery Teams" on page 126	The announcement was well received and we didn't see any quality problems by integrating QA into the teams. Overall, teams reported a major efficiency gain.
Employees lack a sense of purpose	To create purpose we need to define some fundamentals. As the first big step we have to clarify the company's mission and vision.	Now	See *Good Strategy Bad Strategy: The Difference and Why It Matters* by Richard Rumelt (Crown Business) for information on this topic.	Even though it was a good exercise, the resulting mission and vision statements didn't help as much as we hoped.

Issue	Solution	Timeframe	See also	Follow up
Lack of high-level priorities	Define company KPIs and match those to the teams.	Next quarter	"Establish Purpose and Measure Success" on page 132	That worked well for all teams that interacted directly with customer groups, but not for a very project-driven infrastructure team.
Teams lack autonomy	To enable team autonomy we will introduce that at least 50% of each team's time is in the team's control. They can use it for bug fixes, new features, or handling tech debt.	Next quarter	"Embrace Autonomy" on page 128	Balancing roadmap against team-driven work was initially difficult. But after steady reinforcement, it went much better.
Missing one-on-ones for engineers	Introduce regular one-on-ones between team leads and engineers.	Next quarter (training for team leads required)	"People management essentials" on page 62	This led to a lot of great feedback from employees that wasn't visible before.
Lack of awareness of other teams' activities	Introduce demos.	Now	"Company demos" on page 223	Demos were a big success, as each team's progress was now visible to the whole company.
Meetings interfering with productivity	Introduce two meeting-free days a week.	Two quarters from now	"Meeting Explosion" on page 206	Engineers were happy about having two days without interruptions.
Engineers felt they weren't part innovation at the company	Introduce quarterly hackdays so that employees can explore new ideas.	Now	"Models for Encouraging Innovation" on page 99	Everybody was very happy with the results.

Conclusion

In *Scaling Teams*, we've examined five dimensions of growth:

- *Hiring*, to ensure you grow the team efficiently, with the right people.
- *People management*, to provide them with the guidance and resources they need to succeed in their work.
- *Organization*, to coordinate that work efficiently and deliver the products the business needs.
- *Culture*, to ensure that those decisions are aligned with core values, and provide the team with a motivating sense of "who we are" and "how we do things."
- *Communication*, to enable the right information to flow to the people who need it to make decisions about the work they are doing.

For each area, we've covered strategies and tactics for anticipating, avoiding, and reacting to the most common scaling challenges.

In this final chapter, we've given you some practical tools for applying the material, and hope you will try building a scaling plan to help manage your own team's growth. Or take a more surgical approach, tackling one dimension at a time and finding ways to make your team resilient to the challenges ahead. However you decide to apply what you've learned here, we'd love to hear from you about your experience. Please contact us at ScalingTeams.com and share your stories of scaling teams.

Index

About the Authors

Alexander Grosse is currently the VP of Engineering at issuu. Previously, he was the VP of Engineering at SoundCloud and the R & D director at Nokia.

David Loftesness formerly managed engineering teams at Twitter, Xmarks, A9, and Amazon. Currently he is a dad, advises startups, mentors new managers, and writes stuff down.

Colophon

The cover fonts are Gotham Narrow and Helvetica Neue. The text font is Scala Pro, and the heading font is Benton Sans Condensed.

Learn from experts.
Find the answers you need.